THE HELL THAT IS ICE

A Novel By
James Markert

CHICAGO SPECTRUM PRESS
4824 BROWNSBORO CENTER ARCADE
LOUISVILLE, KY 40207
1-800-594-5190

Printed in the U.S.A.

10 9 8 7 6 5 4 3 2 1

ISBN: 1-886094-88-8

Acknowledgments

Special thanks:

—to Jim Stackpoole for editing and proofreading the first few drafts of this novel.

—to Chris Wolf for making things happen.

—to Tori Murden for reading the manuscript and giving me all the details of her grueling journey to the South Pole. All the interesting facts, thank her. Any mistakes, blame me.

—to my typewriter, word processor, and finally a computer for holding up.

—to You, the reader, for doing what you do best.

For my mother and father
— It would be impossible to create a fictional pair that could rival the
goodness of the real thing —
Thank You!

Prologue

December 16th, 1974
Louisville, Kentucky

The outside of the Andersons' home looked very much like the rest of the houses on Bluegrass Avenue—buried under 20 inches of white powder, dumped from last night's blizzard. Officially, the largest snowfall in Louisville history, it eclipsed the previous high of 17 inches back in the late 1940's. Unofficially, it was a disaster, bringing all activity in the city to a halt.

The entire city was eerily still, paralyzed as if embedded in a picture frame. A few adventurous folks took to the snow-clogged streets with skis, snowmobiles, sleds pulled by dogs, and one man even risked it on a horse. Brutalized by the bitter cold, most people stayed inside while the overwhelmed road crews tried to get things moving again. Their job would not come easily. Hundreds of abandoned cars and trucks blocked the interstates. The compacted ice and snow combined with the frigid air to make salting the roads a useless task. Plows broke down and slid off the roads. Tow trucks got stuck in the heavy snow accumulation. Many police officers were excused from work due to the lack of tire chains, and ambulances were getting stuck two and three times on the way to emergencies. Routine medical emergencies were becoming struggles of life or death, and the roads were impassable without 4-wheel-drive.

The National Guard was called in to help haul medical personnel to the hospitals in their 4-wheel-drive vehicles. National Guardsmen were also paired with city and county police so the officers could get through the snow-covered side streets.

Buses were stranded, and all routes were canceled. No planes were able to leave Standiford Field Airport, and all mail was stopped indefinitely. Although most of the city was dead, City Hall was booming with energy as it acted as the control center in trying to figure out what to do with the record snowfall. The Jefferson County Judge-Executive and the Mayor went back and forth from phone to television camera trying to find volunteers with 4-wheel-drive vehicles.

Thousands lost their light and heat as power outages ran wild across the county. Pipes froze and burst, water mains broke, and phone lines were overloaded with frightened citizens. Red Cross shelters were set up for the people without power because the Gas and Electric companies were predicting three to four days before they could get things back on track. Today, temperatures dipped below zero; the wind chill bottomed out at minus 25 degrees. Only the brave or hungry dared to go out.

Fortunately for the Andersons and everyone else in their neighborhood, their lights were on, and their heat was working just fine.

With his head still buried in his pillow and his eyes closed, Bill Anderson stretched his arm over to his wife's side of the bed. He felt the wrinkled sheets, but his wandering fingers couldn't locate Mary's body.

"Must be getting ready for work," he whispered to himself.

After rubbing his eyes enough so that they could stay open on their own, he slowly rolled his legs out from under the warm covers and stretched his arms in the air. He tilted his head to the side. Something popped in his neck, and he instantly felt better. As he stood up from the bed, he looked to the digital clock in the back corner of the bedroom on the dresser.

7:35.

"Oh, shit." He was supposed to be at the bank at 8:00. He hated being a bank teller, but during the worst economic year since the Great Depression, he was satisfied having a job at all. The newspapers reported that the oil crisis in the Middle East was taking its toll on the entire country, resulting in inflation, recession, and high unemployment. Bill had a degree from the University of Louisville in mathematics, and at the age of 25, he thanked God he wasn't coming back from Vietnam like so many other men his age. In many ways he considered himself very fortunate. Working at the bank was better than not working at all. He was married to the most wonderful wife, and their 2-year-old daughter, Amy, added nothing but joy and happiness to both of their lives. For these reasons alone (it certainly wasn't for the pay), he got himself motivated for work. First, he had to see if Mary had left for school. He was already going to be late for work. *Why not take my time and be a tad bit later?* he thought.

Wearing nothing but a white pair of boxers, he slowly made his way over to the bedroom door. Two years of marriage did nothing to impede his need to stay in shape. He was a regular at the YMCA, and he lifted weights three times a week on the average. He didn't have the physique of a body builder, but then again, who wanted to? His stomach was still hard and flat, and every muscle in his body was at least toned. The thing he prided himself the most on was still having a full crop of hair. Mary often teased him that she would file for divorce if he ever went bald. Bill hoped she was teasing. The trait did run in the family.

Bill stopped in the doorway to their bedroom and smiled as he located his wife. She was standing on the right side of the family room, wearing next to nothing, staring through the window at the snow outside. Captivated by her beauty, he said nothing. He just wanted to stare for a minute, and he watched as she slowly rocked from side to side with her arms folded delicately under her breasts. Under her white nightgown she wore nothing. The light from the lamp in the far right corner of the room passed through it easily, highlighting every curve in her shapely figure.

Slowly and quietly he walked towards the right side of the family room, watching. She shifted again. It was a slight movement, but powerful nevertheless. With his eyes, he traced the contour of her 5-foot-10-inch frame in the light, and her legs seemed to run on forever. Only a few feet away, she seemed completely unaware of his presence. She continued to stare out the window as he continued to stare at her. She was beautiful, and even though it had only been an hour since they last made love, he wanted her again. He was so focused on her, that he didn't even notice the snow outside. At 24, she was more attractive than ever. Bill was convinced that she was getting better-looking every year.

With his left hand, he gently moved her sandy blonde hair away from her shoulders. She flinched due to the unexpected touch, and then smiled as she felt his other hand against her hip.

"Bill," she whispered, giggling.

He responded with a soft kiss to her neck. She smelled lovely, like roses.

She felt something hard brushing up against her buttocks. "Bill, we just—"

"Ssshh." With his right hand, he slowly started to lift her nightgown. He whispered in her ear, "I assume you've called in sick for work, so let's make the best of it."

She played along, although she knew they were going nowhere for a good number of days. "Aren't you late for work, honey?"

"Yep."

His eyes never left the soft ivory colored skin of her neck.

"Don't you think you should start getting ready?" she asked, playfully.

"Later."

"Bill?"

"Yeah?"

"Look out the window."

"Mary. You're killing the mood." He let go of her nightgown and it dropped back down to her knees.

"Whoever said I was in the mood?" She wore a sheepish grin. "Just look out the window. I can't believe you haven't noticed."

"Whatever it is, I was distracted."

"I'm flattered, truly I am, but look out the window. I think you'll be surprised."

He did as he was told. Reluctantly, he lifted his eyes from her right shoulder and looked out the window. "Oh, my God! When did that happen?"

"Last night. They predicted three inches. Turns out they were about 17 off."

"Twenty inches? No fuckin' way." He turned completely around and faced the other side of the room. A three-foot-high pile of snow lined the outside of their sliding glass doors. The deck was buried. "This is amazing." His change of emotions was almost scary. One second he was ready for love and the next he felt like sledding. "This has got to be a—"

"A record," she finished for him. "It is. The most since the 17 inches the city had back in 1948. I've been watching the news all morning. The city is totally closed down. That's why I don't have to teach today."

He walked in front of her and stared out the window. "I guess I'm off work, too."

"Your boss called about thirty minutes ago and told you to have the next couple of days off. Then you'd play it by ear from there."

"Excellent." He smiled, staring out at what was supposed to be his driveway. His 1956 station wagon was nearly lost. The only parts showing were the antenna and a small section of the windshield. The snow drifts had covered the rest of it up. He looked as far down the street as he could; his angle wasn't the greatest. Their neighbor's house was only 20 feet away, and it blocked most of his view.

The snow weighed heavily on the cars, flower beds, shrubs, and bushes lining every house in the neighborhood, and it was prepared to stay there for a while. Frozen power lines drooped from the weight of the snow and ice, and brittle, fallen tree branches stuck out of the surface of accumulation. The streets couldn't be distinguished from the lawns, yards, and driveways. It was all one large sea of white, and for now it was beautiful.

Standing naked except for his boxers, Bill started to get chilled looking at the snow. He felt like a kid again, and he couldn't wait to step down in it and measure how far it reached up his legs.

She scooted up beside him and wrapped her hands around his arm and leaned against his shoulder. "It's so neat to look at."

"It sure is," he paused. "Is Amy up?"

"Not yet. I just checked on her a few minutes ago. She's still sound asleep."

"That's surprising. She's usually up and getting into things by now."

"I'll probably give her another half hour or so, and then I'll wake her up. I think you tired her out last night riding her on the knee horse for so long."

"You think she was tired. My leg was about ready to fall off. It still aches."

"Poor baby," Mary said in a childish voice. "You should have told her."

"I couldn't stop. She was having too much fun. I like to watch her laugh."

Mary smiled. " Me, too. " After a brief silence, Mary said, "On the news earlier, the Governor declared a state of emergency. The only traffic allowed on the interstates is for emergencies. I think they're even starting to ticket people that are trying to drive without a good reason."

"I'm certainly not going to be one of them," Bill said. "My car will probably be there for at least a week, if it starts at all. I'm not crazy. I'm awfully hungry, but not crazy enough to drive out in this stuff."

"Which reminds me." She pulled her arm away from his and softly patted him on the chest. "We need some milk and bread for breakfast."

He laughed. "Let me guess. You want me to walk up to Food Mart and get them?"

"Bingo."

He grabbed her around the waist and pulled her close. "And what's in it for me?"

She gave him a quick peck on his cheek. "French toast." Laughing, she released herself from his grasp and walked towards their bedroom.

"French toast it is," he whispered, watching her until she disappeared.

After hiking his way back to the shed for their shovel, Bill was ready for the journey to Food Mart. The store was less than a mile down the street, but because of the terrain, he estimated his round trip, if he didn't collapse along the way, to be less than an hour.

He wore long underwear from his neck to his ankles, a pair of blue jeans, a heavy sweater and turtle-neck, a wool hat, scarf, and two pairs of wool socks. He was barely able to slide his boots on because of the thickness. Mary made sure he was dressed appropriately, even if it meant that his mobility would be severely restricted. He felt like a statue. He could barely move. She even insisted on his wearing stupid black garbage bags taped over his boots and legs to keep them from getting too wet; and so he did with limited argument and set out on his way.

He had planned on shoveling the front porch before he left, but after looking at it, he decided it could wait until he returned. As soon as he stepped out on the porch, he was knee-deep in snow. The scene fascinated him. It was so quiet. The entire neighborhood was a desert of snow, drifts blowing wildly, unmarred by any footprints or tire tracks. It seemed none of his neighbors had appeared yet.

Mary wiped away the frost and peered out the ice-covered living room window, watching and laughing as her husband took his first step into the snow. He looked like a little boy, and he seemed to be enjoying himself. Each step would be an obstacle overcome, and walking would become increasingly difficult as the trip went on. Mary was glad that he was going instead of her. She preferred to stay inside where she could be warm and keep an eye on Amy. After watching Bill for a few minutes, she walked into the kitchen to fix a glass of orange juice.

Amy was usually up and running at the crack of dawn, but not today. Mary welcomed the extra time of peace and quiet, something she was lately missing. The kids in her fourth grade class were bouncing off the walls with excitement for the up-and-coming holidays. Deep down inside, Mary was, too. Physically and mentally she was drained, and the kids were driving her crazy. She was relieved to learn that the last two days of school before Christmas vacation had been canceled due to the storm.

Mary took the orange juice into the family room, sat down on the couch facing the sliding glass doors, stared at the picturesque white ground outside, and waited.

On his way back from the store, Bill found that he could not stop thinking about Mary. Not the Mary that looked so lovely standing in the window's morning light wearing next to nothing, but Mary the person, his wife, lover, and best friend. To her he owed everything. It was Mary who turned his life around. She had changed him from the drug-using alcoholic he was in college, to the successful family man with a completely satisfying life. It started when they were in college at the University of Louisville. He was a sophomore with no direction in life, and she was a freshman with the maturity to carry them both. He was not perfect, but she saw the potential, and most importantly, she loved him. At the time, she didn't know why she loved him, but as the facade of vices and irresponsible actions faded away, his true colors bloomed in full, and she took pride in knowing that she was the reason for it. She was not only happy with herself, but for both of them. They were making it. It wasn't easy at the beginning, but it wasn't long before he began showing that he was a changed and responsible man, and he owed it all to her. With a different perspective on life and a new group of friends, Bill was able to kick the addictions, and within a year he was clean and sober. He hadn't smoked a joint or touched a drop of alcohol in all their days of marriage, and there hadn't been a day gone by that he didn't thank God for her showing up in his life.

No more than a hundred yards away from his house, he stopped to catch his breath. The errand was more difficult than he had thought, and the store was nearly empty when he got there. Digging past his thick coat, sweater, and long underwear, he located his watch. It was 8:40, and he'd been gone for nearly 35 minutes. *Not bad,* he thought. From where he stood, he was able to see his home; and yes, from the outside the Andersons' home looked very much like the rest of the houses on Bluegrass Avenue. Inside the house was a different story, a story of chaos that would haunt the Anderson family members for the rest of their lives.

Inside the house, a huge black bird flew from room to room in a claustrophobic panic, watching out the windows and standing guard as its master did his thing. Its master did his job in the family room, a bad type of job. The screaming woman proved that. The bird stayed on the lookout for anyone approaching the house, and it was to warn its master about the time.

The bird's name was Zoro, and so far, it had seen nothing through the front windows except snow. Zoro wanted the freedom of the outdoors. It didn't like being trapped inside, but it was obligated to the master.

At the back of the house, to the right of the deck, was the Andersons' beat-up storage shed with its doors wide open. The back wall of the shed was lit up a bright tint of green, almost neon, and it was shining outward, illuminating the back side of the house and passing through the broken glass doors into the left side of the family room.

Death-gripping cold and neon-green light swarmed Mary as she fought the struggle of her life. Glass fragments from the overturned china cabinet stuck out of the beige carpet like tiny spears, furniture was turned on end, the glass end-table beside the couch was lying sideways, and the room was deathly cold and getting colder. Allowed in, the wind brought both the snow and cold into the wide-open family room.

The intruder was powerful and huge, clawing and shredding Mary's skin with his fingernails, as she strained to keep his arms away. Through tear-and blood-smeared eyes, she could see the sharp object in his hands. It was a knife. The shards held upward by the carpet ripped her skin as she writhed to avoid the blade. She was oblivious to them. Mary's body weakened as her blood settled into the carpet and slowly spread outward. The fight for her life came to an end as the intruder brought the knife down on her chest for the tenth and final time. Just when the intruder thought his job was over, he heard the high-pitched cry of a baby from an upstairs bedroom. The frigid air had found its way through the rest of the house, passing from the family room into the kitchen, through the living room and up the staircase, until finally reaching Amy's bedroom.

Two-year-old Amy was fidgeting in her crib, screaming as if she had felt the final plunge of the knife dig into her mother's chest. She was too young to understand what was going on, but she heard the breaking glass, her mother's screams, and the unnatural sound of a creature she couldn't see. It was bad, and it was coming after her next.

Zoro heard the first cry and immediately responded by zooming to the stairs leading to the second floor.

The intruder moved from Mary's bleeding, mangled body and listened carefully to the baby's cry. The cry was different and special. The intruder heard a voice. *Spare the child.* A voice in his head, its guidance and knowledge, the voice of his ancestors, *She is the one, but now is not the time.* He didn't understand why, but he knew he should trust what both the baby's cry and his inner voice were telling him. The temptation to kill was hard to resist, but he had to wait until the time was right. When or where that was, he did not know.

Knife still in hand, the intruder left the family room and entered the kitchen. After turning on the faucet, he placed the bloody knife under the strong flow of water. Fresh blood turned the stream of water to red as it poured off the knife and swirled around at the bottom of the sink like a whirlpool, eventually vanishing down the drain into the pipes below.

The knife was not clean, but the intruder turned the water off and rested it on the edge of the sink to dry.

She is the one.

The intruder passed through the kitchen and into the living room, slowly approaching the staircase next to the front door.

But now is not the time.

He stopped short of the stairs just as Zoro had entered the girl's room.

Amy's scream intensified as Zoro crashed through her wooden door and into her room, resting on the edge of her crib. It let out a shrill cry of its own, paralyzing the baby with fright, bringing her cry to an abrupt halt. Zoro tip-toed around the outer edge of the crib, talons clicking together, creating a melodic tick-tock noise that nearly hypnotized Amy. Zoro's bright, fire-red eyes beamed down on her like rays of light, infusing her with a memory that would inhabit her for years to come. Young and helpless, she slid into some kind of trance put on her by the bird's overwhelming presence. The trance would not easily be broken. Staring down into Amy's eyes, Zoro extended its wings, engulfing the entire crib in a blanket of the darkest of shadows. Amy could see nothing but two red dots swimming in an infinite pool of darkness.

She heard the wings, the terrible leathery sound of those wings moving all around her. Everything was black except for the eyes. She could hardly breathe. She tried to scream, but couldn't. The bird's closeness was suffocating. But time was running out, and the bad thing down stairs was no longer after her.

Zoro flew from Amy's room as quickly as it had entered, leaving Amy to the more familiar surroundings of her room.

The intruder left the living room. Zoro followed behind as he moved through the kitchen and out the broken glass doors in the family room, quickly heading towards the dimming green light in the back of the shed. The doorway was closing.

Zoro followed as far as the shed, but did not follow through. After its master was gone, Zoro flew up into the grayness of the morning sky where it could see a man retracing his steps towards his home.

Bill Anderson struggled through the deep snow in his front yard, anxious to reach the front porch. Even though he thought he was in tremendous shape, he was now ready to collapse. His legs were weighted down by the snow, and each arm held a brown bag of groceries, one of which was ripping at the bottom. The last hundred yards he had to carry it in an awkward position to keep it from ripping the rest of the way, so underneath his glove his right hand was cramping badly. He couldn't wait to put it down and straighten out his fingers again.

What little the store had left, Bill had grabbed. Every shelf in the store had nearly been empty because of the panic created by the storm. Most people were afraid of being locked inside with no food to eat. Bill knew what many couples would be doing, locked up in their houses for the next few days, waiting for normalcy to return. He suspected there would be a nice spurt of babies about nine months from now. The thought brought a smile of enjoyment to his frozen face. He and Mary had talked about having another.

Finally Bill reached the front porch, and for a minute he stared at the door. He had a problem. *How in the hell am I going to get the door open without dropping the bags?* He hoped it was unlocked so he could just kick it open, but first he had to get the screen door ajar. As if he wasn't in enough of a hurry to get inside, he heard Amy screaming from upstairs, and his pace quickened. It wasn't her normal cry. The harshness of her voice frightened him to the point that he forgot about his cramping right hand.

With the middle finger of his left hand, he pulled the screen door open and quickly shoved his knee in the opening before it closed. The bag in his right hand ripped another inch and tilted to the right, but he somehow managed to hold on. With his knee now in the door, he inched himself closer to the wooden front door and pushed it slowly with his forehead. It opened, and within seconds he was inside the door standing directly in front of the staircase.

"Honey, I'm home," Bill said, stomping the snow off of his wet boots, sprinkling the dirty welcome mat with fresh clumps of slush. He immediately set the bags down next to the door and pulled his gloves off, bending and flexing his cold fingers. "You should have seen Food Mart. There was hardly anything left on the shelves. Bare as a baby's butt." He took off his coat and hung it on the rack next to the front door. Next, he untaped the garbage bags and slipped them off his boots. *Mary was right,* he thought, *the bags worked.* "I got the last gallon of milk, and the only bread left was some generic brand. Better than nothing, I guess."

He waited for Mary to respond, with a 'That's nice, Bill' or 'Oh, really,' or at least a 'Who gives a shit, Bill,' but she didn't respond at all. The house felt eerily cold.

"Mary?"

Nothing. He walked over to the thermostat near the door and tapped it.

"You asleep?" He waited and then started up the stairs. "Don't get up. I'll check on Amy." Amy's cry was getting more hoarse and broken.

"Okay, Amy. It's okay. Daddy's coming." He leaped the steps two and three at a time. His legs were already throbbing from his trudge to the store, so each step created its own little pain. When he reached the top of the stairs, he quickly realized that something was definitely wrong. At the top platform next to Amy's door, Bill saw a foot-long black feather with a white mark on the tip, surrounded by several splinters of wood. He looked up and saw the hole through his daughter's bedroom door. He turned cold.

"What the hell?" Bill mumbled, staring through the door. The hole was about a foot in diameter; not a clearly-defined circle, but much more rough and jagged, as if something had busted its way through the wood.

"Amy! My God!" He flung the door open and stepped inside the room. Her sobbing was painful to his ears. Several more splinters from the door covered the hardwood floor, and another feather rested just inside the threshold.

He wanted to see if she was okay, but horrible thoughts of his baby, bruised and mangled, clouded his mind. Something was wrong. He sensed it in the air. It wasn't just the hole in the door or the feathers on the floor, but the air was bad and getting colder. Nothing made sense. At the moment he wasn't thinking clearly, and he was totally confused.

Knees shaking, he made his way over to the crib. His eyes moved over the baby as if he were following the flight path of a gnat, checking her for cuts and bruises. Amy's eyes were wide open as if she hadn't blinked for hours, or wasn't able to do so. Her little body was trembling, and the blanket underneath was wet from her urine. Her cry softened as her father lifted her out of the crib and into his comforting arms. He wiped the tears and mucous from her face. He held her tightly against his chest, patting her back gently, telling her over and over that everything was going to be okay. He was afraid to let go.

Bill whispered into her ear, "Thank God, you're okay." He rocked her back and forth with a slight twist of the hips. "Sssshhh. It's okay. Daddy's here now. Ssshh."

Bill saw a trickle of blood on the top of Amy's head. He wiped it off with his finger, exposing a red dot about the size of a pinpoint.

"What's going on here?" he whispered, glancing at the debris from the busted door and then at the spot on Amy's head. Her crying stopped. He held Amy close and headed out of the room. "Let's go find mommy," he said with intensity.

Amy seemed to be fine. Bill's attention now turned to his wife. He needed to see her. He needed to hear her voice. *She has to be okay. She's sleeping, and she just couldn't hear what was going on.* Quickly he ran down the stairs with Amy in his arms.

Bill feared the worst. Mary was his lifeline, and he couldn't get to her soon enough. His adrenaline was shifting to overdrive, and his rattled nerves nearly sent him tumbling down the stairs.

"Mary!"

No response. The first floor was really cold, colder than it had been only minutes before Bill entered the house.

He hurried through the living room and entered the kitchen. Dishes and glasses were shattered and scattered all over the tile floor. A hardening pile of bird dung was on the counter by the sink. He spotted the knife. It looked mottled and a little dirty, but Bill picked it up anyway. He couldn't tell what was on it, nor did he care. His mind was set on finding his wife. He wanted to gaze into her beautiful green eyes, hold her close, and never let go.

He wasn't sure why he picked up the knife; but by the looks of the house, he felt he needed it for protection. The knife helped him feel more secure and safe.

"Mary!" He inched his way into the family room with Amy cradled in his left arm. Despite the cold, a bead of sweat trickled down his left temple and around the back curve of his unshaven jaw.

"Mary!"

No response. Bill gripped the knife. His palm was damp and sticky from his perspiration and the re-wetting of his wife's dried blood on the handle.

The family room was in shambles. The antique china cabinet was face down on the floor in the far left corner of the room. Broken dishes and glasses were smashed into the carpet. The curtains were torn away from the wall and were lying on the floor beside the couch. The air was freezing cold. Bill saw the broken sliding doors and watched as the wind blew drifts of snow into the room.

Leaning against the front of the couch was another feather. *The bird was in here, too,* Bill thought, *but it wasn't the only thing. The bird alone couldn't have done this kind of damage. It'd be impossible. Someone was in here. But who?*

His breathing became heavy. He clutched Amy to his chest with his left arm and held the knife out with his right. Slowly, he circled the room.

Bill looked down at the beige carpet and saw a dark red trail of splotches leading around to the back of the couch. He wanted to put Amy down, but was afraid she would get cut on the glass. He forced himself to follow the trail of red spots behind the couch.

Mary was there, lying in a pool of her own drying blood. Her blank eyes gazed at the ceiling, and her mouth was slightly parted.

"MARY!" Bill screamed, bending down to his wife. His heart dropped like an anchor. Their framed reprint of Van Gogh's *Starry Night* had fallen off the wall, landing on what was left of her chest, covering much of her torso. He lifted the picture. His worst fears were confirmed. She was dead; brutally beaten, torn, and shredded. The breasts that he had fondled and caressed playfully a few hours before were now ripped, red and mangled.

Bill was in shock, and without thinking, he put Amy down on the floor. Luckily she was placed in a spot relatively free of glass. Fury was building, and he felt like he could explode. Then as suddenly, leaning over his wife, a tear trickled from his eyes and landed on her forehead. He placed his fingers over her eyelids and closed them for one last time.

It was senseless. Shock and disbelief quickly changed to reality; he would never speak to his wife again.

"Nooooo! Damn Youuuuu!" Bill slumped down on his wife, pleading for her to come back. He wanted to snap out of this nightmare, but he knew it wasn't going to happen; it was all too real now.

Gently, he closed her lips and kissed her cold forehead. As he leaned, tears dripped off of his face and onto hers, leaving wet lines racing down her cold, pale cheeks.

Amy seemed confused, and for the moment she had stopped crying. She was too young to understand. Bill was 25, and he didn't understand. She sat on the floor amidst the shards of broken glass, staring at her parents, wondering why one of them wasn't moving.

The surprises weren't over for Bill. He looked over his right shoulder to the back lining of the couch. What he saw and read only added to his confusion. The word—SNOWMAN—was written in smeared blood. Mary's blood. Bill couldn't understand how life so precious could be taken away so quickly. She was only 24 years old. Their lives together had just begun.

He felt so alone, and empty.

He cried.

He wept.

Amy joined him. She too was cold.

Mary Anderson was not the only person to die during the Louisville blizzard of '74; she was one of seven. A 60-year-old woman died of a heart attack the first day of the storm. She was trying to shovel her front porch, but the heavy snow was too much for her, and hours after she started, neighbors found her lying face down in the snow, frozen and blue.

A young male college student was killed while skiing down one of Cherokee Park's most famous slopes—dead man's curve. Going close to 30 miles per hour, he lost control and collided with a tree. A sharp branch sticking from the lower part of the tree punctured his chest and heart; he was instantly killed.

An elderly man was found frozen to death on his kitchen floor. With the loss of electricity, he was unable to call for help and physically unable to help himself after he had fallen and dislocated his right hip. Lying there for nearly a week, his death was slow and painful.

A young couple was killed when heavy snow caused the roof on their mobile home to collapse. Both were crushed and not found until two days later. They had been married for only a month.

A young girl, age 11, was killed when her house caught fire and burned to the ground. Left alone while her mother worked the previous night shift at the hospital, she took it upon herself to light the kerosene heater, accidentally catching the living room curtains on fire. Snow barricaded the doors, both front and back, and after she was already weakened by the smoke, she was unable to push the snow away so she could get the doors open. She was trapped, fire on the inside and snow on the outside.

Out of all the deaths that occurred during the storm, Mary Anderson's was the only one that went down as murder. There was something else about the Anderson case that made that day special for the intruder. It had finally found the *ONE*. Amy was the *one*, but then wasn't the time.

Part One

December 14th, 1994
A Winter Remembered

Two evils, monstrous either one apart,
Possessed me, and were long and loath at going;
A cry of Absence, Absence, in the heart,
And in the wood the furious winter blowing.

John Crowe Ransom, from *Winter Remembered*

Part One

Chapter 1

South Pole, Antarctica 6:30 A.M.
Amundsen-Scott Station, Science Building

Three separate buildings were sheltered by the aluminum geodesic dome of the research station: a communications room, a dining hall, and a science lab. The dome itself was not heated, but all the buildings underneath were well-insulated and warm. The dome was only 15.8 meters high and 50 meters in diameter, but it served its purpose of keeping the deadly Antarctic winds away from the scientists, making it the heart of the research station.

Inside the science building, David Johnson, the head scientist of WHITE OUT, a top secret project of SCARE (Strategic Center for Antarctic Research and Exploration), bounced a tennis ball off the wall and into his meaty right palm. It was only the middle of the summer in Antarctica, but the stress of being in charge was already starting to show. The entire SCARE team was falling apart, and tensions were flaring. Some were starting to ask questions, and David was doing his best to keep them working and at the same time keep them in the dark as to what was really going on with the project. Two men had been lost already, and a growing fear was burning among the remaining researchers. David was constantly being pressured by the government to keep the morale and questions under control, so as he sat there squeezing the tennis ball in his right hand, his mind was searching for ways to stomp out what could possibly become a raging fire of controversy. The weather was also at fault. The climate was getting to everyone. Some more than others.

David leaned back in his roller chair and threw the ball against the wall again. Before it reached his hand on the rebound, Sampson Colebridge knocked it out of the air, ricocheting it off one of the computers.

David straightened out in his chair and glanced up at the skinny young man standing over him. "Problem, Colebridge?"

Sampson sighed. "Where is everybody? Austin should have been back by now."

David shifted his 250-pound frame in the chair and smiled. "Easy Sampson, Austin will be here in time. I know he's your little brother, but try and take it easy. He's a big boy. They're all still out in the field." He paused, staring into Sampson's worried eyes. "Get some sleep. You look like shit."

"Fuck off." Sampson turned, picked up the tennis ball and tossed it from hand to hand in quick, jerky motions. His brother had been due back more than an hour ago. It was obvious that he was worried about Austin, and he felt himself trembling. He felt like he was going crazy, as if he and the crew were never going to make it back to the States safely. Sampson bit his lower lip as his eyes glanced nervously around the room.

"You sure are on the edge," David mumbled.

"They should have been back by now."

"It happens, Sampson. It's not like they're returning from the damn grocery store. It's Antarctica, remember that. Shit happens and . . . things get in the way." David took a deep breath and shook his head. "For your information, Austin radioed in about a half hour ago. They're only three miles away. They ran into a little trouble with the weather and an unstable snowbridge, but—." He was cut off.

"Snowbridge? We've already lost two like that," Sampson said, raising his voice. His face reddened.

"Don't bring it up again, not now."

"I sure won't forget it."

"Dammit, Sampson," David raised his arm. His voice was strong, boiling with an anger he could hold back no longer. "It was a tragedy, but they were careless. They crossed a weak snowbridge, and the crevasse swallowed them. There was nothing we could have done yesterday."

"Bullshit. We could have showed them some respect. Tried to fish them back out, or hell, at least tried to contact their families. They both have . . . had a wife and kids."

"Don't you think I know that?"

"You act like you don't even care, like it didn't even happen."

"Because it didn't!" David screamed, slamming his fist down on the top of his computer. Spittle flew from the corner of his mouth. "You better get that through your head now. It didn't happen, not here."

"You're a SCAB (the name created by the scientists concerning the Stupid Cocksucking Administrative Bureaucrats of SCARE) just like the rest of the bastards behind this project. We're always in the dark."

"Back off." David shifted in his chair again, somehow restraining himself from breaking Sampson's neck.

"You're going to try and cover it up, pretend it didn't happen? That's what is going on here, right?"

"I'm warning you. It was a tragedy, an accident!"

"Just like all the other accidents over the years. All these unexplained accidents, yet the damn SCABs still send us down here to this hellhole, risking our lives. All for what? We've lost 20 scientists now in the past 20 years. Not a very strong percentage."

"Sampson, you're starting to sound like that crazy old writer, that . . . Leroy McCalister. You've been reading his shit about the snow beast that lives here, haven't you? Damn fairy tale if I've ever heard one."

"That's probably what we're really researching. I've read about his theories, and what if they're true?"

"They aren't," David said loudly. "We shut that old fool up years ago." He shook his head in disgust. "Trying to spread that garbage, screwing up our initial plans with his warnings of the 'beast' or 'monster' or whatever the shit he called that creature that was supposedly roaming the ice. It's all false."

"But—"

"They were accidents!" David yelled, standing up. "Unfortunate accidents!"

Sampson backed away, but didn't back down. "It's funny we never find the bodies. People seem to die and . . . and just disappear. How can we do this? During the summer months only ten years ago, there were close to 50 scientists per year working out of this station, but now we're down to 17." He paused. "Oh, I'm sorry, only 15. Shit man, even I'm forgetting about them now."

"We are forgetting no one." David took a step closer. Sampson stepped back.

"They cut down the personnel, yet they still send us here. Do they want the minerals and resources that badly? Is it the space program they want to keep secret, or a secret form of defense? Nuclear testing? Something is going on here, and we are all just decoys."

"Budget cutbacks, nothing more. That's all I can say. The bottom line is we can't afford all the workers. And the board is a hell of a lot more selective now. Psychological testing. They increased it so loonies like *you* wouldn't let the climate make 'em crazy. God only knows how you slipped through the cracks."

"Excuse me for being human."

A brief awkward silence filled the air. David took a deep breath, clenching his hands into fists, trying to calm himself. "Look, your brother's team should be back soon. Lucas and his team are only a mile away taking core samples. Nothing is going wrong. Both teams are safe. Now quit fucking causing me stress."

Sampson took a couple of steps backwards, shaking his head. "Bunch of lying bastards. How many more are going to slip through our fingers before we terminate this thing."

David pointed towards the door. "Get out."

Sampson started walking away, then stopped. "There's something bad here, something really bad."

Just as David was telling Sampson to get out again, Brian Conners, their communications expert, hurried through the door. "David, get in here, quick. We've got trouble with one of the teams." Brian was out of the doorway as quickly as he had entered, leaving David and Sampson no time for questions.

They followed him to the communications building.

Running from one building to the next, the change in temperature was noticeable. The inside of the dome was protected from the wind, but the air outside the individual buildings was well below freezing. The urgency of the message left them no time to bundle up. Each wore a pair of white Gore-Tex pants, black plastic snow boots, and green synthetic shirts with the letters SCARE sewn into their right breast pockets.

Once they reached the communications building, Brian started flipping switches on the computers. "Austin radioed in a few minutes ago, but I lost him."

Sampson stepped up to the row of computers against the wall. "My brother, is he okay?"

Brian shrugged his shoulders. "I'm not sure. He mentioned something about a whiteout, and then all I heard was static."

David's face solidified with intensity. "Find them," he demanded.

Just when Brian reached for another button, a voice flared through a background of static into the communications room.

"Somebody!" The voice was stressed and broken. "David. Brian. This . . . is . . . Austin." The static was breaking his speech. " . . an . . any . . ody . . . hear . . . me?"

David grabbed the radio transmitter. "Austin, this is David. What's going on? Where are you?"

"Don't . . . know."

Sampson listened nervously. His heart was settling in his throat. His brother was in trouble.

"Austin, report!"

"White . . . .out."

"Where are you?"

" . . . on't . . . know. . . . an't . . . see . . an . . . hing . . . like . . . wal . . king . . n . . cloud."

They heard voices screaming in the background.

"Don't panic, Austin. You know what to do in a whiteout. Tell them to stop screaming."

"Can't."

"What do you mean, you can't." David was losing his cool, not that he was filled with it before. "Tell them to fucking shut up, Austin."

The screaming was louder, more intense.

"My . . . team . . . dy . . ing."

Static held the line for about ten seconds before Austin's voice cleared through again. "So . . . white . . . som . . one . . . .else . . ."

The screaming stopped.

David yelled through the radio. "Are they okay?"

"Dead . . . all . . .dead."

Sampson kicked over a table and howled, reaching for the radio transmitter. David pushed him away.

"Austin, stay cool, and get out of there."

" . . . hear . . ome . . thing . . br . .eathing."

"What is it, Austin?"

Austin screamed. "It's . . . got . .mee . .eee . ."

Static filled the room.

Contact was lost.

David stared blankly at the radio and dropped the transmitter to the floor. He whispered, "Oh, my God."

Just then, Sampson came flying across the room with his hands ready to attack. He jumped at David and clamped his hands around David's bulky neck. He squeezed hard and pressed his thumbs against David's adam's apple. "We're all going to die. ALL GOING TO DIE!" he screamed.

Brian tried to step in, but was unable to separate them.

David's back was pressed against the row of computers. His face was fiery red and his tongue lolled in the corner of his parted lips. He gasped for air, struggling desperately for a breath, but couldn't find one. In a last-ditch effort to save his life, David brought his knee up and landed it in Sampson's groin. He felt something crunch on impact. Sampson let go and stumbled backwards, arms spinning like helicopter blades. He hit the far wall and slid to the ground.

Gaining his composure, David moved off of the computers. Rubbing his neck, his breathing somewhat returned to normal. Slowly, he walked over to Sampson and lifted him off the ground by the collar of his shirt. Sampson was fragile, weighing next to nothing.

Grimacing in pain, Sampson spat in David's face.

Without bothering to wipe it off, David rammed Sampson's head into the concrete wall.

Sampson immediately saw stars. The back of his head was cut and bleeding. Brian ran out of the room for help.

Repeatedly, David rammed Sampson's head into the wall. He was oblivious to the sounds the skull was making on impact with the wall, a thud and a crunch, thud and crunch. Sampson was unable to talk. He was unconscious, and blood poured down the back of his head and neck. His skull was crushed.

When David saw that Sampson was no longer moving, he let go. Sampson's body slumped to the floor like a sac of potatoes. He was dead. Another accident.

The reality of what David had just done set in. Shaking his head slowly, he backed away from the victim, staring at the crushed skull and spreading pool of blood. He stared in disbelief. He had just killed a man. He stared with increasing guilt. He was in a temporary, uncontrollable trance, and he reacted in a way anyone would have after killing a man for the first time.

David ran.

8:05 A.M. AMUNDSEN-SCOTT STATION, COMMUNICATIONS BUILDING.

With Sampson's body stored away under the cargo arch, Brian Conners made his way through the underground network of tunnels, past the generators and biomedical facility, and back under the dome. Three remained in the station (four counting Sampson's body). With one of them being a cook and another a biological assistant, Brian was pretty much left in charge of the crew. He took it upon himself to dispose of the body. Not knowing what else to do with it, he had wrapped it in a couple of wool blankets and carried it down to the cargo area. He'd never touched a dead body before, so carrying it was a bit awkward. It had frightened him walking with the dead baggage over his shoulder, but he had to be respectful of Colebridge's corpse. He couldn't have just left it where it was in the communications room, leaning against the wall, so he had stored it quickly with the cargo, being careful not to bang it against any stairs, railings, ceilings, or walls.

When Brian entered the communications room, Christopher Livingston, the young biological assistant, was hard at work on a computer in the far corner of the room. His freckled face was intense, focused on the task at hand. Brian could see the seriousness in the kid's eyes, even through the thick glasses. Christopher may have been trying to hide it, but Brian could tell he was worried. *Who wouldn't be,* Brian thought.

Christopher turned as soon as he heard someone enter the room. "Did you store the body?"

Brian quivered slightly. "Yeah, down with the cargo. Any sign of David yet?"

"Lloyd is looking for him now. I think he's long gone." Christopher took off his glasses and rubbed his eyes roughly. Brian could hear them popping in their sockets. "What exactly happened?"

Brian raised his arms and then dropped them back to his sides. "Sampson was going crazy after he heard what had happened to Austin and the rest of the crew. He blamed David, attacked him, and then—"

"David just killed him?" Christopher finished.

"More or less. I don't think it was his intent, but . . . man, it was the damnedest thing I've ever seen. They were going at each other pretty good, and then I went running for help. I came back and Sampson was dead, and David was gone. They both just totally flipped out."

Christopher put his glasses on and stared at Brian. "What *did* happen out there?"

"Honestly. I don't know. Something weird. Something very weird." He paused, staring at the computers and radios. "Did you contact the core drilling team?"

"Yes, I talked to Lucas about 15 minutes ago. I gave him the message, just as you said, but I still don't think he understood the urgency."

"Are they on their way back?"

"He said that they were getting some great samples. The digging is going really well."

"Are they on their way back?" Brian asked again.

"Not exactly. He said that they were going to finish up some samples first, and then they'd return."

"We can't afford to lose anyone else. They better be back soon. I don't know what the hell is going on out there, but it's bad, and it's killing us. We are not going to lose any more men." He stopped, counting the numbers in his head. "Two with the snowbridge incident. We may have lost seven in the whiteout, Colebridge killed, and now David has flown the coop. We've got 11 people either dead or missing and three more very vulnerable out in the field." Brian took a deep breath. He was feeling the pressure. He wasn't sure what to do. "What are the readings now?"

Christopher checked the computers. "The barometric pressure is at 695. Wind is at eight knots. Negative 25 degrees. Storm approaching from the southeast."

"Shit. Chris, get them on the radio again. I don't care if they've found gold, I want them here." He pointed down to the floor. "Now!"

Christopher jumped up from his chair and walked over to the radio.

Lloyd Plummer stormed into the room, breathing heavily. Perspiration beaded on the hairline of his afro. His large hands were shaking. "David is not in the station. I've checked everywhere."

Brian rubbed his temples with his fingers. "Okay. Lloyd, sit down for a second. You look like you're preparing yourself for a heart attack. Thanks for looking."

"No problem," Lloyd whispered, slumping down on the floor, leaning with his back up against the wall next to the doorway. He was still breathing heavily.

Brian turned to Christopher. "Get a hold of them yet?"

"Not yet."

"Keep trying. I hope to God they've already left."

"Me too."

As Brian and Chris labored over the radio, Lloyd closed his eyes. His breathing was slowly returning to normal. He tried to relax, but the events of the last few hours were not allowing him to do so. He was sweating from running around the station, and he was beginning to get cold chills as the cold air from the dome slid through the open doorway. The mixture made him nauseous. Outside, the wind was picking up. Lloyd listened as it swirled around the dome, whispering like phantoms in the night. He was scared.

Lloyd felt a slight breeze, silent and soft, and then something grabbed him around the neck. His eyes popped open as the hands clamped down tighter. The grip was freezing cold, clammy, and inhuman. Lloyd tried to make a noise, but was unable to do so. He couldn't breathe. From across the room, Brian and Chris noticed nothing. The intruder was silent. The freezing touch sent quivering shock waves through his arms, and it stimulated his muscles like an electric current. Lloyd reached out for help, but found nothing. His legs buckled and kicked as he struggled for air. He then felt another hand on the top of his head. The fingers stretched from ear to ear, to his forehead, and all the way to the bottom of his neck. The intruder palmed him like a basketball, easily, and then twisted Lloyd's head 180 degrees to the right. Lloyd felt nothing. His lifeless body slumped to the floor.

The sound and sensation of Lloyd's body hitting the floor grabbed the others' attention. Chris turned in shock and then charged towards the intruder. His attack was too slow. He was grabbed by the throat, kicked in the stomach, and thrown to the floor. Chris swung and kicked wildly, but didn't connect. His glasses had fallen off, and he could see only a massive blur approaching.

It was all happening too quickly for Brian to react. He couldn't move to help.

Two large hands, like packs of ice, pressed against Chris's ears as he was lifted off the floor. The monstrous intruder ripped into his face, gnawing, chewing it beyond recognition. It threw Chris's body against the wall and turned towards Brian, who was backed against the computers with the radio in his hand. He had finally gotten through to Lucas.

"Lucas, this is Brian." His voice was weak and cracking. "Don't come back. Hide. Stay where you are and hide. Something has happened. The station isn't safe." Without waiting for a response, he dropped the receiver and backed himself into the corner, trying to get as far away from that *thing* as he possibly could. Brian knew he had no chance.

Good God, he thought, *is this what we've been chasing?* He watched as the intruder slowly closed in on him. Brian climbed up on one of the computers. It approached slowly, jaws chomping through flesh, opening and closing like a machine. Pieces of skin stuck between its teeth, and blood poured out the corners of its mouth.

Over the radio, Lucas yelled, "Brian . . . Brian. What is going on? What's happening? Brian?"

Brian said nothing. He couldn't. He could only watch *it* approach. He squeezed himself as close to the corner as he could go, and waited for the attack. In the background, Lucas called on. Confusion reigned.

Brian closed his eyes. He knew there was no way out of the research station alive.

He was right.

Chapter 2

2:28 P.M. River City High School, Louisville, Kentucky.

Bill Anderson carefully balanced himself on the top step of the ladder, twisting the eight-foot hallway light into position. He rotated it one last notch to the left. It clicked, and the fixture was filled with a bright burst of light. After snapping the clear lid covering over the fixture and securing it tightly, Bill stepped down off the ladder and folded it up.

Even though it was well below zero outside, the halls were quite warm. After Bill wiped some sweat from his forehead, he glanced at his watch: 2:28 P.M. In a few minutes school would be dismissed. He was very aware of what happened in the halls at the end of the day and knew that because of Christmas vacation the students would hurry even more. After 18 years as maintenance man at River City High, he compared the hallways before Christmas break to the running of the bulls in Pamplona. He made it his goal to stay out of the way.

Just as Bill hung the ladder in the first floor storage closet, principal Mike Greene's voice came over the intercom for closing announcements. After a few minutes of messages that were more than likely falling on deaf ears, Mike wished everyone a good and safe vacation, warned the kids to be careful driving home in the snow, and lastly, told everyone to buckle up. The last was his usual line, something he reminded the students of daily, regardless of the weather.

Realizing he didn't have time to run for cover, Bill slurped a quick drink from the water fountain and backed against the wall across from the principal's office and waited.

Every classroom door opened simultaneously like a faucet, with a flow of students pouring out from each room. Within seconds, the halls were filled with the school's 500 students. All of them ran to their lockers and then scampered for the closest exits, pushing and shoving with excitement.

Everything was running fairly smoothly until, right in front of Bill, one of the jock football players knocked the books out of a freshman's hands, spraying them across the hall and under every passing foot. The tiny, zit-free kid looked more like a fifth grader than a freshman, and his weight hovered just under the century mark. Bobby, nicknamed "Little Boobie" by his classmates, attempted to catch his books in mid-air, but was unsuccessful. Too many legs and larger bodies were in his way. He felt lost in a wilderness of redwoods. Bobby looked up and around, and all he could see were legs and hips of students that were much further along physically than himself. *Damn my parents for making me short,* he thought, *damn them.*

He saw that his algebra book was within reach, and he grabbed for it. While reaching for the book, someone's leg nudged him off balance. He watched as a big, chunky kid seized the opportunity to kick a freshman's book down the hall, and so the boy did with a smile. The boy's meaty leg, which alone probably weighed more than Bobby, reared back and punted the algebra book. It ricocheted off of some other kid's shin before stopping, pages showing, against the far wall next to the main office.

Bobby was mad enough to curse, but he held back. "Dang it," he whispered, now on both knees, reaching for one of his three scattered notebooks. His eyes and cheeks were red, and his mouth and lips tightened with an escaping squeal. He heard hooting and yelling, and even though he wasn't watching, he knew that they were all pointing at him. Worst of all, he heard the laughter, and it hurt. He was afraid to look up as students passed him on both sides. He was frightened and didn't want any of them to see his tears. It would only make matters worse. He couldn't stand to see their faces, none of them. He hated them all, and he hated school because of it.

His notebook was open to the middle, and the pages showing were bent and wrinkled from the traffic, with dirty footprints marking each page. Then Bobby felt a sharp knee connect beside his spine, and the blow sent him down to the floor, causing him to bump his nose against somebody's foot. He looked up, only to see another kid plant both feet on the notebook, one for each page, shuffling them down the hall.

Bobby could hold the tears back no longer. He felt like such a moron, bursting out in tears, sobbing like a baby, right in the middle of the hallway. He was so embarrassed. If it were possible for him to melt like a candle down into the terrazzo floor, he surely would have done it. He wanted to be gone from the school as soon as possible.

Then, out of nowhere, he felt himself being lifted off the floor, as if he were floating up to the ceiling. He felt a strain and a pull under each armpit. When his feet touched the floor again, he was standing with his back up against the wall next to some man he'd seen before, but didn't really know. Regardless, Bobby stared at the man and grinned.

Bobby remembered where he'd seen the man before. It was every day in school. He was the janitor, Bobby was sure of it. Next to Bobby, the janitor man was a giant, standing over six feet tall.

To Bobby, the man didn't seem or look like a janitor at all, but more like a teacher. He was fit and looked fairly strong. He was wearing brown work boots, jeans, and a black-and-white, checkered flannel shirt. Bobby couldn't tell for sure what color his hair was because it was mostly hidden under a red-and-white Cincinnati Reds baseball cap. His sideburns were graying, and his rough face was sprouting with stubble. His hands were strong and thick from years of building, sanding, cleaning, and working with machines.

Bobby liked the janitor man, not only because he came to his hallway rescue, but he was just one of those people that looked pretty cool. Like so many think Harrison Ford is a cool actor, Bobby felt the same for the janitor, although he *was* a bit uncomfortable standing next to a stranger.

The hallways were now relatively clear.

"Thanks, mister." Bobby sniffled and wiped his nose and cheeks, leaving a fresh, slug-like trail of mucous and tears running down the cuff of his white shirt. His voice was high and soft, a voice immediately tagged by fellow students as pre-pubescent.

"My pleasure," Bill said in a deep voice, patting Bobby on the shoulder. "Bunch of punks, aren't they?"

"Yeah." Bobby looked down to the floor. "I'm starting to get used to it though, Mr—"

"It's Bill. Bill Anderson. And you are?"

Bobby wiped his nose against his sleeve again before answering. "My name is Bobby Bates."

"Well, Bobby, it's nice to meet you." Bill shook his tiny hand. "And don't you pay any attention to those losers; they'll get what's coming to them in the end. They'll be working for you some day."

"You gonna beat them up?"

Bill chuckled, thinking to himself that he used to be one of *those losers* in high school. "No, no, no. I'm just saying that what goes around comes around. It's a bit of a cliché, but I believe it to be fairly true."

"If you say so," Bobby mumbled, bending over to gather what was left of his school supplies. Bill picked up a few books for his new friend and handed them to him.

"Here you go, Bobby. I'll get the rest of it when I clean the hallways a little later."

"Thanks. I'm not going to worry about the rest of my stuff. It's just old notes anyway. Now if I had lost a book or two, then my momma would have been steamin' mad. Books aren't cheap."

Bill enjoyed talking with the kid, but work was calling. "Okay, Bobby. The halls are clear for you now. I better get to work so I can get out of here some time tonight."

"Thanks again."

"You're welcome, kiddo. Pleasure meeting you."

"You, too." Bobby smiled from ear to ear. It took him four months, but he'd finally found a friend at school. It wasn't a fellow classmate like he'd hoped, but it was better than nothing. His mother would be proud.

Bill started off in the other direction, but turned back around when Bobby called his name.

"Yeah?"

Bobby was obviously excited about something. Bill could tell by the way he was bouncing on his tiptoes, staring out the window. "Look outside, Bill. Look at the snow. Cool, isn't it?" He couldn't wait to get home and play in what little had fallen. The best thing about it was that he had no homework to spoil his time.

Bill looked out the double-glass front doors, and it was starting to fall fairly hard. "It sure is cool, Bobby," Bill lied. "Bet you can't wait to get home now."

"Nope."

"I hear there's a huge storm coming this weekend, so don't get sick of it too soon. It's looking like it might be around for a while."

"Fine with me," Bobby said with a smile. "I think I might go ice-skating."

Bill forced a smile. He hated the snow and was almost scared of it, but he didn't want the kid to know. To the kid, hating snow was probably a sin. Bill felt like telling Bobby how he really felt about the snow. *Look here, you little weasel. Bad things happen in the snow. My wife was murdered, mangled, and shredded during a snowstorm, and I was accused of the crime, and because of it I've been working as a damn janitor for the past 18 years of my life. They said I stabbed her ten times with a steak knife. My wife, kiddo. I would never. I started drinking again, too, all because of the fucking snow, that annoying white shit that sent my life to hell after years of putting it together. Bobby, I'm always going to be a recovering alcoholic, and the bad years can never be taken away.* Bill felt like telling the kid everything, but held back. His years of depression were over. The nightmares, dreams, and visions were gone. The trials and interrogations were over, but it was still impossible to let go of the memories. He felt like picking Bobby up and shaking some sense into him for jarring up those dreaded memories, but he held back. *The poor kid is excited,* he told himself, *give him a break.*

"Hope it snows 100 feet," Bobby said, spreading his arms out wide, as if he were actually giving an accurate display of 100 feet with his hands. "I'm gonna build me the biggest dang snowman you ever seen. I can't wait."

SNOWMAN.

Bill's face went blank, and he said nothing. Backing against the wall, he could see the bloody word written on the back lining of the couch. He remembered. He could never forget the unexplainable. The bird. The feather. The cold. Blood, her blood, running, dripping, drying . . .

"What's wrong, Mr. Anderson? Don't you like to build snowmen?"

Bill hesitated before answering. "Y . . . yeah, Bobby, great. That sounds like fun."

Bobby turned back and ran for his locker.

Bill watched him run, so innocently and carefree, down the hall. He wanted to leave and get home before the snow got too bad. It was already 3:00, and the school still needed to be cleaned. He was glad that the building was clearing out. He didn't feel like speaking to anyone, not now. An urge was building. A need. He wanted a drink, and for the first time in many years he felt he needed one to drown his sorrows.

Fight the memories. Resist the temptation. He was disappointed in himself for feeling the *need,* but the *need* and the *want* were uncontrollable at times. The actual *doing*, he had learned to control and resist. He took a deep breath and closed his eyes for a few seconds. *Fight it, Bill.* It wasn't as if he had a stash hidden in the school, but he did at home, and the *need* he felt now was more powerful than any he had felt in the last 18 years. He had to rid himself of the *need* before he got home. *The past is not an excuse,* he told himself. *The bad memories can't win. Resist. Settle. Push away.*

Bill grabbed a dust-mop out of the storage closet, sprayed it with Endust, and walked down to the end of the hall. He was worried. For nearly 18 years his disease had improved, and for the last few, the sight of alcohol was not the temptation it used to be. He thought he was almost fully recovered, but the sudden *want* was again uncontrollable. His past. His memories. His need. His medicine.

He pushed them away, for now.

Chapter 3

11:55 A.M. Core Sampling Site, South Pole, Antarctica.

Only 50 yards away from the geographical south pole, Lucas Bergman and his two assistants, Roy Robbins and Phillip Heismann, took the advice from the research station, and they stayed put. They weren't exactly hiding; their work was going too well to stop, but they were more cautious after hearing the message. First it had been urgent for them to return, and then only minutes later, Brian was demanding that they stayed where they were.

Why? Lucas didn't know. Hide from what? He didn't know that either. There were a lot of things he didn't know about project WHITE OUT. He was sure that he was involved in a valid aspect of the project because core sampling was a very standard part of gathering scientific and biological research, but he had his doubts about exactly *why* he was doing the research. He was doing the same type of research that the NSF (National Science Foundation) had been doing on Antarctica for years before SCARE had pushed them out, but Lucas couldn't help but wonder whether his work was only a decoy for something else. The leaders of the project were always so secretive, always hiding something, and now, Lucas wondered if that *something* was causing the problems that were breaking the project apart. There was only one way to find out.

Lucas had tried calling them back on the radio, but couldn't get through. The connection sounded fine, but no one answered. He was not only confused, but now deeply worried. With each passing minute his mind was wandering further away from the results of their samples and closer to a possible problem at hand. Something had happened at the station, but for too long his mind didn't allow him to believe it. Now he did, and he felt guilty for not responding earlier. He would not stay put. He would not hide. The time to return was now.

Lucas ducked under the portable canvas shelter and jumped down into the 3-foot-deep drilling pit. The slightly warmer temperature under the shelter helped to protect the drills, but it was also cold enough to prevent the melting of any ice cores. To his right, Roy was moving a core off the balance and into the storage freezer. Phillip was at the front of the pit, carefully extracting a core from a 10-cm. hole in the ice.

Phillip heard Lucas next to him and looked up. He stared at a mirror image of himself. With all three dressed in orange polar gear, black toboggans, brown boots, goggles, and black gloves, they all looked the same. Phillip saw that Lucas was staring around the pit, thinking. Something seemed to be troubling him. Lucas turned away from Phillip and walked over to Roy, who was now securing the ice core in the freezer.

"Roy," Lucas said, touching him on the shoulder.

Roy jerked around and looked up. "Yeah?"

"Start packing up, we're going back to the station."

"I thought they said—"

"I know what they said. I'm asking you to listen to what I'm saying."

Roy was startled.

"Sorry, Roy. Didn't mean to jump at you like that, but really, we need to get going."

"Sure, right away."

Lucas turned towards Phillip. Unaware that he was being watched, Phillip pulled the wireline drill from the hole and removed a meter-long ice core from the heated annulus at the tip of the drill. Slowly he placed the core to the side and dropped the drill back into the hole. "What's the depth?"

"Ten meters." Phillip sat down on the ice with his legs wrapped around the opening of the small hole. "Nothing like the Russians at Komsomolskaya, but hey, we only have a little under 900 more meters to go if we want to catch them."

"Believe me, we don't. It's incredible how much time and money they're wasting digging that far. It's not worth it."

"I hear at Vostok station near the Pole of Inaccessibility they've reached more than 2100 meters."

"I don't doubt it." He shook his head. "I don't know what they're trying to do, digging for the center of the earth, trying to find frozen and preserved dinosaurs from the Great Southern land mass, or just simply seeing how far that thing will go, but there *are* better ways to study climatic and environmental history. Nobody with a brain goes more than 500 meters anymore." He paused, and his voice decreased to a whisper. He spoke to himself. "Unless they're searching for the same thing we are, whatever *it* is." *Probably a bunch of nothing*, he thought.

"You say something, boss?" Phillip asked.

"Uh, no, just talking to myself." Lucas watched as Phillip started to ease the drill back into the ice. He held up his hand. "Wait. We're packing up."

The drill hit the bottom. Phillip looked up. "Now?"

"Yes."

While he was talking, the drill was extracting another core. It dug into the ice slowly and then suddenly sunk down as if something had pulled on it from below. The top of the drill slipped in Phillip's hand. "What the—"

"What is it?" Lucas leaned over the hole.

"The drill, it slipped. It was digging a fresh core and then—" he stopped to pull the drill back out of the hole, "—and then it went down, as if there was nothing left to drill into."

Lucas knelt down. "Air pocket?"

"I think so." Phillip pulled the drill completely out of the hole. Only a quarter of a core was positioned in the annulus. He stared down into the hole. "It's an air pocket all right. A damn big one at that." He moved away from the hole, allowing Lucas to look.

"Jesus." Lucas sat back up. "Looks deep. Come on. Let's take a look."

Roy saw Phillip and Lucas climb out of the pit and out from under the shelter. After placing another ice core in the freezer, he followed them.

Outside the digging site, the three of them circled the shelter, looking for anything out of the ordinary. On the south side of the shelter, a small hill of ice stood about seven feet high. A jagged hole, about a foot-and-a-half in diameter, was located near the bottom. Darkness was held within.

"How didn't we see that before?" Phillip asked.

"We weren't looking for it. We never came over to this side," Lucas said.

"What's wrong?" Roy asked, approaching them from behind.

Lucas answered. "We found an air pocket underneath the pit. A big one."

Phillip shined his flashlight down the hole. "It's not the same hole. I was over 30 feet into the ice when I found the pocket. This one is only about ten feet down, if that much. We'd also be able to see some light from our hole above, but I don't see any." He paused, shining the light inside, checking out the bottom or floor of what appeared to be a room of some sort. "Looks like a cave. Not natural though; someone made this puppy. The floor appears to be smooth, and as far as I can tell, it has four perfect corners. Looks like the work of a pretty damn good carpenter, or sculptor in this case." He slid his feet down the opening. "I'm going in."

Before Lucas could say a word in protest, Phillip had already fallen into the cave. Immediately he called up. "Send down the flashlight."

Just then, Lucas slid down the opening and crashed to the floor of the cave, nearly landing on top of Phillip.

"You have the flashlight?"

Lucas shook his head. "I thought you had it." He felt the walls with his hands. Even through his gloves, he could tell the surface was uneven. They were smooth in some places, but rough and jagged in others. He looked up through the opening. "Roy, don't you dare come down here, or we won't ever be getting back up."

Roy didn't answer.

"Roy."

They waited but heard nothing.

Phillip walked under the hole. "Roy, send down the flashlight. Don't leave us, you sack of shit."

They saw his feet drooping over the edge of the opening. Lucas raised his arms. "Roy, what the hell are you thinking? Don't come down here without hooking up a rope or something, and why aren't you answering?"

The legs looked lifeless, and they were suddenly removed from the opening as if they had been pulled.

Lucas sighed. "Roy, the flashlight."

Roy didn't answer. After waiting a few more seconds, they saw something rolling from the opening, descending quickly into the cave. It wasn't a flashlight. It was too large, too round. Lucas caught it in his outstretched hands.

Using the light coming from the opening above, he was able to see what he was holding. The object was covered in blood. It had hair, ears, a nose and mouth, and two eyes. Lucas screamed, quickly dropping Roy's head to the floor of the cave. He stumbled backwards, covering his mouth with his gloves.

Phillip sensed what it was, but asked anyway. "What is it?"

Lucas didn't answer. He fell into the corner, knocking his head against the back wall.

The flashlight came down through the opening and hit the ice below. Trembling, Phillip picked it up and turned it on. He shined it in the corner closest to the hole. Roy's head rested in the corner with his eyes open and staring. Muscle tissue, arteries and veins stuck out from the top of the neck. The head hadn't been severed or cut, but torn, viciously torn. Roy's goggles and toboggan had been removed. Phillip screamed. He stopped when he saw two legs in the opening again. The legs wore boots, but they were not the same kind Roy had been wearing. The legs were larger, longer, and they swayed in the lit opening.

Phillip backed away, slowly looking around until his back hit a wall. He heard noise and then laughter. It was Roy. Roy's severed head was laughing. The eyes stared at him from the corner of the cave, and the mouth was dripping blood. It spoke. *No place to run to now, Phillip. No place to hide. He's coming. HE'S COMING!* Roy's eyes closed, but the mouth was still producing a blood-choked laughter.

Phillip couldn't believe what he was seeing. He thought he was hallucinating. He had to be. The walls sounded like they were moving. He looked down towards Lucas.

Lucas stared blankly ahead, in a daze, saying nothing.

Something then emerged from the opening, landing perfectly on the ice. The figure had long hair. Phillip could see that it had on a black hat and goggles. It approached slowly, methodically.

Phillip stepped to the side, tripping over Lucas's legs. Falling to the ground, he supported himself with his right elbow. He shined the flashlight with his free hand. The light gave him brief glimpses of the walls. They *were* moving.

"Oh, my God."

The figure stood directly above them.

The voice returned from the corner, Roy's voice. *He's no longer coming. He's here. HE'S HERE. GET OUT WHILE YOU STILL CAN!*

Lucas was in a trance, staring at Roy's head in the corner of the cave, watching as the lips moved. Lucas seemed to be hiding in a world of his own, hiding in a world that was just not as frightening as the one he was presently in, and he was sure that nothing was real anymore. *Roy's head cannot be talking,* he repeatedly reminded himself.

"Lucas, the walls," Phillip cried, "look at the walls."

Lucas didn't look.

"Th . . . they're alive."

An enormous shadow covered them both, as the figure closed in. Lucas continued to stare at Roy's head. The lips were no longer moving. The laughter had stopped. The eyes were now closed. Phillip screamed, but only for a second. A cold hand squeezed against his neck. Death quickly followed for both of them.

A hundred yards away from the cave, David Johnson could hear Phillip's final scream. Then it stopped. The thing with the long white hair had entered the cave and killed them. David was sure of it. It had killed everyone now. For nearly 30 years agents of SCARE had been searching for ways to locate, test, study, and possibly control this beast, and finally, David was the first person ever to see it. Until now, even though he believed in his work and trusted the ideas behind project WHITE OUT, he had never truly believed it to be anything more than a myth. The project itself was strongly based on myth, but now he had his proof. The beast was reality, and David's ambition for the project's success was gone. The writer, Leroy McCalister, had been right after all. The snow beast was real. After seeing what it had done to Roy's head, David no longer wanted to capture, test, or control it. Nothing could ever control it. He saw what had happened at the science station. Project WHITE OUT was over. He was the only one left now. He was sure of it. He had no place to go. Nothing seemed safe.

He felt like a madman. He felt strong and powerful, but at the same time weak, hungry, and vulnerable. He could still feel Sampson's swollen neck in his grip. He could see the bulging eyes. He could hear the skull cracking against the wall. *Why couldn't I stop myself? Why didn't I let go of him, and let him live. I didn't want to, though, not at the time. I think I really wanted him dead. I am now a killer, a murderer, no different than the thing with the long white hair. What is happening to me?*

Alone. David felt alone, and it scared him. The beast scared him and was only 100 yards away. Out of touch with reality, his feelings and emotions, David acted on pure instinct. He was a killer. He felt like one, but wasn't sure now if he liked it. He had to get away from this place, far, far away. His lips were chapped, cracked and bleeding. His hair and eyebrows were crusting hard with snow. His skin was tight and ready to crack and bleed.

Severely under-dressed, without skis, food, or water, David set off across the ice, running. Where? He didn't know. He wouldn't last for long. He couldn't. Not with that *thing* out there. He just ran to get away. He had to get away from everything; the station, the death, the cave, the beast, himself. He was going crazy, trying to run away from what he was becoming.

Chapter 4

5:20 P.M. River City High School
1 Inch

Bill finished buffing the lobby shortly after 5 p.m. It was the last job on his agenda, and finally, it was time to go home. The squeaking wheels echoed off the walls the entire way as Bill pushed the buffer machine down the hallway. After cramming the buffer into the storage closet, he headed down to his office to get his things.

The work was soothing. Boring at times and a bit monotonous, but soothing nevertheless. Working alone, he was left to nothing but his own thoughts. It gave him time to himself, and so he used the last two hours to settle down after what had happened after school. The memories were still in the front of his mind, but the need and want for his medicine were gone. He was calm.

Located on the basement level with the cafeteria, Bill's office was almost hidden from the regular school crowd. It was actually the school's workshop, or as everyone called it: The Shop.

Bill walked past the gym lobby and down the cafeteria stairwell. At the bottom of the stairs, the cafeteria was on the right, and the shop was through a few more doors to the left. Passing two more storage closets, Bill stopped in front of a huge yellow door marked Boiler Room. It was the room where the normal school scenery turned dark and grim. Bill pushed the heavy door with his right shoulder and entered the boiler room. It was divided into two different levels, an upper level used for storage and a lower level where the boiler was actually located.

The room was very hot, poorly lit, and cluttered with junk. The wall just inside the door to the right was stacked high with empty beer kegs, Coke and Pepsi cases, mop buckets, an old stripping machine, and God only knew what else hiding back in the corners. Bill was always afraid to check.

A layer of dust about a quarter of an inch thick covered the concrete floor on both levels. To the left and down a small flight of stairs was the lower level and the boiler itself. It was loud and cranky as it pushed massive amounts of heat throughout the entire school. It was the size of a tank, with dozens of thick pipes shooting out like cannons into the heating system. Two 50-gallon drums lined the far wall like giant bales of hay. One was filled with floor wax and the other with stripper. Broken desks, mops, an old scoreboard, and scattered pieces of wood were spread out all over the floor. Bill was willing to wait to clean the boiler room until he really had to, or at least until the fire marshal came to inspect.

The room beside the boiler room was filled with paint and broken desks, all covered with a thick layer of dust. The Shop was the next room to the left.

After pulling the doors and entering his office, Bill was immediately hit with a fresh smell of wood chips and a cool breeze. The smell of the wood was normal, but the cool breeze wasn't. After turning on the lights, he walked past his desk and work tables, staring straight ahead at the double doors to The Dungeon. They were open. It wasn't a dungeon as one would picture during medieval times, but simply the name given to the underground tunnels and storage areas below the school. There were three sections to The Dungeon: a front section that was filled with decades of old junk and hills of broken desks, a corridor running north-south, and a corridor running east-west, both of which ran parallel beneath the hallways of the school. The north-south corridor met the east-west at a 90-degree angle, giving the school the shape of the letter 'L'.

The Dungeon was Bill's least favorite place in the school. It wasn't that he had favorite places in the school, because none of his work was really *fun,* but work in The Dungeon was always saved until last, if gotten to at all. The work he had to do down in The Dungeon was definitely not soothing, but very stressful. It was dark, damp, dirty; it smelled of mothballs, and as Bill would honestly admit, it was downright scary at times. The darkness, the smell, the leaky pipes, and various other unknown noises were enough to drive one crazy if working alone. At night, Bill avoided

The Dungeon at all costs. Fortunately, he only had to work down there a few times a year, whenever he'd have to go searching for something lost, or fix an underground pipe or radiator line. Grabbing something out of the first section was quite common, but he only entered the corridors during emergency situations.

Rats. Bill hated rats, and he'd seen enough of them rummaging around the dark shadows of The Dungeon to know to always keep the doors locked. He wasn't about to let The Dungeon scum scamper out of its boundaries and into the school. He always made sure The Dungeon doors were locked, but for some reason, now they were both wide open.

Bill walked slowly up the four concrete steps and looked inside the first section. It was dark and a bit colder than normal, but he noticed nothing strange or unusual. Given the bitter temperatures outside, it was not at all surprising that The Dungeon, too, was colder. Everything seemed untouched. The junk was still junk, and the broken desks remained broken. He prayed that no rats had escaped. Then an idea popped into his head. *Maybe the rats pushed their way out.* He quickly dismissed it. It was stupid. Nonsense. *Those doors would be way too heavy*, he thought, *unless there were hundreds of them. No, that is stupid, too.* Bill turned around and scanned The Shop for rodents. Finding and hearing nothing, he locked The Dungeon doors, pulled on them just to make sure, and jumped off the small set of steps.

At his desk, Bill pulled the middle drawer out. His keys slid, jingling, to the front. He picked them up, shoved them into his jeans, and then reached for his coat.

It wasn't there. He remembered hanging it on the back of his chair in the morning, but it wasn't there now. His red Land's-End ski jacket he'd gotten last Christmas from Amy was gone, vanished.

What the hell? Bill thought, scratching his head under the bill of his cap, wondering how he was going to tell Amy that he had lost the jacket. Visually, he retraced his steps. *I put it right here this morning, went to work in the cafeteria, haven't been down here since lunch, when I remembered seeing it, and now it's gone.* He shook his head. *Doesn't make a damn bit of sense.*

He pulled his chair out from the desk and noticed that his brown leather gloves were on the seat. *Somebody stole it. Why would someone take the jacket and leave the gloves? They were inside the pockets. Why would they take them out?* The thought of him losing the jacket was frustrating, but the thought of someone stealing it roiled him even more. He couldn't figure it out. He had images of a hoard of rats carrying it off, scurrying down one of the dark corridors of The Dungeon to their secret haven or hideaway.

"Strange," he whispered.

He checked and rechecked under and around his desk, but the jacket was nowhere to be found. After giving The Shop a quick glance, he gave up, locked the doors, and walked back upstairs.

Principal Mike Greene closed the door to his office and jiggled the knob to make sure it was locked. He placed his beige Sherlock-Holmes hat on his bald head and buttoned his black overcoat all the way up to his neck. After sipping a drink from the water fountain and wiping the dribble from his lower lip, he turned towards the main office and flipped off the hallway lights.

Mike heard footsteps coming from behind, so he turned around. "Jeez," he mumbled, stumbling backwards with his hand against his chest. "Bill. I didn't know you were still here."

"Actually, I'm on my way out, too."

"You startled me."

Bill laughed. "Sorry. Didn't mean to. I thought you heard me coming."

"I wish I would have." Mike opened a set of wooden doors, and they walked into the front foyer of the school, just inside the glass double-doors. He looked at Bill, noticing that he had on a pair of gloves, but no coat. "Is this a new fashion statement?"

"Pardon?"

"It's 12 degrees outside, and you're hardly wearing anything. Those are nice gloves, but they are limited in what they can do for the rest of the body."

"I can't find my jacket. That red jacket I got from Amy last year. Gone."

"You lose it?"

"I must have. I don't understand how, though. I wasn't downstairs all day to move it, and I remember leaving it on the chair this morning."

"Maybe someone stole it."

"The thought crossed my mind, but I could have sworn I had those doors locked all day." He paused, staring out the front doors at the falling snow. The rats again popped into his head, running down one of the corridors with his jacket. "And who would go down to the basement, anyway?"

"You'd be surprised. The smokers would sneak anywhere to light one up. Maybe they were tired of freezing their balls off outside and went searching for shelter."

Bill shrugged.

Mike asked, "Is there any way into The Shop other than those doors?"

"You can get in there from The Dungeon, and those doors were open, but—"

"Maybe a student got in that way."

"No, that'd be impossible. The only way into The Dungeon is from The Shop."

"I don't know what to tell you, Bill. You've looked everywhere?"

"I think so."

"It's colder than a witch's titty out there."

"I'll be fine. I don't have far to run to get to my truck, and, hey," he clapped his gloved hands together, "I still got my gloves."

Mike unlocked the door and smiled. "Good point." He started laughing.

"What?"

"Oh, I just remembered something that happened this morning."

"With one of the kids?"

"No."

"And it was funny?"

"Well, now it is, but at the time it was pretty damn weird."

"Well?"

Mike chuckled again, leaving the keys to dangle in the lock. He leaned against the foyer wall and told his story. "You know that old street-man that hangs around here every once in a while?"

"Snaggletooth?"

"Yeah. I was getting out of my car this morning, oh, I'd say about seven, and out of the blue, he came up to me. He was drunk as a damn skunk, and those two teeth he's got growing out of his upper gum were showing more than normal. I think maybe they're growing. Well, anyway, he was wearing a bandanna around his head and nothing but rags from head to toe. He stunk something awful, too. Man, I could have smelled the alcohol on his breath from a mile away. Scary." Mike shook his head, reliving the incident.

"He looked worse than normal?"

"Well, he always looks like shit. We all know that. But this morning he was acting extra strange. As usual, I felt sorry for him at first. That is until he decided to talk."

Bill was shocked. "Snaggletooth talks?"

"There's always a first time for everything. He talked, and boy, did he have a mouthful. He ran up to my car. I guess he had a wild hair up his ass, and it was itching him pretty good to talk to someone. He was yelling and screaming things, crazy things about the world coming to an end. He was yelling about the devil coming to rule the world, and that he'd seen him, and Armageddon, and you know, just a bunch of stupid crap like that."

Bill tried not to laugh. "I can't believe he talked. I thought he was a mute. What did you tell him?"

"I was afraid he was going to wake up the whole neighborhood, so I calmly told him to leave the school's property or I was going to call the police."

"I'm sure my brother would have enjoyed answering that call," Bill said.

"He backed off after that."

"What a mess."

"He was walking away, and then he turned around again and let out a few more choice words. He started yacking about the coming of the year 2000, the millennium, and how the fires of hell are going to boil over."

Bill laughed and shook his head.

"And then he told me to start preparing for Doomsday. He told me to start praying."

"Did you?"

"Not yet. I think I might wait until I get home." Mike pushed the front doors open. "Let's get out of here."

"Good idea."

Mike flipped the collar up on his coat and locked the door. "Can't wait to tell my wife about this."

"I bet Kathleen will get a kick out of his expert opinions."

The sky was cloudy, gray, and quickly turning to night. The temperature was flirting with the single digits now that the sun was going down, and the wind-chill was well below zero. Bill was immediately covered with goosebumps as the bitter, stinging wind slithered in and out the openings of his shirt. His heart ached, and the hairs in his nose turned to little slivers of glass.

"Mike, I'd love to stay and chat, but I'm freezing to death." He rubbed his hands up and down each arm, trying to keep warm. It wasn't working very well.

"Okay, Bill. You have a good break and give that lovely daughter of yours a hug for me."

"The same to Kathleen."

"Will do." Mike walked over to his white '92 Pontiac Grand Prix. The parking lot was getting slick. "Oh, Bill. Don't forget about the Christmas party here Friday night, weather pending, of course. You coming?"

"I'll have to wait and see. Amy is coming in town with her roommate on Friday, so I'll have to play it by ear."

"Bring them along."

Bill waved and jogged to his truck.

Mike ducked inside his car and started the engine. His windshield wipers struggled over the thin sheet of ice at first, but after a few seconds it broke it down and cleared it away. He backed out and pulled away to the sound of crunching snow under his tires. A large rectangle of pavement could be seen where his car had been parked.

Bill made it to his truck without falling. It was the only vehicle left in the parking lot, and everything was covered with an inch of snow. The lot was a solid sheet of white, and the grass all around was quickly disappearing under the covering.

Chapter 5

5:20 P.M. University Of Michigan, Ann Arbor
Helen Newberry Hall, Central Campus

Its bright blue eyes were cold and piercing, shining down on her body, cutting like knives. She tried to free herself from its vice-like grip, but its hands would not budge. Icicle fingers dug deeply into her fleshy biceps, pulling her closer, and closer, and . . . She tried to scream, but nothing came out. It laughed an evil laugh, and her naked body went numb. A smile formed on its pale face, and its razor-sharp teeth sparkled like diamonds in the pulsing green light that surrounded them. For the first time she heard it speak, and the voice was scratchy and deep. Don't bother screaming, Amy. All voices are mute down here in Iceville. I'm all you've got. Inside a cave of moving shadows, the walls seemed to be shifting. Her head was spinning. She felt the ice pressing and sticking against her bare back, but at the same time she felt the fire within and all around her. It pulled her close and whispered into her ear. Sssshhh. Give in to your fears, Amy. She screamed a silent scream, but couldn't resist its strength and power. Rolling on top of her, it forced her against the cold, icy floor. Strands from its long white hair tickled her exposed neck and chest, like ants running wild. Don't be afraid, Amy. This won't hurt a bi . . .

Amy Anderson snapped out of her nightmare, smacking the back of her head against the hard, stone wall of her dorm room. She caught herself before falling off her bed. Her hands shook, and her body trembled, inside and out. She could still feel the hands as they flowed like ice-cubes across the curves of her body. She could still hear the voice. *All voices are mute in Iceville, Amy.* She looked up, and through her blurry eyes, scanned the room for her roommate. To be alone right now would drive her insane. She felt better after placing her feet on the floor, and running her toes through the loose entanglements on the gray carpet. Sitting on her bed with her hands resting in her lap, she was breathing much too rapidly to be considered normal. She was not alone though; Kathy Harris, her roommate of four years and best friend, was standing beside the bed, confused and concerned.

"Amy?" She placed her hands on Amy's shoulders. "You okay?"

"Y . . . yeah," she whispered, wiping tears from the corners of her bloodshot eyes. Her voice was weak and broken.

"You sure? You don't look okay."

"I'm fine," she insisted, although her tone of voice was not convincing. "Just a nightmare."

"Must have been pretty damn rough to get this reaction out of you. I've never in four years seen you this rattled before."

Amy stood up from the bed and took a deep breath. "Haven't had one that bad in a while," she said, blowing her nose in a tissue.

"Do you want to talk about it?"

"No," Amy said quickly. "No, thanks. I'd rather not." She forced a smile and wiped her face again. "I'm fine, really."

"What about your head? You smacked it against that wall pretty hard."

Amy felt for a bump. She found a small one forming near the back of her skull, but there was no blood. "It's fine. I do have a headache now." She put her left hand on top of her head. "Got any aspirin?"

"Yeah, just a second." Kathy walked over to her desk and searched the drawers for her bottle. When she turned back around to Amy, she held two white tablets in her palm. "Here you go."

"Thanks." Amy gulped them down with a can of flat Pepsi, and then closed her eyes as the pills slid down her esophagus like pebbles. She took another deep breath that grew into a yawn. "What time is it?"

"Almost 5:30 P.M."

"It's that late? Why'd you let me nap for so long?"

"I figured you needed it. You were up until four last night studying for organic."

"Don't remind me," Amy sighed, "I bombed it."

"Bullshit," Kathy said, laughing. "Don't even give me that crap. You've never bombed a test in your life, and you know it."

"Neither have you."

"Right, but I'm not the one who after every test *thinks* they failed it and then ends up getting an A. I always *know* that I'm getting an A. You see, I'm confident, and confidence is the key."

"Well, I wish I had it, but I don't." Amy tossed the Pepsi can into the garbage basket beside her bed and walked over to her desk. "We going to the library?"

"Definitely. I've got that damn anatomy final tomorrow morning at 8:30. I'll be up all night."

"Isn't that your last final?"

"Yes, thank God. What time is your physics final?"

"Nine."

"Aren't you lucky. Get to sleep an extra half-hour."

"If I get to sleep at all. I don't think I'll ever be ready for this exam."

"There you go again," Kathy said, shaking her head. "You know, other students hate people like you."

"Oh, well." Amy looked into her mirror above her desk. She pushed her shoulder-length blonde hair out of her face and tucked it behind her ears, securing it in place with a purple-and-red Mickey-Mouse baseball hat. She stared at herself momentarily, disgusted with what she saw. Her blue eyes were glossy, and the bags under them were getting heavier. She needed sleep. Finals were hell, she was convinced of that. Her face was a little pale, but other than that she was okay. She didn't feel it at the moment, but she was very pretty.

"You look fine, Amy." Kathy waited by the door with her school bag hanging over her right shoulder. "Let's go." Kathy had on a pair of gray sweatpants and a blue Michigan sweatshirt. Her coat was old, long, and blue, with the texture of a rug. Fashion was not her main concern.

"I feel gross."

"Amy, you look gross, too."

"See."

"I'm kidding." Kathy shook her head. "Amy, you're one of the most attractive girls on campus. You look fine, like always. Or at least that's what *he* said."

Amy picked up her school bag and coat and walked towards the door. "Who's *he*?"

Kathy ignored the question. "Now if you looked like me, then you might have something to complain about. Let's go."

"And *you* were telling *me* about confidence."

"How can I not feel insecure. Look at me. I look like a guy." Kathy closed the door to their room, and they moved down the hall.

"You *don't* look like a guy."

"Never mind that. Let's grab a bite to eat before we hit the books."

"Sounds good. I'm starving."

Amy and Kathy were both 22 years old and ready to graduate in the spring, Amy with a degree in biology and Kathy with one in chemistry. Although their personalities were quite different, they had been friends since the first day they'd met freshman year.

Kathy was extroverted and never shied away from telling what was on her mind. Straight from the streets of New York City, she arrived in Michigan on a full academic scholarship. Orphaned at the age of four, she spent much of her childhood in and out of different foster-homes, always ending up at the orphanage. It was a rough way to grow up, but she was determined to do something positive with her life. Forced to mature at a young age, she stayed clear of the vices of the streets and buried herself in the books. After graduating valedictorian in a class of over 500 students, her lifelong goal of college was realized.

Kathy fidgeted in her uncomfortable library chair, looking up from her anatomy notes at Amy. Amy was two chairs down. Her physics book was open, but her eyes were elsewhere. She stared blankly into the rows of books across the room.

It wasn't all that unusual for Amy to stare off into the distance and bury herself in her thoughts. Kathy would have given much more than a penny for Amy's thoughts, many times in the past four years.

Amy was an introvert, very shy, and comfortable with keeping to herself. There was a lot she had to hide and a lot that others didn't need to know. It wasn't that she was ashamed of her past, but she *was* frightened of it at times. The memories haunted her. They were memories that no one knew she had, and she preferred to keep it that way. She knew much more than her father thought she did and remembered what no one had ever seen or fully believed. She was the only witness, but she was also only two years old. She wasn't *supposed* to remember, but she did.

Like Kathy, Amy had a rough life growing up; in fact, that was their bond; they were both survivors. Unlike Kathy, Amy had two loving parents, that is, until one was suddenly taken away from her. Struggling through the alcoholism and court trials for the next two years after Mary was killed had been difficult for both Bill and Amy, but despite the dysfunctional environment, Bill had been able to raise Amy with love. She was very young and often confused with her father's mood swings, but had learned to be supportive in her own right. Like Kathy, Amy had also matured quickly. Growing up, Amy didn't know what it was like to be addicted to a drug or to crave something that was not allowed, but she knew and understood that the feelings were real because they were happening to her father. She understood that he was struggling and in need of support, so she stood by him every step of the way. She was the crutch that her mother had been for him only years before. Amy realized that her father was not perfect, and she liked him that way. She loved her father for the man he was and the man he was becoming. The periods of sobriety lengthened, and as Amy grew older, their bond strengthened. She supported him and helped him during his recovery, and he did his very best to give her every opportunity to succeed in life.

For Amy, growing up without a mother had been difficult, but Bill had tried to display enough love for the both of them, and for that, Amy was ultimately grateful. She had helped with the lawn, the leaves, cleaning and cooking, and they worked together on everything as a team. She had helped take care of their dog, Gus, and Bill helped her with her homework. They had laughed and cried a lot, trying hard not always to *forget* the past, but rather, learning to live with it. They enjoyed spending time with one another, playing board games, watching television, renting movies and eating buttered popcorn, talking, and living. Bill had raised her with limited finances, but he had raised her well and couldn't have been more proud of the person she had become.

Many of Amy's fellow college students thought she was conceited because she didn't talk all that much, didn't like to do all that much, and wasn't involved in a sorority, but it wasn't vanity at all. She simply had learned to accept being alone or with her own little clique of friends. Before college, her father had always been her closest friend. Being cheated out of the special mother-daughter relationship, she cherished the relationship she had with her father, never taking for granted the fact that she only had one parent left. Bill was not perfect, and never would be, but he was the most important person in Amy's life, and *always* would be.

As Amy stared off into the thousands of books, Kathy wondered what was on her mind. They were on the fourth floor and nobody else was around. "Hey, Amy."

Amy jerked her head to the side. "Yeah?"

"What's on your mind?"

"Just thinking."

"About what?"

"Ah, it's nothing really."

Kathy was far from convinced that it was nothing. "Amy, come on. You can tell me anything. You *know* that. You've been acting strange ever since you had that nightmare, and you won't tell me anything about it. You said you were starving earlier, yet you never touched your food in the cafeteria." She hesitated. "Sure you don't want to talk?"

"Yes, I'm sure. Let's just forget about it."

Kathy paused, and then looked back down to her notes, wishing that she could crack Amy's shell or get her to lower her defenses. It wouldn't be easy. Kathy focused her attention back to the muscles of the cat. Her mind wandered.

"Kathy."

Surprised, Kathy looked at Amy, who was now sitting in the seat right beside her. "Yeah?"

Amy stared at Kathy for a few seconds before speaking. "Do you believe in . . .," Amy stopped. "Oh, never mind. You'd think I was crazy."

"Dammit, Amy. Spill it. I'm not going to think you're crazy, and I'm not letting you off the hook this time. Talk to me."

"Okay," she paused. "Okay. Do you believe in hell?" She asked it quickly, still not totally sure what had possessed her to start the conversation.

Kathy chuckled, a little stunned by the question. She hid her smile, realizing that Amy was quite serious. "Well, actually I do. Why do you ask?"

"What do you think it is?" Amy asked.

"This is really bothering you, isn't it?"

"It has been on my mind a lot lately, yes. What do you think hell is?" she asked again.

Kathy closed her notebook and turned in her chair so that she was now directly facing Amy. "I needed a break anyway." She glanced up to the ceiling and rubbed her hands through her short, brown hair. "What do I think hell is? Oh, boy, let's see."

"You don't have to answer if you don't want to."

"I'll answer it. Just had to think for a second. This wasn't in my notes, you know."

Amy wasn't amused with her making light of the subject.

Kathy saw that she was serious, worried about something, and so she answered. "I think hell is the place that we fear the most. It's a place or state of existence where all of our fears climax, and we can never escape. Never, no matter how hard we try. Day after day you'd be surrounded by things that you hate and fear the most."

"Example?"

"An example?" Kathy was starting to feel a little uncomfortable. "I don't know, maybe if you hate to do homework, that's all you do in hell is non-stop papers and homework."

"Be serious, Kathy. Describe what you think hell is."

"Okay, okay. I guess I'd have to go with the obvious description of hell and say it's a very hot place with fire. Lots and lots of boiling fire and devils and stuff."

"Why fire? Why is it *obviously* fire? Why does everyone assume it's fire . . . and . . . and hot."

"I guess because of what we hear growing up." Kathy felt like she was on the defensive, bombarded by all the odd questions. "The term—burn in hell—comes to mind. Shit, Amy, I don't know. Why all these questions all of a sudden? I feel like I'm being attacked."

"I'm sorry, it's just that . . ." she trailed off.

"Just what, Amy? Why this sudden infatuation with hell?"

"Not infatuation, Kathy. Believe me, talking about this scares me to death. I hate it. I'm just looking for some answers, that's all."

"To what?"

Amy said nothing.

"Look. I can give you my views and my opinions, but to the question 'what is hell', that's something I don't think we can give a concrete answer for. Like I said, I think hell is different for everyone, and for me and I'd say most other people, we think of fire when we hear about hell. I'm not sure what else you want me to say."

Amy buried her face in her hands briefly and then slowly raised her head. Her eyes were red and wet. "Kathy, please don't think I'm going mad. I didn't expect that you'd understand."

"Understand what?"

"Hell is not fire at all. It's real, and it's a place covered with ice. Hell is ice, Kathy. I've seen it, and it's real. I don't know where it is for sure, but I've seen it and even been there in some way, and, my God, have I felt it." Amy broke down right there on the table, sobbing in her physics book.

Her words were muffled. "I've seen it, and nobody can hear me. Nobody."

What is going on, Kathy thought. *What do I say to her. She's breaking down right in front of me, and I'm clueless of what to do or say. This is all so sudden and weird.* Kathy closed her notebook and shoved it into her backpack. She was trembling, scared to death that something was seriously happening to Amy, emotionally. She hadn't been herself lately. Kathy tried to remain calm, but her heart and mind were racing. She had to be supportive and strong. Helping Amy to her feet with her left arm, Kathy used her right to gather Amy's books. "It's okay, Amy. Everything is going to be okay." She didn't believe that it was, but she knew of nothing else to say. She felt helpless and stupid.

"Sorry," Amy whispered.

"Don't apologize to me. Let's get you back to the dorms. We'll straighten all of this out later." *Hopefully,* she thought. Kathy walked Amy over to the elevator and pushed the down button. When the door opened, they stepped inside. Kathy hoped no one else would get on. She couldn't handle any questions. Everything was happening too quickly, and she had too many questions of her own to deal with first.

Chapter 6

6:00 P.M. River City High School
I Inch

Bill closed the heavy door to his red 1980 Chevy truck and hung his keys in the ignition. His organs felt like they were cracking from the cold, and his heart was pounding against them, almost painfully. The temperature inside the truck wasn't much better than out, but at least he was out of the wind. He was breathing heavily. His lungs ached with every inhale, and his mouth and nostrils blew tunnels of steam with every exhale. He prayed his heater was working.

Bill turned the key and pumped the gas pedal. The old truck wasn't very responsive. It hissed and growled briefly, but then went back to sleep. He turned it again, holding it a bit longer as the frozen engine shook and rumbled.

"Come on, come on, come on."

The growl was growing steady, almost continuous. His foot aggressively pumped.

"Come on, baby. Don't do this to me now."

Something popped, and the truck came roaring to life. He felt like he was riding a roller coaster. It shook for a few more seconds, working out the final kinks, and then finally turned over. Once Bill heard the humming of the engine, he relaxed and let loose of the keys. After pressing the gas pedal another time, he let the truck idle for a minute before moving out.

Relieved that the truck had started and he didn't have to sit in the parking lot freezing, he patted the dashboard and leaned back in his seat. "I knew you'd come through." Really, he didn't know. With the 14-year-old truck, it was hit or miss nowadays. With the engine now running smoothly, he turned his attention to the heater. It hadn't worked in the morning on his ride to school.

He reached for the heat switch and pushed it to HIGH. The first burst of air through the vents was cold, but seconds later the heater was pushing out warm air. He couldn't wait to get home and nurse his body with some warm clothes and a hot bowl of tomato soup.

Switching the gear to reverse, he slowly backed out of the parking space. A thin layer of snow covered the windshield, so he turned on his wipers to clear it away.

The black cat sitting on the hood caught him by surprise. Startled, Bill slammed on the brake, and after sliding back a few more feet on the fresh snow, the truck came to a halt.

"Get outta here," Bill yelled through the glass.

The black cat was the size of a baby tiger. It had a slender body, large paws, and two fiery red eyes. Walking closer to the glass, it focused in on Bill. Its tail slithered like a snake across the hood of the truck, leaving tiny grooves in the snow, marking its path.

Bill honked the horn. The cat didn't move or even flinch. Instead of jumping off, it hunkered down on its rump and hissed. The glass protected Bill from the wicked sound.

The light coming from the cat's eyes penetrated through the glass as if it were slowly chiseling it away. Bill pressed the horn again and held it for a few seconds.

The cat meowed loudly, standing back up on all fours. It started pacing from side to side across the hood, keeping its eyes focused on Bill, trying to tap into his mind and drive him crazy. It was doing a good job of it.

"Okay, asshole." Bill slid the gear to drive. "You asked for it," he mumbled through clenched teeth. He floored the gas pedal, and the truck darted across the parking lot. After about 20 feet, he slammed the brakes in hopes that the devilish feline would fly off. The truck did a doughnut and came to an abrupt halt. The cat stayed put.

"Son-of-a-bitch!" Bill screamed, smacking the steering wheel with the palm of his gloved hand.

The cat stood, staring with its long black tail swinging like a pendulum from side to side. Bill extended his middle finger towards the cat and then reached for the door. He was ready to physically remove the cat from the hood if that's what it was going to take. Just as Bill opened the door, the cat gave him one last domineering stare, grinned, and then took off into the trees surrounding the school.

Bill slammed the door and shook his head. *That thing grinned at me. That arrogant piece of shit grinned at me.* He'd never seen a cat grin before, but it did, sure enough. He couldn't scrape the sight from his head—with those gray, gummy-worm lips parting open, exposing those pointed teeth for him to see.

Bill turned out of the parking lot. Looking beyond the houses on Loftlin Avenue, he saw the last section of the sun behind the woods of Iroquois Park. He turned his headlights on and turned onto Kenwood Drive. After a few minutes, the inside of the truck felt like a furnace. He was finally starting to thaw out.

During Bill's drive home, the snowfall dwindled to scattered flurries, but the streets were getting slick, freezing quickly. His house was located in Iroquois Park in a secluded area on the southern tip of the woods. He pulled into his long gravel driveway and cruised. The tall trees overhead protected it like a tunnel, leaving it relatively untouched by the snowfall. The path of the driveway went uphill, curving and bending around the hundreds of skyscraping trees. Everything was extremely dark, but as Bill neared his house, he saw glimpses of light coming from the front porch.

Bill heard the crunching of the rocks give way to the smooth pavement as he pulled onto the slab of blacktop directly in front of the house. Pink Floyd's *Wish You Were Here* was finishing up on the radio. He waited to hear the song out. He put the truck in park, but left the engine running. His enjoyment was interrupted when 101.9's obnoxious D.J. cut into their supposedly half-hour of uninterrupted music.

. . . Wow! Was that nice? It just doesn't get any better than the Floyd Boys. This is Wild Chickenman kicking it to you from Louisville's favorite Rock-n-Roll station, 101.9 WKL. It's a bit after 6:30 in the P.M. folks, and boy does this weather bite. And it's only going to get worse. They're calling for light snowfall and temperatures in the teens for the next couple of days, before mother nature drops the bomb on us for the weekend. They're calling for a blizzard. Yes, you heard me right. A blizzard is being predicted for the River City area starting this Saturday, possibly even Friday, and lasting well into

*next week. I've heard anything from 30 to 40 inches when all is said and
done. We haven't had anything of this magnitude since 1974. I was only a
pup when that storm came roaring in, but from what I'm hearing, this one
coming will make the '74 storm look like a mere dusting. If you can remember
back to the blizzard of '74, the stores were . . .*

Click.

Bill hastily turned the engine off and stepped out onto the frozen blades
of grass in his front yard. The grass crunched under his weight, seemingly
echoing through the stillness of the surrounding woods. Tiny flakes of
snow escaped through the covering of the trees above, sprinkling down
on him softly, whispering through the silence of the crisp air. Instantly, he
was freezing again, but glad to be home.

It was a two-story, white, wooden house, built back in the '50s by a
World War II vet and his family. Its black shutters and large front porch
gave it a homely country appearance. His closest neighbors, besides the
animals in the woods, were more than a mile away. He welcomed the
isolation and cherished the privacy.

Bill put a bid on the house in March of '78, and moved in a month
later. Living in and out of jail and various apartments for four years after
Mary was killed, the house came as a blessing. It was exactly what he was
looking for—a place to start over. Those four years had been the worst of
his life. He lost his wife, his daughter, his job, and his sense of stability.
He lost his life, and slowly, his mind. With the pressures from the tragedy,
lawyers, cops, the media, and a growing sense of guilt he felt for not being
there to protect his wife, he turned to the bottle again. Alcohol. It was
what he craved and quickly had become addicted to when he was in college. What started off as the coolest way to fit in, quickly became the
easiest way to forget his problems. He never believed it could happen.
Not to him. He was too young and invincible. But it did, and what was
once enjoyable and social, became necessity and medicine. After Mary
was killed, that same need he felt in college returned.

In his college days, one drug led to another and one party blended into
the next, until his nights were consumed by them. Experimentation led
to habit, and the nights he wasn't taken in by the bottle, he was flying
high on pot, tripping on LSD and acid, swimming and floating around
in a cartoon world of hallucinations that set his mind ablaze. His life was
declining rapidly, rolling down the spiral to death, until one afternoon,
an afternoon where he was sober for once, he met the love of his life. He
met Mary, and from then on he was a changed man. It was the freedom of
college, being away from his parents for the first time, and immaturity

that turned him into the lifeless, mindless waste he was becoming. It was Mary that helped him turn all of that around.

Seeing her that day was like running straight into a brick wall. Instantly it seemed as if his miserable life had come to a screeching halt. The lightning bolt of reality struck him in the head that afternoon on campus. He wasn't sure how or why, but he liked the feeling. He wasn't a bad person, but he realized that his lifestyle was making him into one. He realized he was troubled, and he needed help. Then, there she was.

He sat alone on a wooden bench in front of the library on that April afternoon in 1970. The sun was shining brightly, and the birds were singing beautiful songs of spring. Skipping yet another English class, he sat like a slug without a purpose, watching squirrels scamper across the grass and climbing up the trees. Then she came out of the library unexpectedly. He had seen her before in the cafeteria, but had failed to meet her. Now he had a second chance. As she walked down the steps and onto the sidewalk in front of him, his focus shifted from the squirrels to her. His palms were sweaty, and his mouth turned dry.

He stared. She was beautiful, wearing her short, white shorts and silky dark-blue blouse. The sun glistened off of her tanned legs. In the slight breeze, her shirt ruffled like waves, foamy waves rolling silently up the shore. He was captivated by her. A lump started to form in his throat as she slowly turned her head his way. To him it was in slow motion. They made eye contact. It was inevitable now, he would have to say something, although he was totally clueless of what that might be. It will probably come out stupid. Maybe I won't say anything after all, but…

The initial eye contact. The turning away. The double-take. The smiles. They were all good signs. Bill stood on two nervous legs and introduced himself, and the conversation that followed was a good one. He didn't make a fool of himself. He wasn't drunk for some reason that day, maybe fate, but he didn't really believe in that garbage. For a week they talked and really got to know each other, and then they started to date. The relationship took off from there. His recovery and turn-around had begun. He finally had a reason to quit. She was the supportive force that turned his life around, away from the parties, drugs, and alcohol. Although the addiction for alcohol would always be there with him, his needs and wants changed. More than anything in life, he wanted and needed her.

He wanted and needed her now and always, but it couldn't be the case. She was gone, and as much as he wished her back, he knew it could never happen. The memories were all he had.

Bill wiped the tear from the corner of his left eye. The snow was starting to pick up again, and he was getting wet. Putting the memories of Mary on hold, he made his way to the front door. He could hear his 10-year-old golden retriever, Gus, barking and scratching the front door.

When Bill opened the screen door, he heard the heavy paws smacking against the door and sliding back down to the floor. "Hold on, Gus. Let me find my keys."

Gus barked.

Bill turned the key and pushed the door open. As soon as Gus saw a path, he shot out through the door and into the front yard. After circling the yard twice, he stopped by a tree about 30 yards away and hiked his leg up in the air.

The snow was coming down hard, adding quickly to the thin covering that had already fallen. There was a 30-yard radius around the house that was relatively free of trees, so unlike the long driveway, his house wasn't protected from the snowfall.

The snowflakes were falling like quarter-size puffs of cotton, silently, and Bill had trouble seeing Gus off in the distance. He could tell that he was shivering, and while doing so, he was turning a patch of snow to yellow. Bill was surprised that the stream of urine wasn't freezing on the way to the ground. After Gus had finished, he shook the snow from his back and turned towards the house.

"Gus, come on, boy." Bill smacked the side of his jeans. "Come on," he smiled, "I'm freezing." Gus stopped in the middle of the yard and stared.

"I'm closing the door in five seconds, Gus."

Gus stared.

"Are you in or out?"

Gus scratched behind his ear, but didn't move any closer to the house.

"Four . . . three." Bill slowly started to close the door. "Two." That got his attention. Gus sprinted up to the porch, shook all the snow from his back, head, and ears, and then ran inside. "One."

Once in the house, Bill immediately took off his boots and gloves. Gus danced around the front room with his tongue hanging out, panting and breathing heavily. *Feed me. Feed me.* His paws made a clickityclack noise on the hardwood floor.

Bill walked into the kitchen and returned with a large bag of Purina Dog Chow, beef-flavored. Gus towered over his bowl, waiting for the food to be poured so he could devour it in seconds. Bill poured a heaping bowl and then checked the water. It was filled to the top. "Now don't be spilling any of that on the floor." He patted Gus on the top of the head. "Or you'll be cleaning it up this time."

In the kitchen, Bill grabbed a can of tomato soup out of the cabinet, mixed it with a can of water, and placed the bowl in the microwave for three minutes. When the timer sounded, Bill poured himself a tall glass of milk and sat down at his kitchen table. From the front room, he could hear Gus tearing into the food. The crunching and chomping echoed through the house.

The first swallow of soup was hot, but it felt soothing going down. He grabbed the sports section from the newspaper and started reading. Before taking the second swallow, Bill glanced out the window next to the kitchen table and noticed that the snow was coming down even stronger than it had been only minutes before. Bill was disgusted with the solid white scenery. He leaned across the circular table and closed the curtains to the window. "Not while I'm eating," he mumbled, plopping back down in his chair.

He hoped that the blizzard would miss and blow right over. He dreaded another major snowstorm and the implications that would come along with it. Winter was here again, and there wasn't a thing he could do about it.

The '74 blizzard not only took away Bill's wife, but also his entire life. Accused of murdering his wife, Bill was in and out of jail and the courtroom for most of the next two years, until finally, the matter was resolved. During that time, he was forced out of his home, and Amy spent her days and nights with Kathleen and Mike Greene, longtime friends of the family. He was able to see his daughter on a limited basis, twice a week for an hour per visit. The Greenes brought her to the courtroom during the numerous trial days, and he was able to at least see her there, but it just wasn't the same. He needed to hold her and touch her, not simply look at her. He took what he could get though, and his miserable life puttered along. Amy was too young to understand what was going on, but was at the age where she was starting to ask questions and wonder why she wasn't living with her daddy. The questions were not easy for the Greenes to answer. Bill was nearly a stranger for two years of her life. So many nights Mike and Kathleen tucked her in, read her bedtime stories, and kissed her good night. Not Bill. In the mornings they fixed her cereal, dressed her, taught her, and basically raised her. Not Bill. Amy was confused and became more so the older she got. Who were her real parents? Where was her father? Her mother? Why was she living with other people? They were loving and caring people, but they were not her mommy and daddy.

In a way, Bill's mind had been put at ease because he knew the Greenes, he trusted them, and he knew that they were going to raise her well, but at the same time he felt cheated. He missed some very crucial stages of Amy's childhood, stages of her life that he could never get back, and it was through no fault of his own. He was cheated out of Amy's early childhood, all because he was wrongly accused and nearly found guilty of a crime that he could have never dreamed of doing.

The prosecution had a case against Bill, a strong one. His fingerprints were the only ones found, and they were found all over the victim and murder weapon, so the cops were quick to accuse. The steak knife used for the kill was not like any other knife that was found in the house. It was from an older set of knives that had been stored in a box in the shed since their wedding. Bill's fingerprints were found on the top of the box. Bootprints were found leading from the broken glass doors of the family room to the shed and back. They were the only footprints found around the house, and the indentations in the snow exactly matched the markings on the bottoms of Bill's winter boots. The investigation was handled poorly. Too many things were left unexplained and not looked into thoroughly. The bird feathers. The writing on the back of the couch. The hole in Amy's door. The cops had questions, too, but they had no other leads. With the evidence they had, Bill was their man. They were weak on motive, but the fingerprints were strong enough in their minds. The bootprints in the snow were the exact same size as Bill's boots. If anyone else had entered the house, different prints would have been found.

Fortunately for Bill, after suffering through the long battles and verbal attacks in the courtroom, his lawyer was somehow able to plant the seed of doubt in the minds of the jurors. His lawyer attacked the validity of the fingerprints, stating that simply because Bill lived in the house, his fingerprints *should* have been found everywhere. They were found all over the victim because he had embraced and touched her several times after locating her behind the couch, already dead. The bootprints were left from when he went out to the shed to get a shovel earlier that morning, before he had even left for the grocery store. Reaching for the shovel in the back corner of the shed, he had braced himself by placing his hand on the top of a box, the same box that contained the murder weapon. He wasn't wearing gloves at the time, so his prints were left.

Bill's lawyer couldn't explain the lack of another set of bootprints in the snow, but he never gave up in what increasingly became an uphill battle in creating a defense. In the closing weeks of the trial, just when it seemed as if the prosecution was gaining a definitive advantage in the minds of the jurors, the defense received some very helpful information. The source of the information was a 36-year-old weather analyst from Colorado, Leroy McCalister, who was gaining popularity (mostly from controversy and criticism) across the nation because of his research on the negative and evil aspects in the worldwide history of snowfall. Leroy strongly supported the idea of the "Snowman" as the killer when he'd heard of the story, giving evidence in his research that this "figment of Bill's imagination" (as the prosecution had termed it) was, indeed, a real entity. Leroy was eager to testify on Bill's behalf, but the night before he was supposed to appear in court, everything came to a halt, and what had been up to that point a very open and public trial, suddenly became extremely secretive and hush-hush. Leroy never showed up to testify, and because of it, Bill's last minute hopes of acquittal were seemingly thrown out the courtroom windows. In Bill's mind, he had already lost, but his lawyer had different feelings. His lawyer seemed more confident than ever that they would win, but refused to tell Bill why. Actually, after Leroy's no-show, Bill's lawyer told him next to nothing. It was as if their lines of communication had been totally severed. Both the prosecution and the defense hurried through the last week of the trial as if the outcome didn't even matter to them, and the judge seemed oblivious to their actions. Bill was not. He noticed everything. He was worried that his case was doomed, and that his lawyer had given up, throwing him to the wolves. He was left in the dark and furious with his lawyer for the sudden loss of communication. He didn't know what to do. He didn't know what he *could* do. Nothing was going right. The trial was rushed to a conclusion, but to almost everyone's surprise in the courtroom, Bill was acquitted. After nearly two years of what Bill called "completely ludicrous" hearings, he walked out of the courtroom a free man.

Bill's lawyer left town as soon as the trial was over, and Bill never heard from him again. Bill wished he knew more about Leroy McCalister's part in the outcome of the trial and his lawyer's whereabouts, but he was so filled with joy about being free and with his daughter again, that his wishes never panned out to be more than a dwindling curiosity.

Something had happened near the end of the trial that Bill couldn't quite put his finger on, something dirty, but he didn't waste time trying to understand or uncover what may have gone on. He was finally free and very anxious to start rebuilding his shattered life.

He was free, but at the same time broke, emotionally drained, jobless, and he'd been away from Amy for nearly two years. He had trouble finding work. He was cast aside by the local citizens, and employers had a hard time wanting to hire the "wife killer." Regardless of what had been decided in the courts, the people of Louisville were convinced of his guilt. It took most of them years to tolerate him.

After months of job searching, a janitorial position opened at River City High School. Even though he was overqualified, Bill knew he needed work. The principal, Mike Greene, hired him on the spot. Being a janitor (janitorial engineer as he liked to jokingly call himself) was not his ideal job, but it did clear $17,000 a year, and after a few years he became quite comfortable with what he was doing. Mike Greene gave him the break he needed during a time in his life when he felt he had no one. He credited the Greenes for saving what little he had left of his life, and it wasn't just because of the job and their help in taking care of his girl. They believed in him, trusted him, and Mike's wife, Kathleen, saved him from going crazy.

With Kathleen's help as a psychiatrist and caring friend, he again was able to push himself away from the bottle. His life was on the rebound. He was back with his daughter. He had a job. He was sober and feeling good about himself again. He bought Amy a golden retriever and set his sights on the house in Iroquois Park.

Shortly after the house was bought, the dreams, visions, flashbacks, and hallucinations surfaced, and a life that had been running smoothly for months was again experiencing rocky terrain. Kathleen took him on as a patient early in her career and met with him often, free of charge. They weren't like the hallucinations he had experienced in college. They were different, much more frightening, and they consumed him to the point where he thought suicide might be the only way to escape the horror. He refused to let the alcohol be his escape valve, and Kathleen helped him to stay strong. It was difficult, and the temptations were often there, but he continuously pushed them away.

For a few years, the flashbacks and dreams occurred almost daily, but through numerous sessions, Kathleen was able to help him in driving them away. After 10 years of therapy, Bill's hallucinations, dreams, and visions were totally gone, removed from his system. The fears and the horrors of what had happened to his wife were replaced with the good times and pleasant memories.

During the height of his worst years, the visions dug deep into his mind until they nearly drove him to his death. He dreamed about that day, December 16th, 1974. He had visions of Mary, the snow, Amy, and worst of all, the Snowman, even though he had never seen the killer. It got to the point where he couldn't distinguish his subconscious from reality. He couldn't sleep at night, afraid of what he might see if he did close his eyes for too long. He was afraid to live. During the first years of work, Bill walked the halls at River City High like a zombie, sleepwalking from task to task. Slowly, he was losing control of his mind and body.

As Amy grew older, Kathleen included her in a few of their sessions, but nothing promising was found. Amy swore she didn't remember a thing from that day, and that she wasn't haunted by the same dreams and hallucinations as her father, so Kathleen reluctantly didn't push her any further. She realized that Amy was only two years old when it had happened, but it was hard to tell what a baby could or couldn't hear and remember. Kathleen wondered if Amy really didn't remember or she was too afraid to talk about it. The questions went unanswered.

Amy turned out to be a beautiful young woman, seemingly unscarred by her screwed-up childhood. That's really all Bill had hoped for, his daughter's happiness. Over the past decade, Bill's life had taken a turn in the right direction. He was financially stable, his daughter was about ready to graduate from college, and most importantly, he was finally happy with himself again. He was content with his life, even though he was a janitor and had been so for the past 18 years.

After the last drop of soup was gone, Bill washed his dishes and left them to dry. Out of the corner of his eye he noticed that Gus was out cold, snoozing next to his bowl, and every last nugget of food was gone. Bill dried his hands on a dish towel and walked into the TV room near the back of the house. In the corner by the far window, he saw a bright red, flashing light, and the first thing he thought of was the cat. He could see the cat's eyes again, and they were in the back corner of his house, beeping and flashing, and beeping . . . then he realized it was only his answering machine. Two quick flashes, a pause, and then two more flashes. Two messages. He turned on a lamp next to the window and flipped on the machine.

BEEP

. . . *Bill, this is Ralph, give me a call when you get in. It's about a surprise birthday party for Dad next weekend. Bye.*

BEEP

. . . Dad, this is Amy. It's about 12:30 Wednesday afternoon. Um . . I'll call back later tonight. Love ya. Bye.

CLICK

Bill smiled. Hearing his daughter's voice had a way of doing that to him. He turned away from the window and took his hat off his head. As he tossed the hat over to the couch, the answering machine beeped again.

Bill turned back around to look at it.

It clicked and started playing. The red light was flashing. An unfamiliar voice whispered from the machine . . . *I knew you'd pick up the knife, Bill. I think that was your worst mistake, but don't you worry about a thing cause as you've probably noticed, the wheel of snow has landed on Louisville yet again. Unlike the circumstances then, now is the time. I'm the worldwide traveler, you see, and it ain't too often when I'm able to hit the same place twice in one century.*

BEEP

Just as it had turned itself on, the answering machine clicked off. *That wasn't real*, Bill told himself. *That message wasn't on there.* He ran his hands through his hair and bit down on his lower lip. He pushed play again on the machine and listened to the messages. The one from his brother played, and then the one from Amy followed. The third message was not on there. It didn't exist. But he had heard something coming from the machine.

Bill placed both hands against the window pane and stared out into his backyard. The pane was cold. He could feel a draft. He thought of the message. *You're hearing things again. It was just a vision. Just your mind playing tricks on you, nothing more. The message was only in your head. How could I create a message like that in my head? And why? Why now? Someone else must have done it. Something else must have brought the words along. But why? And how? It's been eight years since anything like this has happened to me. It can't be happening again. It can't.*

Wind blew flakes of snow against the window. The snow was mounting quickly. He watched it. He saw every flake hit the white blanket covering the ground. The snow was growing. He looked past his yard and into the wilderness of darkness beyond the trees. The voice on the last message. He recognized it now. It *was* all in his head. The voice; he remembered it. It was back. He felt alone, searching for answers as he gazed out the window. *Could it be? Not again. Why me?* He felt chilled.

His phobia of snow was returning.

Chapter 7

7:30 P.M. 1994 South Pole Overland Expedition
Thirty-Seven Miles To Go

On the 52nd day of a scheduled 54-day expedition, the Antarctic Overland Team reached a safe stopping point for the night, roughly 37 miles away from the geographical South Pole. For 52 days, the team of nine (two women and seven men) had skied across nearly 750 miles of barren snowland in sub-zero temperatures, en route to becoming one of a very elite group of adventurers to travel overland to the bottom of the earth.

On December 14, 1911, Roald Amundsen from Norway was the first human ever to reach the South Pole, and he did so with four men-and-dog teams. He had won the race to the Pole, but only one year later, Captain Robert Scott reached the Pole from Ross Island with four others. They located Amundsen's tent, but no one from Scott's party survived the trip to tell about it. The international quest for Antarctica's land was on. Already heavy into Antarctic exploration, the United States in 1959 was joined by 11 other nations in the signing of an international treaty, suspending any territorial claims for the next 30 years. The continent was reserved for research.

The countries studied the continent and sub-Arctic islands. They studied meteorology, oceanography, glaciology, geomagnetism, the ionosphere, and by 1962, the first nuclear power plant began operation at McMurdo Sound. It was a scientist's dream to study the vast, previously unexplored areas of the great southern continent. Advances in research increased yearly, and new and amazing findings were made consistently through the following decades. Overland expeditions were being made, and on January 17, 1989, two Americans, Victoria Murden and Shirley Metz, became the first women ever to reach the Pole overland. They traveled with nine others, covering 740 miles in 51 days. Before the '88-'89 team, only 13 people, none of whom was American, had ever gone to the South Pole on foot. Five of the 13 died on the way.

This current team, all Americans, was well aware of the history of overland travel and the dangers and risks that went along with the glory; but the nine weren't about to let the stories make them reluctant or give them cold feet. Every expedition was different; and, so far, this one had gone off without any glitches.

Isolated from all human life for so long, the team knew of nothing else but ice and snow. The trip was taking its toll. They were exhausted from the harsh climate and by their means of travel, and their tempers often rested on short fuses. They all swore never to touch a ski again once they returned to the states. Around the middle of the trip, spirits sagged—the type of feeling one gets in the middle of a marathon when reaching the finish line seems unrealistic. As of late though, their moods were changing, booming with a newly-found optimism and thoughts of reaching the Pole and relaxing on the flight home. Physically they were worn out, but it was difficult not to get excited. They knew that in two days their trip would be over, and then they'd be able to return to civilization.

At 7:30 in the evening, the sun was a blurry ball of white and yellow fire, glowing through the thin layer of ice crystal clouds. Two smaller mock suns were suspended on each side, and all three were surrounded by haloes as the sun's rays were reflected and refracted by the ice crystals in the atmosphere. The optical phenomena were beautiful and spectacular. All through the summer months, day and night, the sun hovered in the sky as if suspended by invisible strings. It hung above the horizon as the earth rotated.

After measuring the wind's speed, Brice Campario shoved the anemometer back into his coat pocket. At age 40, Brice was one of the older members of the team. An expert in mountain travel, he was the leader of the expedition, which meant that he also carried the burden of responsibility on his shoulders. This was his first time in Antarctica, but by no means his first experience with a sub-zero climate. With 15 years of glaciology under his belt, he was twice picked to lead expeditions into the Arctic and North Pole. He had experience with freezing weather, and he knew how to deal with it.

This was his first major expedition since his Arctic tragedy eight years earlier, so he had a lot to prove about his leadership, although mostly to himself. It had happened when one of his men lost balance and slid into a crevasse. It was close to the water's edge, and the Arctic Ocean pulled him under the ice. They had searched for days, but the body was never found. Brice took it hard, and the incident played on his conscience for years, to the point where he refused to ever lead another team. He had dreams of the dead man's blue and bloated body breaking through the ice, sneaking up to him at night, strangling him until he stopped breathing. It was the same dream, over and over again. Brice knew the death had been beyond his control, an accident, but he couldn't help but take it personally, and for several years he did.

Eight years of nothing but research and the boredom was killing him. So when he was approached in early June and asked to lead an expedition to the South Pole, he jumped all over the offer without hesitation. He felt ready again, ready to take on another challenge. He looked at it as his chance to prove to himself that he was not a failure.

"Brice!" He heard someone scream his name from behind. The voice was weakened by the wind. Brice turned around and saw that his assistant leader and mountain guide, Gabe Mulloy, was standing by his side. He wore a black ski mask and a pair of red goggles. "What did it read?"

Brice adjusted his goggles. "Twenty-four miles per hour, from the south."

"Twenty-four?"

"Yeah, it's fluctuating though."

"That's still better than the readings in the 50's last week." It was almost useless to mention days and weeks, simply because it was so difficult to keep track of them. With the days and nights running together and the sun never setting, time lost all meaning.

Brice glanced up at the sky and pointed at the sun. "Look at those two sun dogs."

Under his mask, Gabe smiled. "Amazing. I don't care how many times I see those things, it still is amazing. The good Lord sure paints a pretty picture. The sky here just does some absolutely incredible things."

"Sure does." Brice flipped his hood back over his mask and secured it by pulling the two strings around his neck. "Eric and Magnus here with the snowmobiles yet?"

"They just showed up about five minutes ago. They're setting up the TURD (Transportable Utility Retractable Dome) right now." Gabe pointed to an uneven, jagged wall of ice about 20 yards to his right. It looked like a large, frozen ocean wave. "We're going to set up the tents behind that wall. Does it look big enough, or should we go ahead and build the windbreaks?"

Brice hesitated. "Set up the windbreaks just in case. I don't want to take the chance of getting buried again overnight."

Gabe nodded.

"You get a hold of the guys in the Amundsen-Scott station yet?" Brice asked.

"That's the other thing I wanted to talk to you about."

"Still no answer?"

"Right. I'm getting static and nothing else. I think the lines might be totally wacked."

"Dammit," Brice growled. "We're going to be there in less than two days." He shook his head. "And we can't even contact them to call for our pick-up plane."

"Do you want me to try again, Brice?"

"No, not yet. We need to recharge the batteries with the solar panels again. I'm afraid the radio might be getting drained. Maybe we'll have better luck if we charge it up again."

Gabe couldn't see it, but beneath Brice's mask was a face full of concern. He did see Brice shake his head again. "What is it, Brice?"

"I can't help but wonder."

"About what?"

"I don't know, maybe something has happened."

"Like what?"

"The wind or a blizzard may have knocked the antenna down."

"That's definitely a possibility, but—"

"It concerns me. Our pick-up plane would be flying from Argentina, right?" Brice didn't wait for a response. "And our equipment isn't strong enough to reach that far. Only the Amundsen-Scott station's system can broadcast from that distance, or bounce through our base at McMurdo."

"What exactly are you saying?"

"I'm thinking that unless we can get through to the guys at Amundsen-Scott, we might be here on this damn continent for longer than we had planned. The plane isn't going to pick us up until we call, and if the communication system is working, we *will* have a delay. It might be a day, two days, a week, who knows?"

"I'll keep trying after we recharge the batteries. All we can do is keep our fingers crossed. Hopefully we'll get through to someone tonight or tomorrow." Gabe turned away, and then stopped. "I'm going to go help with the tents. I'm starving."

"I'll be there in a minute, Gabe."

"Okay." Gabe turned and joined the others. At 25, Gabe was the youngest of the group. He was also the most religious, completing two years in the seminary before deciding that the priesthood wasn't for him. He wanted a wife and kids and a family he could call his own; so he made up his mind that he would become a deacon instead of a priest. According to church law, one had to be 35 years old before joining the church as a deacon. Gabe had 10 years before he could be officially ordained, so in the winter of '94 he planned another vacation (his third of the year), and where else to go for the beginning of winter but Antarctica. His family and friends questioned the logic of vacationing in sub-zero weather, but Gabe looked at it as more of a challenge than a joy ride. Growing up in Elk City, Idaho, Gabe spent much of his youth hiking the Clearwater Mountains and getting lost in the wilderness of Nez Perce National Forest, just east of the city. With a strong and solid 6-foot frame, Gabe loved to rough it in any wilderness. Despite his youth, he had already climbed nearly every major mountain in the world, from the Alps to Mount Everest, without injury. An expert at every move, he was always looking for the next challenge. Coming home from a climb over the Nanga Parbat Mountains in Pakistan at the end of the summer, Gabe was immediately ready for his next hurdle—the coldest, highest, and driest desert on earth, Antarctica. Brice knew of his credentials and experience and quickly latched onto him as his second in command.

Brice stared into the distance. Most of the rough terrain was behind them. He was amazed at how flat the land seemed, although he knew how much higher they were now than at the beginning of the trip. He could hardly tell they were on an incline. At the start of the trip they were at sea level, but in skiing to the Pole, they would be roughly 9,300 feet above. It was quite an altitude, but stretched over 700 miles of land, it is hard to realize the climb.

Brice was pleased with everything thus far. The communication loss with the research station worried him, but he tried not to let his imagination run wild. The trip had been an exciting one, but Brice was ready to get back home. The constant cold weather was annoying and frustrating, and the wind made everything that much worse. It took more than physical strength to endure the travel, much of it was mental. The Antarctic was not for the weak of heart. Once they started the trip, there was no turning back. They were not going to get picked up, barring an emergency, until they reached the South Pole.

He remembered the day, late October, when their plane crossed the Antarctic circle and coasted down over the beautiful Weddell Sea. He remembered the sun shining against the partially frozen surface of the sea, giving it an oily appearance. They touched down smoothly on the Filchner Ice shelf of Northwestern Antarctica, just off the Luitpold coast, nearly 800 miles from their destination.

Brice reflected on the memories of that day, stepping off the plane and onto the glistening blue runway. With the Filchner shelf being second in size to the great Ross Ice Shelf in the south, the blue ice seemingly ran on forever. He remembered tasting the bitter wind as it stung his uncovered face for the first time. It was colder than the Arctic, and at the time he felt like running back to the plane to hide. His excitement and anxiety won out over his nervousness. The day remained in his head like a picture, and even now he could still hear the rolling and swishing of the waves from the Weddell Sea and Atlantic Ocean in the distance. He was anxious and a bit nervous then, but now as he stared into the distant miles of ice, he couldn't wait to get home. He was tired, and so were the others.

"Two more days," he whispered, "two more days."

Brice secured his hood around his head and ears again and pulled his scarf back over his exposed mouth. Despite the Everest screen ointment, his lips were starting to crack and chap again. He turned into the wind and joined the others.

Chapter 8

By the time Kathy and Amy had returned to their room, it was after seven. Nothing had been said coming back from the library. Amy used the brisk walk to get her head screwed back on straight. Kathy was full of questions, but decided to wait until they were in their room to ask them.

Kathy kicked the door closed. Amy flopped on the couch with her arms folded. She stared at the wall across the room and said nothing. Kathy sat down beside her, thinking of something to say.

"I'm sorry," Amy said.

"For what?"

"Freaking out like that. It's embarrassing. I'm not sure why I did it, or why I even brought up the subject. I hadn't planned on telling you about *my* hell, it just sort of came out, and . . . and I couldn't stop myself. It was weird."

"You want to talk about it, or give it a rest?"

"It's just that I have a different and very vivid idea and description of hell that I don't think most people could understand. And I don't really know why that is."

"Well, everyone is entitled to their own opinions. Like I said before, there really is no distinct definition of hell. I don't see what the big deal is though. I don't mean to sound like an asshole, but why is this bothering you so much?"

"Because I'm scared."

"Scared? Of what?"

"The man in my nightmares. I think he's real."

"So this *does* have something to do with what happened earlier?"

"Yes," Amy said, reluctant to reveal anything more. Nervously, she moved the arm rest around with her fingers.

"Who's this man?"

"I don't know. He's got long white hair and light-blue eyes."

"And he's in your dreams?"

"Nightmares, not dreams, they're nightmares. They started about a week ago, and they've been gradually getting worse."

"Do they occur daily?"

"No, but I've had three of them now, and they all involve this man. At first I just saw his hair, and the next time I saw his hands and body. Today I saw his face."

Kathy wasn't sure what to say, so she said nothing.

Amy rubbed her eyes and again stared blankly at the wall. "My God, is it cold *there*."

"Where is *there*, Amy?"

"Where my nightmares take me. He calls it Iceville, my own little nightmare world where no one else can hear or see me. It's so cold in Iceville, and there's nothing but snow and ice," she paused, searching for more words. "Snow and ice."

"Amy, this is getting weird." Kathy leaned back on the couch.

"I told you."

"Have you told anyone else about this?"

"No. It only started a week ago. And the nightmares I've had before were different than these."

"What were they like?"

"I'd rather not discuss it. I shouldn't have brought it up. They don't have anything to do with these nightmares; these are so real and ..."

"And they're progressing," Kathy finished the sentence for her.

"What do you mean?"

"Well, from what you're saying, something more is happening in each new dream or nightmare. How far are you going to let this go on before it drives you crazy?"

"What, you think I'm crazy now, Kathy? Is that it?"

"Heavens no. I don't know if it's the pressure of finals getting you or what, but you need to talk to someone about this. It's not doing you any good to hold on to what happens to you in these nightmares. I'm worried about you, Amy."

"Thanks, but there's no need to be. I'm fine."

"You haven't been acting fine though. That's my point, Amy. There's something more to this. What does this man do to you? Does he hurt you? Jump out and scare you? Touch you? What?"

"Please, Kathy, stop. Let's change the subject. I don't want to talk about my nightmares anymore. Not now."

Kathy wanted to dig in further, but realizing Amy's fragile state of mind, she didn't want to send her over the edge. At the same time she didn't want to be shut out. "Sure. Amy, do understand that I'm trying to help."

"I know, and it's appreciated, but this is something I have to deal with on my own."

"Nobody should have to do that, not when there are people that want to listen. I do though, and I will. I'm sorry if I upset you, Amy."

Amy got off the couch and walked to her desk.

"One more thing," Kathy added, standing up. "Is this why you think hell is ice, because of these dreams you've been having?"

"It's part of it, yes, but . . . "

"Go on."

Amy hesitated. "Later, Kathy."

Kathy let it go for now. "Okay, we'll change the subject." If she'd open up a little bit more, Kathy thought, maybe I could help her. But what is she hiding? And why? "What time does our flight leave tomorrow?"

Relieved, Amy said, "We're scheduled to take off around 1:30 P.M. I'll have to check the tickets to make sure though."

"Sounds good."

"We should probably get to the airport at least by 11:30."

"Why so early?"

"Just to be safe. You never know what's going to happen before boarding an airplane."

"Meaning what? Remember, this is my first time flying."

"Well, we have to get our luggage and all that stuff straightened out before boarding; and there will be a lot of people in line, I'll guarantee that. Trust me. Early is better."

The tension was dwindling.

Kathy opened the refrigerator. Squatting, she searched for something to drink. "What time are you getting up?"

"Uh, probably around seven. I'm going to try and study a little in the morning."

"Can you wake me up then after you get out of the shower?"

"Sure," Amy said. "I'll set the alarm now so I don't forget." She stretched across her bottom bunk to reach the clock by her headboard.

The time showed 7:30 in bright red numbers. Her eyes locked on the red dots that made up the numbers. The numbers zoomed in. Suddenly, she froze to the bed. Everything around her turned dark except the numbers, which were blurry. She screamed for Kathy, but couldn't even hear her own voice.

"Amy, you want something to drink?" Kathy asked with her head in the refrigerator.

No answer.

"Amy?"

Kathy turned and saw Amy lying on top of her bed, her face contorted as if screaming, but making no sound. Her hands reached upward, grabbing something that wasn't there. She put the can of orange juice on her desk and walked over to the bed. "Amy, wake up!"

Amy couldn't hear a thing. The blurry, red numbers began bleeding together to form two distinct red dots, glowing like a pair of eyes. The eyes got closer and closer, larger and brighter, red, like blood. She couldn't keep them away. She swiped at them with her hands, kicked with her feet, but couldn't push them away.

Kathy tried to grab Amy's arms but was unable to do so and was nearly punched out in the process. She shook Amy's shoulders to no avail. Amy's eyes were like glass, intensely focused on something not in the room.

Amy heard the sound of a baby crying, and then realized it was she *…two years old again; she could hear the sound of a woman screaming in danger, her mom being attacked…Nooo…please, get out of here!…somebody help me, Bill…*

The two red eyes kept staring. An odd smell surrounded her, smothering her. She felt a breeze.

Whoop Whoop

The flapping wings.

"Amy!" Kathy screamed, near panic. "Please wake up, you're scaring me."

In the background the woman stopped screaming, but Amy could still hear the sound of the . . .

Whoop Whoop

. . . leathery wings . . .

Whoop Whoop Whoop

. . . surrounding her . . . suffocating darkness and wind . . . red eyes . . . watching . . . beaming . . . something grabbing her arm . . .

Amy felt something on her arm. Someone was shaking her.

"Amy! Wake up!"

Amy opened her eyes and saw Kathy hovering over her, calling her name.

Amy leaned up and hugged Kathy tightly. She no longer saw the red eyes, or heard the wings, or felt the breeze, but she needed something real to grab hold of. Trembling and crying, Amy buried her face in Kathy's shoulder.

"I'm right here, Amy, it's okay now."

Amy pointed towards the alarm clock.

Holding onto Amy with one arm, Kathy grabbed the alarm clock cord with the other and yanked it out of the wall. She also felt like crying.

"It's okay, Amy, let it out. Let it all out."

Chapter 9

6:26 P.M., Iroquois Park
2 Inches

Bill leaned with his hands against the sides of the window, trying to clear his head. He gazed out the window to the snow and dark trees beyond. The only light in his back yard was from the small fixture on the front of the shed, which was about 20 yards away from the house, even with the edge of the woods. As hard as the snow had been falling only minutes ago, it was now only flurries.

Despite the two inches that had already fallen around the house, Bill could see the ground in the distant woods underneath all of the trees. The ground was frozen, but free of snow. From the shed's light, he could see the fallen branches, twigs, and dead leaves under the trees, but further back he could only see darkness. He imagined it was much of the same. Everything in the woods seemed protected from the snow except his house. As if the last message on his answering machine hadn't been enough, Bill became more unnerved at the thought of his vulnerability. His house was secluded, yet out in the open as far as the woods were concerned, open for the snow to come closing in until everything around him was buried. The thought of being buried in another snowstorm scared him—buried in a house by himself with no one to save him from the *voice* and his own mind.

The voice. *His* voice. The Snowman. It came from the answering machine, or did it? Bill knew the answer, but was still afraid to admit it to himself. The Snowman was back inside his head. The worldwide traveler.

He hoped the dreams and visions wouldn't return. He didn't understand and tried not to believe any of it could be real again, but the voice *was* so real. It stirred up some thoughts and feelings from his past that had no business coming back. The past he had spent so long trying to overcome was all storming back, all prompted by the voice. He tried closing his mind to the horrible memories, but it was impossible. The switch had now been flipped, the floodgates were open, and the memories of the Snowman had returned.

Bill nervously thumped the side of the window with the palm of his hand, thinking. His thoughts scared him. *The Snowman can't be back. Whoever or whatever he is, he can't be back. Not now. Not after so many years of freedom.*

The window rattled in its frame. Outside, the wind was really starting to pick up, whistling around the house and trees like a kazoo. The light snow and flurries began spinning in a cyclic frenzy. Bill watched as a patch of flurries gathered, swirling faster and faster together, forming a funnel of snow about 20 feet outside the window. It seemed odd. Something didn't seem right with what was happening outside his window. The snow was doing things it wasn't supposed to do. *It's happening again,* he told himself. *The visions, I can feel it, it's happening all over. Come on Bill, gain control before it controls you. Get control before . . .*

The thin funnel of snow, about five feet high, picked up speed, spinning and turning like a top. Gaining more and more mass and width as it bounced around the open space in Bill's back yard, the funnel was solidifying in each rotation, turning into something else, something large with substance.

. . . it controls you. This is not real. What I am seeing is not real. I won't allow this to happen to me again. Stay out of my mind you crazy bastard. Bill closed his eyes. When he opened them again, the tornado was still spinning. He thought he was hallucinating. He tried shaking his head, but it didn't work. The spinning mass remained outside the window, twisting and turning and bouncing and . . . the few inches of snow that Bill knew were really on the ground, now appeared to be about 20. Even in the distance, the ground underneath the trees was now snow-covered.

The tornado slowed until the last few flurries vanished from the air. The wind had built something from the snow. The small light from the shed silhouetted the figure the tornado had made. It was five feet tall. Two huge balls of snow stacked on top of one another, one for a head and the lower one for a body. It was a snowman, the type of snowman a young boy like Bobby from school would have built. The two halves were poorly sculpted, and the top half was slanting to the side, ready to slide off with the slightest push or shove.

Bill had an urge to run outside and knock it down, but he couldn't take himself away from the window. He couldn't peel his eyes away from the snowman, although he badly wanted to. The snowman had a huge red-and-white striped hat on the top part of its head, drooping over to the side from the weight of a furry red ball at its tip. A red-and-white scarf fit between the two balls of snow, its tassels flying in what little was left of the wind. Two large black buttons served for eyes, and a third slightly lower for the nose. Two thick branches, each about three feet long, stuck out from the bottom section acting as arms. The snowman faced directly towards Bill.

Bill stared at the snowman. He believed those buttons were staring back at him, as if they were playing the "try not to blink game." Bill could feel the fear growing within him. Something weird but not foreign was coming over him. He'd felt it before, many times in his past. He was losing control. He tried to fight it but was not strong enough. *He* was winning. The Snowman was the game-master, always in control. Bill's body started to tremble, and now more than ever his eyes were focused out the window. Something was not allowing him to turn his head away. He could only look straight ahead at the snowman sitting there in the shed's spotlight.

Out of the tree tops, a large black bird, vulture-like with long silky black wings, landed on the left branch. The wings had distinct white patches at their tips. The head was bald, the beak, sharp and hooked. Huge talons clutched the thickness of the tree branch as the bird sat silently, looking around the back side of the house, its neck swiveling in quick jerky motions, like that of a robot. The blood-red eyes locked on Bill's.

Without taking its eyes off of Bill, the bird opened its beak and let out a series of screams. The sound hurt Bill's ears, but he couldn't take his hands away to cover them up. His hands were stuck to the sides of the window. The bird was a scavenger, and Bill now felt like the prey. The bird looked away from Bill, towards the snowman, and then back to Bill again.

The snowman's head started to move and wiggle slightly, just enough for Bill to notice. Small clumps of snow sprinkled off from between the two halves. What Bill had thought were buttons turned out to be lids, and they suddenly sprung open revealing two shining, light-blue eyes. It blinked twice and wiggled its nose, loosening the snow underneath as if it were trying to reveal a hidden mouth. A dark line about a foot long cracked through just underneath the nose.

When the mouth opened, the snowman looked like a puppet, but unlike any normal type of puppet, this one's mouth was filled with razor sharp teeth on top and bottom. The teeth were like tiny icicles, glistening in the shed's light.

Inside the house, a furious Gus was jumping up next to Bill, barking loudly, trying to get his attention, but Bill couldn't hear a thing.

Outside, the snowman started to talk. "Whatcha lookin' at? You in some kind of daze? Ain'tcha never seen a snowman before? Or ever hear one that talked?"

Bill didn't respond. He wanted to but it seemed like his words were frozen in fear. They wanted to come flowing out, but couldn't.

"Talk to me, Bill." The snowman paused, blinked, and then spoke again. "Cat got your tongue?"

Bill remembered the cat in the parking lot.

"Who are you?" Bill said hesitantly, surprised that his words were now audible. "You can't be real. There isn't that much snow outside, and the bird isn't really there. Just like the voice from the answering machine. The same voice." Bill shook his head. "All of it, not real."

"Of course I'm real," the snowman said in a deep voice, before switching to the voice of a woman in mid-sentence. The voice was soft and familiar. "Of course we're real, Bill. You don't remember me?"

Bill's mouth dropped and his heart skipped about ten beats.

"What, you don't recognize my voice?"

"Mary?" Bill said, wanting to step through the window and get closer to the soothing words and voice. "Mary, is that you?"

"Oh, you do recognize my voice." She started to cry. "You murdering son of a bitch! Why'd you do it, Bill? Why?"

"But Mary, what are you saying?"

"Why?" she screamed from the snowman's mouth.

"I would never—"

"Was it something I did, Bill? Something I said?"

Bill pressed harder against the glass. "Mary, don't say these things. You can't believe that I would—"

"I believe what I know, you murderer. It must have been a bad connection growing between us. Was I a bad wife?"

"Honey, please. You know I didn't do—" she wouldn't let him finish.

"Don't you call me honey you murdering fuck." It didn't sound like her. *When Mary was alive she never used that word,* he thought. *Something is making her say this.* The voice continued on. "It didn't even bother you that Amy was still in the house. You just went right on with your evil business and…"

"Stop it!" Bill screamed, pounding his fist against the glass.

" … kept on stabbing me…"

"Nooo, Mary! It's not true!"

"…like the killer you are…"

"It wasn't me," Bill pleaded, lowering his voice to a mere whisper. "It wasn't me."

"… and now I'm down here, in the cold… still feeling the wounds…"

Bill let out a loud wail of anger, clutching the wood paneling of the window frame.

"… stab stab stab stab stab…"

The snowman's voice returned, laughing. Bill could see the lower section beginning to shake.

The bird jumped off the branch and hovered directly in front of the snowman's head, knocking the hat to the snow. It looked up into the trees, and then brought its curved beak down like an ax into the snowman's head. Flapping its wings, the bird was fully extended, easily eight feet from tip to tip. Furiously pecking away at the head and face, snow flew in every direction. It chiseled as if sculpting. Clumps of the snowman's head crumbled to the ground.

Bill could see only the bottom half of the snowman. Streams of blood trickled down from the top half and settled in puddles on the snow. The bird finished his work, and while still hovering, turned his head towards Bill, giving him one last look before flying into the dark trees of the woods.

Bill's eyes followed the bird as it flew out of the shed's spotlight and into the darkness. Bill slowly lowered his eyes to what was left of the snowman. What he saw amazed him. The vision was far from over.

His daughter's head was sticking out from the top section of snow. Blood matted her hair down against her scalp, and one of her ears had been chewed off. Skin and cartilage from her nose dangled from the bridge. Lines of blood zigzagged like rivers on a map between and around her eyes, down her mangled nose and cheeks, and down the curve of her neck.

"Amy!" Bill screamed, fooled again by what the vision was showing him.

"Daddy." Her voice sounded young. "It's so cold down here. I can hear them screaming, the voices in Iceville, Daddy, but they don't hear me."

"My God, Amy! What is going on?"

"So cold. His touch is so cold." Her eyes closed.

Bill pushed hard against the window, so hard that he pushed himself free of the vision. He stumbled backwards and fell to the floor. His head bounced against the hardwood.

He felt something wet on his face; it smelled like dog. Bill opened his eyes and saw Gus, his large tongue drooling, dripping, and smacking against Bill's nose and cheeks.

"Oh, God, Gus." Bill nudged the dog away. "What the hell just happened to me?"

Gus barked.

Bill's head was throbbing, but he managed to raise himself off the floor, leaning on his elbows. Pushing himself to his feet, he felt old. He looked out the window.

Everything was back to normal. The accumulation was only a few inches. The bird and the snowman were both gone. Bill stared out the window, thinking. *They've started again. I thought it was all behind me, but I guess I was wrong.*

Gus joined him by the window, placing both front paws on the window seal, panting.

Bill saw something jutting out of the snow about where the snowman had been in the vision. It was long, thin, and black. *The feather. It's the black feather.*

"Oh, my God," he said slowly, backing away from the window, shaking and trembling. Sweat beaded on the top of his eyebrows. *Everything is returning,* he thought. *Now worse than ever. My past is revisiting my present, all aspects of it. The visions. The voices. The snowman. The urge. My old way of dealing with problems. My medicine.* He needed a drink, badly.

After glancing through the window at the feather again, Bill ran through the kitchen and into the front room. He grabbed a coat from the closet and hurried out the front door.

Gus followed him all the way to the back of the house to get the feather.

Chapter 10

6:30 P.M. Ohio River, Downtown Louisville
2 Inches

Ralph Anderson, Louisville's deputy chief of police, pulled his black, unmarked Crown Victoria off River Road and onto the Ohio River's bank. The scene had not been hard to find; ambulances and police cars were beacons of flashing light under the dark, overcast sky. Below the roller coaster highways and ramps of spaghetti junction, Ralph could hear the rolling of cars overhead as he stepped out of his car and onto the frozen, snow-covered grass along the riverfront.

The ground crunched under his feet. Ralph looked up at the raised highway, noticing each passing vehicle as they slowed down to catch a glimpse of what was happening below.

The downtown wind was frigid as it swooped up from the river and along the banks. Ralph adjusted the collar on his brown, London Fog overcoat to protect his ears from the wind and started down the bank's incline to the scene of the crime. About 20 yards in front of him, six officers struggled to keep nosy civilians away from the scene, and several more roped off a large semicircular area next to the river with wide yellow tape. Inside the crime scene perimeter, police photographers snapped pictures of the frozen river and its banks, and detectives searched with flashlights for evidence.

The river was frozen all the way across. For 13 days the temperature had failed to rise to zero. It was only the second time in history that the river had frozen all the way across. The red, white, and blue flashing lights from the police cars glistened off the river's coating of ice. Ralph couldn't help to notice its beauty at first sight, but his feelings soon changed after hearing what had happened out on *that* ice.

At 37, Ralph was the younger of the two Anderson brothers. Even at an earlier age, he had aspired to be a police officer or detective. He had been determined to put an end to senseless crime, rape, and murder, but after serving the force for 16 years, he was convinced that his goals were unrealistic. To totally eliminate evil from society was impossible, and after a while Ralph had learned to accept that reality.

Ralph took small steps down the slick incline, trying carefully not to slip on the snow. Flakes collected in his dark-brown hair and eyebrows like dandruff. At 6-foot-2, Ralph was a few inches taller than his brother Bill, but built relatively the same—both were barrel-chested and strong, with long, lanky arms, and huge hands. Ralph's brown eyes were well-hidden under his bushy eyebrows and separated by his sharp-bridged nose. The small cleft in his chin distinguished him from all the rest of the Anderson men, except for Grandpa Johnny, who had a cleft that was more often referred to as a valley, or canyon. Ralph's was minuscule in comparison.

Approaching the taped-off area by the river, Ralph reached inside his coat pocket and pulled out a pack of Camels. "Here we go again," he said, slipping the cigarette into his mouth and putting the pack back. "Another day, another death." Smoking was a minor habit he'd been trying to break now for years, but the stress of the job made doing without them very difficult. He hated to admit it, but as Lisa, his wife of five years, reminded him of daily, he was addicted. He'd already quit smoking at home, and work would come next. Lisa was now eight months pregnant with their first child, and Ralph was well aware of the dangers of second-hand smoke. He didn't want to put his wife's or the baby's health in jeopardy.

Work was a different story. The temptation was always there. For the moment though, he was quite proud of himself, down to smoking only half a pack a day while working. It still wasn't good enough for Lisa.

He walked through a crowd of people and slipped under the yellow tape marked: POLICE EMERGENCY STAY BACK. He was immediately greeted by a mountainous, black officer in a raincoat, anxious to unleash the news.

"What's the story, Andy?" Ralph asked with his cigarette dangling loosely between his freezing lips.

"Forensics are about finished," he paused. His face was strong, with high cheek bones and a sculpted jaw-line. His 6-foot-7 frame held a massive amount of well-distributed bulk and muscle. His voice was strong, deep, and intimidating. "Looks like another murder."

Ralph took out his lighter and lit another cigarette before saying another word. He took a long drag and blew the smoke into the frigid air. "Go on."

"It was a kid, Ralph."

"How old?"

"Thirteen."

"Christ," Ralph mumbled, looking to the river and back again. The flashing lights against its slippery surface no longer seemed beautiful. "How'd it happen?"

"He drowned, sir." Andy placed his huge hands on his hips. At 28 years old, Andy was already one of the most respected officers of the LPD. When needing a partner for anything, especially something dangerous or threatening, Ralph was always quick to choose Andy Evans. Andy went on. "There was another boy with him. He and his mother are in my car now, trying to warm up. I was waiting for you to question them. The poor boy is scared to death. I could hardly get a word out of him earlier."

"Naturally," Ralph said, squinting against the wind. It hurt his exposed face. He stared at the sign on the southern bank of the river. It read: WARNING *** KEEP OFF THE ICE *** NOT SAFE ** "So senseless," Ralph said, filling his lungs with another drag. "So young." He backed out of the way as an EMS team walked by. The chatter of the onlookers faded as they started to turn and walk away from the crime scene. "How long did it take to retrieve the body from under the ice?"

Andy motioned for him to come down the bank towards the river. "The friend called 911 as quickly as he could. We were at the scene in less than seven minutes, but it took our rescue team more than an hour to even locate the body." Standing next to the river, Andy pointed to a large section of ice they had to knock away to fish out the body. The jagged hole in the ice was about six feet in diameter, and flowing water could be heard and seen underneath. The sound of the running water was chilling.

"This is where we found the body," Andy squatted down to point. "Right around there. His left arm was snagged on that root right there. We were lucky; if he wouldn't have gotten tangled up, he could be in Owensboro by now. This is where we found him, but not where he fell through. He actually fell through the ice about a mile up the river. The currents carried him this far."

Ralph squinted, shaking his head. "I wonder how long that poor kid was unconscious, or how long it took him to die under the ice."

"By the looks of the body, he'd been under for nearly two hours, and luckily, we think he was dead for just about all of it. With the temperature of the water and the strong currents, he couldn't have been able to survive for more than a couple of minutes, a couple of struggling minutes."

"It's painful to even think about." Ralph threw his cigarette down and ground it into the snow with the tip of his shoe. He had lost his urge to smoke.

"Once we'd found him," Andy went on, "it wasn't all that difficult to get him out. The hard part was locating him. The damn ice is so muddy and thick, especially along the banks." He pointed to the edge of the ice. " I bet it's a good five or six inches deep along the sides. We were lucky to finally get a glimpse of him with one of our flashlights. Real lucky. He was lodged up under the ice, his body twisted, and his face was glaring upward, mouth wide open and crammed full of leaves. His face was cut up real badly, too. Terrible sight, both the kid's eyes were still open when we found him. It scared the piss out of me when I first shined the light on him." He paused, taking a deep breath, then exhaling. "For a second, man, I thought he was still alive."

Andy stared down at the ice. "You know, I find it difficult to believe that he simply fell under. The kid couldn't have weighed a hundred pounds. Especially where he went under. It was along the bank, where the ice was the thickest. I couldn't see him cracking through it even if he had tried."

"What are you getting at?"

"Well, I don't know for sure, but I got a look at the body. The kid's shoulders were broken and bruised badly."

"There *was* a lot of pressure under that ice. The impact against the side alone could have caused the injuries."

"I know at this point this is speculation, but I still think someone had to have pushed him under."

"Let's go to your car," Ralph said. "Hopefully the other kid is ready to talk, possibly shed some light on this mess. What was the victim's name?"

"Bobby, as his friend, Jamie, told us. Full name is Robert Bates. He was a freshman at River City High School. He had it all written down with his phone number and address inside a little Velcro wallet."

"Come on, let's get some information."

They walked up the bank towards Andy's car.

Andy jumped into the driver's seat of his car and reached across to unlock the passenger's door for Ralph. Once in the car, they turned around and faced a frightened mother and son who were crouching together in the corner of the back seat, just behind the passenger's side. Jamie and his mother were both crying.

Jamie Kennedy was his name, and his mother's was Beverly. Jamie was 12 years old, with strawberry-red hair and a face full of freckles. His coke-bottle glasses were askew on his nose as his mother's meaty arm clutched him tightly against her breast, holding onto her son for dear life. He wasn't pushing away; he needed to be held.

Beverly was an enormous woman, easily weighing 300 pounds. She smothered him in her grasp. Beverly's face was round and chubby, and even in the darkness of the closed car, Ralph could see the mascara streaming down her face from her tears.

Ralph turned his body so he could talk to the boy a little easier. He stretched his arm over his seat towards Jamie. "My name is Ralph, son, Ralph Anderson, and I just want to ask you a few questions."

Beverly loosened her grip and gave her boy some breathing room. Jamie shied away from shaking Ralph's extended arm, but as soon as he was given some space from his mother he took a deep breath and shrugged his shoulders. He remained silent, but seemed to be much more in control of himself than Andy had seen only 20 minutes earlier.

"Jamie," Ralph said in the most pleasant voice he could, "let's talk about your friend, Robert."

"Bobby!" Jamie blurted out, folding his arms to his chest like a little brat. "His name is Bobby."

Beverly was embarrassed by her son's reaction. Both officers could tell. "Jamie, you watch your tone of voice with these two nice men. They're on our side."

"It's okay, Mrs. Kennedy," Ralph nodded.

"Call me, Beverly, please."

Andy said, "Jamie, we *are* on your side. We are here to help you. You and us, we can be a team. You don't have to worry about anything."

Ralph said, "We know you're scared, and we understand that; I mean, who wouldn't be? It's okay to cry if you feel you have to."

"Okay," Jamie said sniffling, wiping his runny nose down the arm of his coat. He was slowly warming up to them.

Ralph continued. "Concentrate now. What can you remember about tonight? Take your time. No hurry."

Jamie was finally able to look Ralph in the eyes. "Me and my friend Bobby ate supper, you see, he came over to my house after he got out of school. He was all excited because he met a new friend there. Anyway, after we ate, we went outside to play in the snow. Then we got the idea of going ice skating down at the river."

"Had you ever done that before?" Andy asked.

"No, sir. I heard about some other bigger kids doing it though."

"You live close to here then?" Ralph asked.

"Uh huh, just a couple of streets off of River Road."

Beverly could hold her anger in no longer. "Why, honey?" she bellowed. "Why? You know darn well I told you never to go to the river without an adult. What are Bobby's parents going to think of me now?" She started to cry again, putting the saddle of Bobby's death partially on her back.

Ralph placed his hand on her shoulder. "Don't worry about that, Beverly, this was not your fault. You can't take the blame for this. No one can. It was a tragic accident. You know it's impossible to keep track of kids 24 hours a day."

"We'll handle everything with the parents," Andy said.

Beverly gained her composure, allowing her son to finish talking.

Jamie glanced at his mother with a silent apology, and then went on with his story. "I know we shouldn'ta been there, but the ice seemed real strong and solid, so we decided to give it a try."

Beverly closed her eyes with her free hand. She refrained from speaking.

"We skated for about 30 minutes before we started getting really cold."

"So at that point, you were getting ready to leave?" Ralph asked.

"Yeah, I mean, yes, sir. Bobby kept talking about making a snowman. I skated on over to the bank and changed back into my snow boots."

"And what did Bobby do at this time?"

"Bobby decided to stay out there a couple of minutes longer. He wanted to show me how he could spin around real fast on the ice, just like the people in the Olympics can do." Jamie lowered his head, trying to hide his tears. "I warned him not to get too close to the middle cause it hardly had any ice covering it."

"And he went towards the middle of the river?" Andy asked.

"No, he did as I said. He came closer to the side." Jamie looked up. "The *man* came running from the middle."

"The man? What man?" they asked simultaneously.

"A crazy man. He came from the middle of the river, out of the water and ice, and he pushed Bobby under."

"What else can you tell us about him?" Ralph asked, noticing that Andy's speculation had been right on the nose.

"He jumped out from the middle of the river, landing on the ice. He ran towards Bobby, screaming and yelling, waving his arms around and stuff like a . . . a crazy man."

"What was he saying?" Ralph asked.

"He was yelling stuff like, 'watch for the snowman, look at the snowman', and 'I'm the real snowman', stuff like that. He was laughing the whole time."

"Snowman?" Ralph whispered, mostly to himself.

Andy looked at Ralph. "That mean something to you?"

"N . . no," Ralph lied, "no, it doesn't." Ralph was silent for a second. He allowed Andy to go on with the questioning.

"What exactly did this man do, Jamie?"

Jamie hesitated briefly before answering. Remembering was difficult for him, and frightening. "He ran after Bobby, but then Bobby slipped and fell. He grabbed Bobby from behind. Bobby tried to get loose, but the man was too strong. Real strong and mean. He picked Bobby up off the ice and started jumping up and down. I didn't know what to do. I was so scared, I just kind of froze. I couldn't move."

"We know, honey," his mother said, kissing his forehead. "You did the right thing. If you would have gone out there he would have killed you, too."

Jamie went on. "Bobby was crying and screaming, but the man just kept jumping up and down on the ice. He was wearing black boots, like cowboy boots, and each time he landed he'd dig part of the ice away. He just kept jumping . . . until he made a hole." Jamie paused, taking another needed breath. He was now showing tremendous composure and cour-age. "Then the man looked at me with his light-blue eyes."

"Blue eyes?" Ralph asked.

"Not just blue, Mr. Anderson. They were light-blue. He was really scary looking. He looked at me and asked if Bobby could swim very good. I just stood there, saying nothing, watching as he forced Bobby through that tiny hole in the ice. Bobby was much bigger than that hole, but the man made him fit."

Ralph couldn't believe what he was hearing.

Andy was stunned.

Beverly brought her thick meaty palms to her face and cried.

"That was the last I saw of him."

"The man?"

"No, Bobby. Then the river took him away."

"What happened next?"

Jamie shifted in his seat. "After he pushed Bobby through, I yelled something at him. I can't remember what I said, but the man turned back towards me and pointed. The next thing I knew, he was running down the river following Bobby's body, pointing at it and laughing the whole time. He ran under the bridge downtown, and that's when I left to go find a phone and call 911." Jamie broke down into tears.

Andy shook his head. He'd never heard of such a demented story in all his years as a cop. He didn't know what to say. What would he tell the kid's parents? And how would he do it?

Ralph felt sorry for the kid. He was pouring his little heart out. He hated to ask him any more questions, but they needed a description of the attacker. "Jamie, I'm sorry, but one last question and then Andy can take you home."

Jamie looked at Ralph and nodded.

"Can you in any way describe what the man looked like? His size? What he was wearing?"

"He was white, like you Mr. Anderson, and his eyes were light-blue, like I said before. He had real long white hair, down past his shoulders, and I guess he was about as tall as you, Mr. Evans."

"That big, huh?" Ralph asked.

"Oh, yeah."

"Doing just fine, Jamie," Andy said, "can you tell us what he was wearing?"

"All he was wearing was a pair of jeans, boots, and a plain ole white T-shirt."

"It's awfully cold out now, Jamie, can you remember if he was wearing a coat or jacket, or possibly even holding one?"

"No, I'm sure of it. All he had was the shirt."

The questions were over for now. Ralph folded up his note pad and thanked Jamie and his mother for their time. "Andy is going to take you home now, but we'll be in touch."

Beverly hugged her son and nodded. She thanked the two officers as they got out of their car. They waited in the back seat while Ralph and Andy talked outside.

"I'll find this son of a bitch," Andy said over the hood of the car.

"Sounds like a real lunatic, that's for sure."

"You think he might be albino?"

"It's possible," Ralph said, lighting another cigarette. "Who knows? We've got some fairly good information, though. We need to get right on this."

"Hofmann and Littlefield are down there right now finishing everything up. We've got it all under control here. I'll run them home and then head over to talk to Bobby's parents. I'd like to get that over with."

"Good idea," Ralph said, "and good luck. I'm going to drive down River Road and check the spot where he was pushed under. I'll be in touch with you first thing in the morning."

"Okay, Chief."

"Good work tonight, Andy."

"Thanks."

Andy got into his car and drove off the river bank. Ralph watched them go and then jogged over to his car. He felt in his gut that there was another piece to the puzzle, and he was determined to find it. He drove off the bank and turned left, heading east along River Road. About a mile down the road he stopped. The scene was still marked off with yellow tape, but deserted.

He located the hole in the ice and walked all around it, careful not to get too close. The hole was already starting to re-freeze, but Ralph could still hear the strong flow of water below. He just wanted to take a quick look around and then head back to his car. The weather was killing him. The wind swooping across the river was bitterly cold, numbing his ears and nose.

Since the time of the incident, a light dusting of snow had covered the ice, but Ralph was still able to see some indentations or prints in the surface. He followed the bootprints around the hole. What surprised him was the pattern scratched in the ice. Prints from the claws of a bird? He wondered. Jamie never mentioned anything about a bird. Maybe the bird arrived after Jamie had gone. The talon scratches were huge. Ralph quivered at the thought of how large the owner of those talons must have been. Other than the ice and the talon marks, there seemed to be nothing else to see.

Ralph headed back to his car. About five feet away from the river bank, he saw something red at the bottom of one of the trees, buried under the snow. He walked over to check it out. It was obviously out of place.

What he found was a red coat, crumpled and frozen. After prying it off the ground, Ralph shook it hard to loosen it up, and then looked for some sort of identification. Written with a black marker on the tag of the coat was the name of the owner—Bill Anderson.

What the hell? Bill? What is your coat doing out here by the river, in the middle of a crime scene that involves a man that calls himself the snowman? What were you doing at the river?

Ralph was confused. Does Bill have something to do with this? He tucked the coat inside his own and ran, slipping and sliding up the bank to his car. He radioed for an officer to come guard the scene over night and then pulled away. He needed some answers from his brother.

Chapter 11

Brice joined the rest of the team in the tent. They were all gathered around a large pot of oatmeal, each one methodically eating a bowl, savoring every bite. They were all starving, but too worn out to eat fast. They made room in the small tent for Brice to sit down, and Leroy McCalister handed him a steaming bowl.

"Ah, food," Brice said, sitting down Indian-style next to Leroy.

"Dig in while it's still hot," Leroy said between bites. At 56, Leroy was the oldest member of the expedition team. As a retired weather analyst from Colorado, he had set out on the trip to study and research new aspects of global warming and ozone depletion. The rest of the team had yet to see him run a single experiment. They figured out that science and research weren't his real reasons for coming along. The real reasons didn't really matter, though. Leroy was an adventurous man, a writer, and a near expert on the history of snowfall and Antarctic travel, so the rest of the team suspected that he really had nothing better to do with his retirement than journey to the South Pole collecting knowledge. Leroy was as close as one could get to an Antarctic historian, and he never shied away from letting the others in on what he knew about the continent's short history. He always sounded knowledgeable, but with some of his off-the-wall theories about the continent's mysteries and past, the others were often annoyed with his wisdom, especially as the trip was now coming to a close. They knew of his controversial books, and they did their best not to get him talking about what he had written because once he got going, it was difficult to shut him up.

The man on the other side of Brice was 47-year-old Colonel Marvin Shard, a research representative from the United States Air Force. He was the only military man and African-American on the crew, and his main reason for the trip was of an adventuresome nature. He was in it for the Air Force, but mostly he was in it for the rush of doing something completely stupid and dangerous. He thrived on challenges and loved to live on the edge, and his friends from the Air Force would be the first ones to agree. They hated flying with him when his maniac button went off, and his wife hated driving with him. Danger was in his blood.

The two women in the group were Loreda Cranfield, 38, and Pamala Stevens, 27. Sharing the same tent for 51 nights made them very good friends. Loreda was an adventure and thriller writer looking for a new story or idea for her next book. Published twice, she was looking for something excitingly new and drastic for her third book. The adventures they'd experienced so far would surely fit the bill.

The days were long and the nights were non-existent. The only darkness they had was what they could provide for themselves under their sleeping bags. The skiing was hard, treacherous, and grueling with the wind, cold temperatures, and uneven terrain constantly slowing them down. Loreda would never forget the rumbling of the ice as it would shift unexpectedly under their feet. The mountains, sastrugi ice waves, cliffs, crevasses, whiteouts—she would remember all of this and include them in the next book. She couldn't wait to get started.

Pamala was the second youngest of the group. A graduate student of the University of Wisconsin, she was doing hands-on research on the Lost Continent for her senior thesis. She was accompanying her geography teacher, Dr. Mark Moriarity, as his assistant. She was his understudy, and would get a semester's worth of credit for coming along. She couldn't pass up the offer, and she knew the experience would speak for itself in the future.

Dr. Moriarity was considered by many in his field of work to be a genius. His students loved him simply because they thought he had the answers to everything, and many times he did. He was a big, bear of a man, with a bushy, brown beard, his own facial barrier against the frigid air. He was 39 years old, equipped with a boisterous personality, and was able to relate very well with most everyone, especially his students. Married with two kids, an authority in his field, and in a profession he loved, he had absolutely nothing in his life to complain about, except for the Antarctic weather.

To Loreda's right sat one of the two snowmobile operators, 37-year-old Eric Brey, or 'Eric the Red' as they had nicknamed him on the first day of the expedition because of his long mop of red hair. He now had a thick red beard along with it. Sitting next to Eric was 34-year-old Magnus Gustavson, the second snowmobile operator. Magnus was a tall, lanky blonde who was born in Sweden but had moved to the United States 30 years earlier with his family. He was very much an American. Their job as snowmobile operators was to carry the equipment and supplies from camp-site to camp-site. The rest of the crew would take off early in the mornings on skis, while Eric and Magnus broke camp. It wouldn't take them long to catch up on their snowmobiles, eventually pass the crew, and then search for the night's next camp-site. The trip could have been made without them, as earlier expeditions had, but for safety and logistic reasons, snowmobiles were the modern way to go.

As the team sat around the tent in a circle, they washed the oatmeal down with cups of melted ice. It wasn't the best of beverages, but it was better than nothing. They were out of cocoa and Kool-aid, so they made do with what they had. They all tried to lean back and relax the best they could.

Leroy pulled out a small, black, leather book from his coat and started writing, being very careful not to let anyone else see. He was extremely secretive about his journal. He wasn't the only one to keep a journal, most of them kept one of some sort, but Leroy was the only one that protected his like it was a threatened infant.

"Hey, Leroy," Eric said, "you got the answers to all the world's problems in that thing? Ease up a little, old man."

Everyone chuckled or smiled. They showed no interest in what was written in his journal, but deep down they were all dying to know.

"That's very funny, Red, but this," Leroy held up his journal, "is very personal."

Gabe gulped down another spoonful of oatmeal and chased it down with the melted ice. "What can be so damn personal about this place?" He wiped his mouth with the top of his glove. "Unless you've seen something we haven't, or that we may have missed."

"If that's the case, Leroy," Eric said, "I wanna know about it."

You disrespectful youngsters, Leroy thought. Shaking his head, Leroy closed his journal and put it back inside his coat. "I don't know about the rest of you, but I'm beat. Eric, did you and Magnus get the sleep tents set up?"

"Yes."

"Good, because—"

Just then a huge gust of wind smacked the side of the tent, shifting it slightly. The pot of oatmeal shook and bounced. The poles in the corners of the tent started to rattle. The ice underneath moved and rumbled. They were all trembling and vibrating with the unstable atmosphere around them. They held onto each other and whatever they could grab hold of to keep stable. The oatmeal spilled over onto the floor of the tent. A corner of the tent collapsed, but no one was hurt.

The sudden movement of the ice was abnormal, unlike anything they had experienced on their 52 days of traveling. It was a minor earthquake, a tremor, and it lasted about 10 seconds before everything settled down again.

Chapter 12

6:50 P.M., Iroquois Park
2 Inches

Bill sat at his kitchen table, trembling, nervously shaking as he stared at a bottle of Jim Beam. It had been in his cabinet above the sink for three years since he'd won it at a Christmas party. He cursed himself now for not throwing it away then, but swore he was only keeping it to show himself that he could resist temptation. He felt a tremendous amount of pride because of his recovery. He kept the bottle around as a test of his strength and will power, proving to himself that he could live in the same house with his worst enemy and not feel the urge to abuse it.

No one knew about the bottle. He kept it hidden in the back of the cabinet, not because he feared it, but because of what others would think if they stumbled across it, especially Amy. Even though he hadn't had a drink in nearly 18 years, if she were to find the alcohol in the house her mind would certainly wonder and feelings of disappointment would over-shadow the trust.

Bill rubbed his thumb over the unopened bottle top. His unsteady hand shook the alcohol's meniscus around the interior of the glass. The sight of the liquid had a teasing affect, and the more he stared the more he wanted it. *The Snowman*, he thought. *The dreams and visions. The bad luck. Everything is returning. Stay strong.* He never thought he would feel the weakness again. He thought the temptations were long gone, but now more than ever he felt he needed a drink to calm his nerves. The last vision had been so real. The lady's voice had been Mary's, he was sure of it. And then Amy. It had been her face in the snow, mangled and bleeding, all so real.

He couldn't take it any more.

He needed a drink.

Slowly he started to twist the cap. He stopped before breaking the seal. He grabbed the feather he had found in the snow and felt it with his fingers. It was more than a foot long with a white mark at its tip, and its surface was rigid and hard, nearly frozen. Running the feather through the fingers on his right hand, he picked the bottle back up with his left.

His eyes focused on the bottle, the feather, and then back to the bottle again. "Don't let them win," he whispered, "stay strong."

The feather and the alcohol. The would-be cause and effect. The tickets for his return to alcoholism. He had to resist. He stared at them both, yet understood neither one of them.

"Be strong," he hissed through clenched teeth. "Resist." If he couldn't be strong, the memories of one would definitely lead to the indulgence of the other.

Amy. His focus turned to Amy, and suddenly away from the objects he now held in his hands. Unaware that he was doing so, he dropped the bottle and feather down on the table and stood up. He couldn't rid himself of the sight. Amy's head in the snow. Her ear and nose. The blood and confusion. Why? He didn't know.

Slowly, Bill walked from the kitchen to the television room. *She said that she was so cold. What did she mean?* He needed to see her, to talk to her, to hold her. She was supposed to be home in two days, but he didn't think he could wait that long.

He grabbed Amy's high school senior picture from the top of the television and walked over to the couch. He suddenly felt tired. Staring at her lovely face, his eyelids became heavy. He feared sleep, but couldn't control it. Even though he had been wide awake only minutes earlier while he was staring at the feather and the bottle, now he could barely keep his eyes open.

Clutching the picture to his chest, Bill swung his feet onto the couch and rested his head on one of the pillows, all the time thinking of Amy. At least he had control of his thoughts. Within seconds he was sound asleep, and his thoughts were no longer under his control.

Chapter 13

7:40 P.M., Helen Newberry Hall

Amy dropped her legs over the side of the bed and sat upright. She used her shirt sleeve to dry her tears.

"Amy?" Kathy whispered, sitting on the bed next to her deeply troubled friend.

"Yeah," she answered, staring down at the floor.

"You're starting to scare me."

Amy chuckled, forcing a weak smile. "Thanks."

"I mean it, Amy. First that nightmare, then the incident in the library, and now this. What exactly just happened to you?"

"Nothing."

"No," Kathy said harshly, "I can't believe that, and I won't. Something is definitely wrong, and I don't understand why you're not telling me everything."

"It's not something I like to talk about. It frightens me."

"You can tell me anything, Amy. I'm your best friend. If you can't tell me, who can you tell?" Amy slowly turned her head towards Kathy. Kathy said, "I'm not letting you off the hook this time."

Amy looked Kathy straight in the eyes. "I've never talked to anyone about this before. I'm a little scared."

"Please, Amy, maybe I can help."

Amy hesitated. "Okay. Do you remember when I told you that my mother was killed in a car accident when I was two years old?"

"I do."

"Well, she wasn't killed in a car accident. I made that up." It was difficult, but Amy said the painful words. "She was murdered."

"Oh, my God," Kathy said softly, placing her hand over her mouth.

Amy stood from the bed and sat back down on the couch. "My mother was murdered 20 years ago on December 16. I was only two when it happened, and I was the only other person in the house."

"Who? I mean, the murderer. Who was it?"

"For a long time the police thought it was my father. Some probably still do."

Kathy's eyes lit up.

"But he was acquitted. I don't want to go into the details, but thank God he had a good lawyer. My father was innocent. The murder went down as unsolved, and most of it was unexplainable."

Kathy scooted closer to the couch. "They never found the real killer?"

"Nope, and they didn't really try. They were so quick to put everything on my dad that they didn't have any more suspects. To them at the time he was the easiest target."

"That's terrible."

"I know. It screwed our lives up for a couple of years, but fortunately we were able to get back on track." Amy paused, taking a deep breath before going on. "It wasn't easy growing up without a mother, but my dad did a fantastic job. It still wasn't the same though. I never got to know my mom. The only way I can remember her is by stories and pictures."

"I'm sorry, Amy."

"Thanks. I don't really remember her, but I still know her voice," Amy said, glancing back down to the floor. "I heard her yelling for help. I can still remember the screaming like it only happened yesterday."

"I don't understand."

"The only thing I can remember from that day has something to do with what just happened here a few minutes ago."

"What did just happen?"

"A flashback. I can't explain it. Really, no one can explain it, but the day my mother was murdered there was some kind of a large black bird in the house. It's this black bird that I remember most of all."

"I don't follow."

"From what I've learned—my dad tried to keep a lot of the details from me, but I learned them anyway from old newspapers and such—I found out that this bird, sort of the killer's pet I guess, broke through the door to my bedroom."

"And this is what you remember?"

"I can't get rid of it. Those two beaming red eyes looking down upon me, and everything was surrounded by darkness. It perched on my crib and covered me with its wings, suffocating me." Amy shook her head slowly. "The wings," she paused. "I can still remember the wings as clear as the day it happened. Leather. They sounded like leather, like a leather cape, and smelled terribly. The sound of those wings flapping muffled the only words I can ever remember my mother saying. It's sad that through the two years I was with her, I can't remember a thing that could be considered a pleasant memory. All I know of her voice . . ." Amy stopped to gather herself. "All I knew of her voice were the cries of pain and her screaming for help."

Kathy said nothing.

"It was terrible, especially for my dad. He's the one that saw her."

"Get killed?"

"No, but he's the one who found her. He had gone out to the store to get groceries, and when he came back he found her dead behind the couch in our family room. I was in his arms when he found her. He did tell me that much, but of course, I don't remember it. It's just the black bird that causes me trouble. That is what haunts my dreams."

"So this is what the last nightmare was about?" Kathy asked. "This bird?"

"Yeah. It was the first flashback I've had since probably my freshman year of high school. I had nightmares and flashbacks about that bird for years and years, but eventually they went away. I actually believed that they were gone for good, until now. I guess I was wrong."

"What do you think brought it about?"

Amy shook her head. She didn't have any idea.

"What about stress?"

"I doubt it. I looked at those red lights on the alarm clock and went into some kind of trance. From then on out it owned me."

"Wait a minute," Kathy interrupted. "Who owned you?"

"The Snowman. My mother was murdered during the worst snowstorm in Louisville history, so I think this psycho picked up the name from that. Everyone referred to him as the Snowman, and since he was never caught, he'll never have a real name. When my father found my mother on the floor, he knelt down beside her. To his side, he saw that the word "Snowman" had been written on the back of the couch in red lipstick, or so I was told. The papers said it was blood, but then again, I quickly learned to ignore what the papers had said. The things they wrote about my dad were terrible, and so wrong."

"Why did you say he owned you a minute ago?"

"It's as if he owns a part of my mind, or someone does, and whenever he wants he can tap into it. He's the one that reminds me of what happened. He's the reason for my nightmares and flashbacks. Whether it's something supernatural, paranormal, or just totally in my head, he is the one that links me to my haunted past. I thought they were over and that he was gone, but evidently he's back, or something is back, because I don't think I could bring these flashbacks back on my own. Why would I?"

"You wouldn't," Kathy assured her.

"I think that he is the man I saw in my nightmare earlier, he's got to be. Why? I don't know the answer to that, not yet anyway, but until late this afternoon I had never seen the Snowman's face before."

"If it's really the same person."

"It has got to be. He's not a person at all. He's a . . . a monster, an evil monster. My dad sees him in his nightmares, too, or at least he used to. Like myself, I don't think he has experienced anything unusual for many years. For about 10 years though, after my mother was murdered, my father was swarmed, almost possessed, by terribly vivid flashbacks, nightmares, and visions. They were all so unpredictable. There was no controlling when they'd happen. He never liked to talk about the Snowman or what he saw in his visions, but from what little he has described of that monster, I'm almost sure it's the same guy as the one in my last nightmare."

"Amy, this is all so unbelievable."

"I know it sounds that way. But it is very real, and my mother is proof of that. I don't know why it is all happening again, and it scares me to death to think about it, but for some reason I'm now seeing the Snowman, and not only the bird. He owns my mind again."

"Did either one of you get professional help?"

"We both met with a psychiatrist, a friend of the family."

"Did you tell him any of this?"

"It was a her, and no, I didn't."

"Why not?"

"I was so young at the time. I froze up, never said a word. I denied seeing or hearing anything. And why wouldn't they believe a little five or six-year-old, or something like that, who was only two at the time of the murder?" Amy leaned back against the couch and took a deep breath. "You'd be surprised what a baby can remember, and they would too."

"You've never said a word to anyone about this, not even your father?"

"Just you."

"He has no clue that you had, or still have, I should say, these flashbacks and nightmares?"

"I don't think he does, or if he did, he never pressed any further than a few questions. It does feel good to finally share it with someone, though."

"I'm sure it does. Amy, it isn't healthy to keep things like that to yourself. You have to tell your father; he has to know."

"I've been thinking about that too, and I've decided to tell him. I can't go through this alone, not again. I wouldn't be surprised if it has also started with him. I'll talk to him tomorrow."

"Good idea, Amy. And you won't be alone, either. I'll be right there with you."

"Thanks."

"I mean it."

"I know, and I appreciate it. Oh, I just remembered that my dad still thinks we're coming in Friday. I forgot to tell him that we switched our tickets."

"You better call him then."

"I will, later though." Amy got up from the couch and stretched. She walked over to the window and looked out across the snow-covered campus. Her breath clouded a small section of the glass. She turned back to Kathy.

"Does everything have a reason?" Amy asked. "Why was it my mom? She never harmed anyone. I don't understand why she had to die. I'm sure I loved her, but yet, I never really had a chance to love her. Why my family? Was it randomly selected, or did it have a meaning, a reason? I've got the Snowman to thank for everything. He's the puzzle that I have to solve," she said, shaking her head, "and the missing pieces are multiplying." She looked Kathy straight in the eyes. "Even in my nightmares he's getting closer to me. He's coming again Kathy, and for some reason, I'm getting the feeling that this time he's coming after me."

Chapter 14

8:20 P.M., Southern Parkway
2 Inches

Turning onto the access road from Southern Parkway, Ralph Anderson struggled to find his driveway. The snow had started falling again, and with the wind, it severely decreased his visibility. Glancing to his right, he spotted his porch light through the falling snow and scattered trees, and followed it. He slowed down, easing into the snow-covered driveway and pressed the button on his sunvisor. The garage door rotated upward. He drove inside and closed the door behind him.

After turning the engine off, Ralph glanced at the passenger's seat and stared at the red coat. He had thought about it the entire way home, and he couldn't figure out why it had been down by the river, or what Bill had to do with the boy's death, if anything at all. Despite the family ties, questions would have to be asked.

He thought of the Snowman. The man that had supposedly murdered his sister-in-law. The man that was never seen or heard from again. The man that was never found. Ralph couldn't help comparing the circumstances. Two killings, unrelated, 20 years apart, both at about the same time of year, both involving the Snowman, and as Ralph hated to admit, in some way, both had involved his brother. *What does it mean? What have you gotten yourself into, Bill?*

He stared at the red coat as it began to shed its frozen layer of snow onto the seat. The car's heater worked well. He was warm. He debated whether or not to stay in the car and head straight over to his brother's house, but he had to check in with his wife first. He was already much later than the time he had told her he'd be home. He did call, but the guilt would still remain if he were any later than he was now. He needed answers, the coat demanded them, but they would have to wait an hour or so.

Lisa wasn't due for another month, but Ralph was anxious. She was large enough to give birth any time now, so Ralph was always checking in on her. According to Lisa, he was checking on her a little too often. His calls from work, every hour on the hour no matter where he was, were starting to annoy her. It would be their first child, so Ralph was determined to have everything running smoothly when the time came. The coat would have to wait, but now it brought back memories, memories that he was not yet ready to face—the tragedy, the trials, the snowfall, the aftermath, the Snowman.

He remembered the day vividly. Only a senior in high school, he remembered the 20 inches of snow. He remembered being trapped in the house with his parents, everything buried. He remembered the phone call, the harbinger of bad news, and most of all he remembered his father telling him what had happened to Bill. It had hit the entire family hard, making the winter very long, difficult, and depressing for everyone. Ralph had been crushed.

Growing up, Bill and Ralph were not what one would call close. Despite the eight-year age gap, they had fought quite often. Whether it had been over the chores, the television, phone, or sports, they clashed over nearly everything. Although the conflicts had been mostly verbal, both could remember the few times their arguments had come to blows. Bill, the elder, had won them all.

During all the years the two of them had lived under the same roof, not a day went by that tensions didn't arise. It was more than the normal older brother picking on younger brother, and growing up, Ralph had resented it. He wasn't sure why they didn't get along. They just didn't, and still sometimes don't. It wasn't jealousy, or even hate, but a close bond was definitely not there. Deep down, there had been sparks of love for one another. It was an almost forced, family love, but it did exist. So Ralph did care about Bill and was crushed when he'd heard the news of Mary's death.

After Bill left for college, the tensions decreased. Their meetings were a lot less frequent, and when they did get together, calmer emotions usually prevailed. For the first time, Ralph started to look up to his older brother. Bill was out on his own, in college, starting a life for himself. Ralph admired that and was even proud to call him his big brother. For a while, Ralph had started to respect and trust Bill.

And then came the drugs and alcohol, two habits their parents had spent all of their lives preaching to the boys against. To them, it had been like a slap in the face. Bill's addictions in college had turned him away from any family life. The trust was gone, and the respect Ralph had gained for Bill was gone, too. He no longer admired Bill's status in life, and he no longer had thoughts of wanting to do what his big brother was doing. Bill was ruining his life, and Ralph was ashamed of him.

When Mary was murdered, Ralph didn't doubt Bill's innocence, but in his eyes it was another blemish on his personality. The charges alone, no matter how off-base they may have been, made Ralph view his brother in a different light. The one person who had been able to change Bill's life for the better was now dead, and for nearly two years his brother was the one the police had thought committed the crime. The tragedy could have had two outcomes. It could have brought them closer, as it had with Bill and their parents, or it could have driven them further apart. With Ralph and Bill, the latter happened.

With the nightmares, visions, and flashbacks Bill had experienced after the tragedy, his life quickly went downhill again. Ralph had realized that Bill was suffering through some very difficult times, but he wasn't convinced that it had all been because of the Snowman. With the criminology and drug-related classes Ralph had been taking in college to prepare for the police force, he'd concluded that the flashbacks and visions may have been the results of other circumstances. He had learned that the symptoms of alcoholism and the side effects of hallucinatory drugs remain long after they had been used. The idea that the memories of the Snowman alone were causing Bill's flashbacks seemed a bit hokey to Ralph. He believed that the drugs Bill had taken in college were coming back to haunt him when he was emotionally weak and vulnerable. For many years, Ralph hadn't been convinced that his brother had totally stopped drinking. He had always thought the worst of him. In his own little way, Ralph had tried helping, but in the end he had given up. For seven years Ralph had nothing to do with Bill.

It wasn't until Bill was free of the dreams and flashbacks, that Ralph slowly began gaining respect again. Finally, Ralph became convinced that Bill had stopped drinking and taking drugs. He saw that his brother was again starting to turn his life around, and he felt good for him. They were both maturing. He cared, and deep down felt a tiny inkling of guilt for not giving more support over the years. But then again, what kind of support had Bill given Ralph growing up? None.

Ralph had questioned Bill's motivation in not trying to find a different job, but he reminded himself that it was better than nothing, and at the time of his hiring, Bill *was* having a very difficult time of finding any type of work. Ralph was able to see that Bill was content with living a stress-free life, being out of jail, free of drugs, and back with his daughter, even if it meant working as a janitor.

Over the last five or six years, Bill and Ralph had been getting along quite well. They saw each other at family functions and were starting to talk more than they had ever talked before. Their relationship was growing, and the respect and trust between the two was increasing. The idea of friendship was even in the future, possibly, maybe. But now this.

Word of the Snowman. Another death. Bill's coat.

Ralph wasn't sure what to think, and he didn't know how he should feel. He grabbed the coat and was ready to take it in with him when he realized it would raise suspicion and questions with Lisa, and he wasn't in the mood to talk about it. He'd tell her about the boy's death and leave it at that. She didn't need to know the details, not yet anyway. Ralph folded the coat and stuck it behind his seat.

What is it with snow, he thought. *Why does everything seem to happen when it snows? Does it drive people crazy? What is it?* To Ralph it seemed like every year during a snowfall something strange would happen. Even if the death or murder had nothing to do with the snow, Ralph couldn't help but group the two together. *It's cabin fever,* he thought. *It's cabin fever that drives people to do the crazy things they do. They don't like being contained like prisoners.*

Just last year about this time, Ralph had gotten a call one night about a reported gunshot. The incident had been only two blocks away from his house. It was a suicide. The man's name was Jonathan Mobour, 55 years old, his life brought to an end by a shotgun blast through the mouth. Ralph would never forget walking into the house that night. The heat must have been off for hours, if not days, because the house had been freezing. Along with several other pathetic excuses to end his life, at the bottom of the suicide note was written: *Can't take the weather anymore. It's gone and driven me crazy.*

The electricity in Mr. Mobour's house had been off for days, and the inside of the house was silent and dark. Ralph remembered the creaking of the front door when he'd opened it, and if death had a smell, the front room had it. Mr. Mobour sat in the middle of the floor, slumped back in his wooden rocking chair, still holding the shotgun. Ralph would swear to this day that the rocking chair was still moving. The man's head had been completely blown away from the bottom of his chin. The tip of the spinal column was protruding through what was left of the back of his neck. Blood covered the floor and walls: skull fragments surrounded the chair like scattered rocks. Possibly unrelated to the suicide, but relevant in Ralph's mind, it had been snowing heavily that day.

In the winter of 1979 Ralph had experienced his first homicide case, and it was one he would never forget. A 29-year-old man, depressed over losing his job, decided to take it out on his family. That evening, after clearing the driveway of snow, he beat his wife and eight-year-old boy to death with a shovel. He then turned the shovel on himself and beat his head with it until he could no longer grasp the tool. He was found with severe brain damage, but he lived, spending the next two years of his life in a hospital before finally dying. Ralph remembered everything from that day, too, including the exact snow accumulation—13 inches.

Of all the deaths Ralph had witnessed through his many years on homicide, the strangest and goriest always happened during the winter months. Ralph, like his brother, hated the snow and winter. It was one of the few things they agreed on. Snow and winter. Ralph couldn't help linking the two with tragedy, accidents, crime, and death. It seemed natural to him. He believed that there was something about snow that leads people astray; something that causes people to do things that they wouldn't ordinarily do.

Ralph finally got out of the car and closed the door. It echoed loudly through the garage. His wife was waiting for him in the doorway. She wore a solid purple maternity dress and a pair of red house slippers. Her brown hair was made up in a bun on the top of her head, and her face seemed long and tired, worn out from another strenuous day of being eight months pregnant.

As Ralph approached her, he noticed she was wearing her oven mitts. "Hey, Lisa, I didn't see you there."

She smiled. "I've been standing here for about five minutes, wondering if you were ever going to get out of the car. Were you afraid to come inside?" she joked.

"Ah, no, I was just listening to the radio."

"Must have been a good song."

"Yeah," he hesitated, "one I hadn't heard in a while."

"Well, come on in here. I just took a meat loaf out of the oven."

"I'm starved." Ralph walked up the three concrete steps leading into their house. Standing beside her on the top step, he brought his hand down and felt her large belly. "How's my boy doing?"

"You mean girl, Ralph."

"We shall find out soon enough, won't we?" Resting his arms on her shoulders, he gave her a quick kiss on the lips. "Let's eat." He took off his overcoat and hung it on the rack next to the door. He was anxious to get to the kitchen.

"Ralph?"

"Yeah, babe?" he said, turning around.

"Have you been smoking again?"

Ralph grinned. There was no point in lying. "Yeah, I guess so. How could you tell?"

She shook her head and followed him into the kitchen.

Chapter 15

9:15 P.M., Iroquois Park
3 Inches

Bill felt lost. Everything around him was blanked out by an eerie darkness, yet the smell of the surroundings was vaguely familiar. The air was dank, muggy, and stale. Bill brought his hand up in front of his face and was relieved he could see it. His eyes were slowly adjusting to the dark.

Afraid of taking steps, Bill shuffled his feet across the floor, hands out in front like a blind man, searching for a wall. He was sure to bump into something sooner or later.

Where am I? he thought. *How did I get here?*

Finally he did run into something. He had expected to run into something, but he didn't plan on it being painful. The object had a funny shape to it. It hit him both high and low, smacking him directly under his kneecap and above his hip.

"What the…" Bill felt around, knocking something over in the process. He felt a dusty platform and ran his fingers over the surface. It was connected to some sort of a seat.

"A desk?" he whispered.

Bill pushed the desk backwards and heard the rumble and crash of several more desks falling over. He knew exactly where he was now. He was in the front section of The Dungeon. But how did he get there? He didn't know. He sure didn't remember leaving the house to come back to school, and of all places, ending up in The Dungeon would not have been his first choice.

Bill slowly made his way around the large pile of broken desks, feeling the wall for a light switch. The air was freezing cold. Now in front of The Dungeon's entrance, he found the lights and flicked them on.

The fixtures buzzed and the lights flickered stubbornly, but stayed on. It wasn't very bright, but it was better than total darkness. Bill was cold, confused, tired, and a little scared to find himself in The Dungeon alone, at night. He pushed against the doors, but they weren't opening. He nudged with his shoulder, but they wouldn't budge.

He backed up a few feet to think about the situation. Just a couple of years ago he had fixed these doors so that no one could ever get locked in, but for some reason now his preventative measures weren't working. He rammed the door again with his shoulder. It didn't work, and now his shoulder hurt.

Convinced that the doors would not open, he decided to step back and punt. He tried to remain calm, turning in slow circles, surveying the surroundings. He was standing in the first section of The Dungeon, the storage area. Mountains of desks covered the walls in every direction. Further back behind the desks were old festival supplies; spinning wheels, tarps, booths, number boards, and countless other knickknacks from past generations. In the far corner was even older junk, behind which Bill never really cared to check because it was a perfect hideaway for rats, and Bill hated rats.

Bill looked down at the concrete floor which was covered with a thick layer of dust. Lines zigzagged through the dirt like trenches from the shuffling of his feet in the dark. To his left was the small, five-foot entrance to the corridors. He hated the creepy corridors, but for some reason now, he was being drawn closer to the entrance.

Just inside the entrance Bill saw a large, brown rat. It was gnawing on something in the front corner of the first corridor. When it heard Bill's approaching footsteps, it looked up at him. Its tiny mouth nibbled quickly and its long, black whiskers shook from the motion. Its two beady eyes of coal stared at Bill briefly, and then it took off scurrying down the north-south corridor.

His curiosity overwhelmed his fear, so he hunched over and ran into the corridor. He had nowhere else to go. The lighting was scattered in patches on down the corridor, because many of the light bulbs were either burned out or missing. Bill had never really felt the need to change them.

Now he wished that he had. He saw the rat at the very end of the corridor. It stopped and turned back towards Bill, and then darted off to the left, out of Bill's view and into the east-west corridor.

"Little bastard," Bill grumbled, straightening his back out the best he could in the cramped quarters.

"Shit!" Bill yelled as he smacked the top of his head on one of the pipes above, forgetting that the ceiling was only five feet high. He felt his head for a bump, but nothing had surfaced yet.

He bent lower to look up at the pipe. It had a warning sign attached to the bottom of it with the black skull and crossbones insignia at both ends: ASBESTOS. DO NOT DISTURB WITHOUT PROPER TRAINING AND EQUIPMENT. Everything about The Dungeon frightened him— the corridors, the smell, the darkness, the coldness, everything. But still, he continued to walk.

"Bill," someone called from somewhere down the corridor. It sounded like it had come from the east-west wing, echoing off of the walls.

Bill stopped dead in his tracks.

"Bill," the voice called again.

"Hello," Bill said hesitantly, "who . . . who's there?"

No answer.

"Somebody down there?" he asked again. The rat was out of sight, but he knew *it* wasn't talking, or at least he hoped not. He had seen some crazy things in his life, and was now to the point where he couldn't rule out anything.

Bill took about ten more steps before stopping again. At the corner of the two corridors, an animal suddenly appeared. It was much bigger than the rat he had seen earlier. He moved closer to see what it was, but it was difficult because the light in the corner was missing.

The animal walked closer to Bill, passing into one of the patches of light. It was a cat, a black cat with red eyes. It was the same cat he had seen on his truck. He recognized the glowing red eyes and the cocky swagger. Bill stopped as the cat approached and began rubbing up against his jeans, purring loudly with its tail sticking straight up in the air.

Bill bent over and reached down towards the cat. It hissed and quickly scratched the top of his hand. Bill pulled his hand away, raising it high in the air. Four scratches lined the top of his hand. One of the larger ones was starting to bleed.

The cat immediately backed away, frightened, and gave Bill a cold, lonely stare.

Bill looked down at the cat and noticed its attention was no longer on him. It was as if the cat had totally forgotten that Bill was standing there. Bill reached down again, this time snapping his fingers, but the cat didn't even give him a look.

The light above Bill formed a shadow directly in front of him. Bill noticed that the shadow was moving slightly, be he was not. He stared at the cat. *What are you looking at you stupid animal?* Bill was afraid to turn around. His shadow seemed to be growing, getting taller and wider. Then all of a sudden his shadow spilt into two bodies, and the cat took off down the corridor, quickly peeling around the corner in the same direction that the rat had gone.

Something scared that cat away, Bill thought, *and I don't think it was me. That something is breathing down my neck.* The breath was cold and chilling, even colder than the air. Bill felt the hairs on the back of his neck stiffen. The second shadow started jumping from side to side, but Bill still didn't hear a thing, not even the slightest hint of a footstep.

Finally Bill turned around to face the silent shadow, and as soon as he did he was greeted with a fist to the face. It was a crunching blow to the bottom of his chin. It easily broke the skin. Bill's head ricocheted backwards. The impact sent him flying back five or six feet before landing on the cold, damp floor of the corridor.

Bill hadn't noticed it before because the lights had been out, but the temperature was cold enough that his breath was clearly visible. Supporting himself on one elbow, Bill brought his right hand up to his chin. When he pulled it away he had a handful of blood, and his chin was still dripping like a leaky faucet. Bill looked up just as the man was starting to speak.

"I'm back, Bill," the man with the long white hair hissed, coming closer. He was wearing brown leather cowboy boots, and each step produced its own echo.

"Who the hell are—"

Before Bill could finish, the man landed one of his boots in Bill's crotch. Bill rolled back a few more feet, doubling over in pain. He felt nauseous.

"Didn't want to do that, Bill, but you left me no choice. I'm the one that does the talking here, not you. This is my world. Remember that."

Bill was lying on his side, pulling himself up with one elbow. His other arm was down comforting his groin. He felt numb down there now and dizzy. He glanced up at the man with the long white hair. His face was pale like an albino and very wrinkled and dry. His two, light-blue eyes were like tiny diamonds, looking coldly down on him.

The man reached down towards Bill, offering him his long, ghostly white hand. It too was very dry, and the thin skin around the bones seemed to be cracked and peeling. "Bill, I don't think we've officially met. I'm the Snowman, and I killed your wife."

Bill didn't move. He couldn't. He wasn't about to shake the extended hand.

The Snowman didn't appreciate being left hanging, so his hand quickly clenched into a fist, and he punched Bill just above his right eye, knocking him back down to the floor. Bill was lying flat on his stomach, arms sprawled out in front. He slowly raised his head up so that he could keep an eye on his attacker. Blood, mixed with beads of nervous sweat and tears, trickled down through the corner of his squinting right eye.

The Snowman squatted down on one knee. "The appropriate thing would have been to shake my hand, Bill, don't you think?"

Bill nodded his head in agreement.

"The snow is coming again, Bill. Real soon. What do you think about that?"

Bill swallowed hard and tried to say something, but nothing came out. His mouth was dry.

The Snowman flicked the cut over Bill's right eye. "Answer me, dammit."

Bill screamed out in pain, holding his hand over his eye.

"You are not going to fuck things up for me, are you, Bill?"

Bill shook his head no. His vision was blurry, and his head was throbbing from the abuse. The Snowman winked at Bill and reached for his face again. He swiped his long finger nails across Bill's bloody chin, opening the wound even more. Bill screamed again, lifting himself off the cold floor. He leaned against the wall.

The Snowman came closer. "I've got to finish what I've started, Bill."

Bill started to say something, but was interrupted by a ringing noise.

"Sounds like the telephone, Bill."

"There's no phone down here, you bastard."

The Snowman smiled, raising his arms in the air in praise. "He can talk. He can talk. For a while there I thought you'd turned into a deaf mute."

Ring Ring Ring

"Answer the phone, Bill."

Ring Ring Ring

"No phone down here, asshole."

"No time to get testy with me, Bill. What's wrong? Don't think I'm real, do you. Is that it? You think this is a dream, don't you?"

Ring Ring Ring

The Snowman reached around and pulled something out from behind his back. "Look, what do we have here? Looks like a phone to me." It was shaking and vibrating in his long, skeletal hands. The Snowman took the receiver off and held it out to Bill. "It's for you."

Bill didn't grab the phone. "You are not real."

"Answer the phone, Bill. I think it would be the polite thing to do."

Bill didn't move.

"How rude!" the Snowman said, banging the receiver down hard on Bill's head.

Bill hit the floor with a thud and instantly opened his eyes. The air was much warmer, and he felt carpet underneath him. He noticed he was lying right next to his coffee table in front of his couch in the television room. He had fallen asleep.

He took a deep breath. *Only a dream,* he told himself. *It was all only a dream.* He had fallen off the couch. He felt the top of his head. It ached, but he had no blood on his face.

Ring Ring Ring

He glanced to the end table next to the couch and sat down to answer the phone.

Ring Ring Ring

He was scared to pick it up. What if it was *him* on the other end. *Oh, Bill. Quit being a chicken shit and pick up the phone. It would be the polite thing to do.*

Bill grabbed the phone, fumbling it in his trembling hands before answering.

"Hello," he said softly.

"Daddy."

"Amy?"

"How many other people call you Daddy?" Amy asked. She faked her excitement. She didn't want to worry him.

"I'm sorry. I just got up from . . ." he ran his hand through his hair, yawning, "excuse me, from a nap. My mind is still a little muddled."

"Did I wake you up?"

"Actually, you did."

"I'm sorry."

"No, no, no, your timing couldn't have been better," he insisted. "I really needed to get up anyway." *More than you could possibly imagine*, he thought.

"Look Dad, I can't talk for long because I need to get back to the books. The reason I called was that—"

"You don't need a reason to call me, Amy."

"I know, but anyway, are you going to be home tomorrow afternoon?"

"I can be, why?"

"Could you pick Kathy and me up at the airport?"

"Tomorrow?" Bill asked, surprised.

"Yeah. I changed the flight. It's tomorrow instead of Friday. That okay?"

"Absolutely. This sure is a pleasant surprise. What time?"

"Let's see here," she said, looking at her itinerary. "It says here we should be arriving in Louisville at 1:20 P.M."

"Great. I'll be there with bells on," he said.

"And you're sure you're not busy?"

"I've got a few things to take care of in the morning at school, but no, it shouldn't be a problem at all."

"It's a date then."

"Count on it," Bill said. "It's good to hear your voice again, Amy."

"Yours too, Dad. How are things going?"

"Okay, I guess," he lied. He didn't sound very convincing.

"And Gus?"

"He's fine, too. He's sleeping right now, or otherwise I'd let you talk to him."

"Oh, bummer."

There was a brief pause.

"What airline are you flying?"

"That might help, wouldn't it? Continental Airlines."

He scribbled the information down on a yellow note pad by the phone and repeated them aloud to confirm. "That's Continental at 1:20, tomorrow afternoon."

"Correct."

"Can't wait, honey. I've missed you."

"I've missed you too, very much." She paused. "Look, I've got to start hitting the books now."

"Yeah, I don't mean to keep you."

"I'll see you at the airport then," she said.

"Will do, Amy. Love you."

"Love you, too. Bye, bye."

Bill gently hung the phone up and buried his face in his hands. *What the fuck is going on here?* He ran his fingers through his hair. His head was pulsing with pain. It felt like little micro men were running around the folds of his cerebrum digging in with pick-axes. He got up off the couch and walked into the kitchen to get some aspirin.

In the cabinet above the sink, he grabbed the bottle of aspirin. When he started to twist off the top, he was startled by a knocking on his front door. *Won't the excitement ever end?* he asked himself.

He looked quickly to the front door. His heart raced as Gus came running down the steps from upstairs. Bill dropped the bottle of aspirin in the sink, and they scattered, half of them down the drain.

Reluctantly, Bill walked out of the kitchen and into the front room. Gus was right up next to the door, barking loudly. "Who is it?"

No one answered.

Bill nudged Gus away from the door with his right leg. "Quiet, Gus."

Gus continued to bark ferociously as if he sensed something evil and bad on the other side of the door.

Bill stepped closer to the door and grabbed the door knob. It was cold.

The knocking was louder. His heart pounded. Gus was barking.

Finally he unlocked the door and opened it.

"Ralph?"

"Bill." The greeting lacked enthusiasm.

"What's wrong?"

"We need to talk. Let me in."

Chapter 16

The ground settled. Everything was silent.

"What *was* that?" Pamala asked.

Brice helped himself to his feet and eyed the collapsed corner of the tent. "Some kind of tremor, or maybe even an earthquake."

Marvin stood up to help Brice with the broken pole. "You've got to be kidding me. An earthquake, here, in Antarctica?"

Leroy turned the kettle of oatmeal back on end and wiped off his hands on his pants. "Like I've been telling you all along. It's getting warmer here. It's been slow and gradual for a very long time, but now it's . . . it's speeding up."

Brice turned his head away from the corner of the tent and stared directly at Leroy. "What the hell are you talking about, Leroy?"

"Internal warming. Yeah, scientists are right on track with their studies on increased global warming and ozone depletion, but this is something different all together, something even beyond their imagination." His eyes raced around the tent, darting from person to person, hoping that they would finally start believing in him. "This is all very different and dangerous I think for the future of this continent. It *is* getting warmer here, and it's coming from under the ice."

Gabe chuckled. "It was a damn tremor, Leroy, that's it, old man. Quit reading stuff into it."

Leroy continued. "I hesitate to even mention this theory, but what the hell, most of you think I'm nuts anyway." He paused. No one protested. "There's something going on in this place that none of us can really understand. There's something about it here that is . . . not right."

"Is this what you've been writing in that diary?" Gabe asked.

"It's a journal, not a damn diary, boy. This may be difficult for you to believe, but I'm not filling you all up with a bunch of crap here. I wouldn't waste your time like that. You fail to see it because you don't know what I know. You do not know the history like I do. In 1819, no human record of this continent existed. We are still feeling this place out. It's still new to us, and the secrets to this place are phenomenal. Some of the stories are unbelievable. The failed expeditions, missing navigators, the . . . the Robert Scott expedition, missing pages in journals and diaries that could tell us, oh, so much more. The bizarre reports coming from our own Richard Byrd from 'Little America'. They say he was mumbling from being poisoned by carbon monoxide, but who really knows for sure what happened to him out here. Who knows what he really saw out here in the icy wilderness, all alone, totally isolated and—"

Gabe held up his hand. He was the youngest of the group, but not afraid to voice his opinion. "Leroy, I know you know your stuff, but ever since you've been here you haven't given us one iota of evidence that anything you've been saying is true. Increased global warming on this continent only? Something internal? All these mysteries? Come on, man. Why don't you wake up and smell what you're shoveling us."

"Okay, guys," Brice said, "let's cool it down." He looked at both Gabe and Leroy.

Loreda spoke up. She hated to see any of them arguing, and they had been doing a lot more of it of late. "Brice is right. It's been a long journey. Don't start cracking up on us now."

"Tell that to the land beneath us," Gabe said.

She wasn't sure whether to smile or come back with another remark. She smiled and said nothing.

Silence. Cooler heads prevailed.

Brice hadn't been able to fix the broken tent pole, but he positioned it in a way that it would at least hold for the night if they didn't have another tremor or increase in the wind.

"Leroy," Eric said, "what did you mean by something is not right?"

Brice gave Eric a look of disappointment for dragging the subject on.

Leroy looked around the group as if silently asking their permission to speak again. He shook his head. "Nothing, Eric, it's nothing. It's just that . . . that . . . ah, never mind."

"Actually gang," Mark Moriarity said, shifting his bulky body, leaning on his right elbow. "I think I can shed some light on this. What Leroy said is partly true. The ice *is* moving and shifting. It's natural though," he said, scooting closer to the group. "Let me explain."

"Please do," Gabe said with a smirk.

"I know there has been some times during our days here where you've heard the snow settle. It's almost like the distant sound of thunder. I know I've felt it a few times myself, like the ground was moving under my feet."

"Doesn't the ground always do that when you're walking on it, Mark?" Eric asked.

"Very funny, Red." Mark took a drink of water. "As you've probably noticed, the outer surface here is a level of very hard, wind-blown snow, like ice really. Two miles of permafrost. Underneath this hard level is a much softer level of snow. Because of the wind, the freezing temperatures, and us skiing over it, large sections of this outer layer are actually breaking down and settling into the soft layer beneath it. That's why every once in a while it feels like the ice is shifting, or," he folded his hands, "a slight tremor."

"But how can you explain the severity of the one that just happened?" Brice asked, genuinely concerned. "I've felt what you're talking about, too, but this seemed totally different. This was worse, much worse."

Mark smiled. "Honestly fellows, I don't know the answer to that. Maybe Leroy is on to something. Yes, it's far fetched, and not explained fully, if at all, but at least it's something."

Gabe stood up and stretched as high as the ceiling of the tent would allow. His arms were bent, with his elbows scraping the ceiling. "I just hope it doesn't happen again."

"Or get any worse." Marvin said.

"Both," Mark said, "I think may be possible."

"Very possible," Leroy said, standing up now. "And trust me, very probable." He got up and walked towards the door to the tent with his journal in hand. "I'm going to sleep."

They watched him go, and no one said a word.

After a brief silence, Brice said, "I think it's a good idea. What do you say we all call it a night. Long day tomorrow. I think we all need the sleep."

Everyone agreed.

Chapter 17

9:25 P.M., Iroquois Park
3 Inches

Ralph let himself in the front door, staring at the floor as he walked inside. He wiped the flakes of snow from his hair and looked at Bill.

"Ralph. What's the problem? You look worried."

"I am." Ralph unbuttoned his overcoat and handed Bill his red coat.

Bill grabbed it slowly, almost cautiously, checking it all around. He found the tag and saw his name printed in black ink. It was still very stiff and partially frozen, but starting to thaw out. "Where did you find this? It was stolen from me earlier today at school."

"I found it frozen on the banks of the Ohio River."

"I don't get it."

"You sure?"

"Yeah, I'm sure, Ralph. You think I'm lying?"

Ralph didn't give an answer to that. "A couple of hours ago I got called down to a crime scene on the river."

"What happened?"

"Young boy got murdered there tonight. We found him stuck under the ice. Somebody pushed him under, and that's where I found your coat, frozen to the grass right under a tree, about 20 yards away from where the boy went under."

Bill got defensive. He didn't like how Ralph was looking at him. "What? You think I did it or something, because if you do, you can wipe that crazy idea right out of your clouded head. Jesus, Ralph, what do you think I am?"

"I don't know *what* to think. For the record, no, I don't think it was you. It was stupid to even take the evidence, but initially I thought of protecting you."

"From what? Am I a suspect?"

"Not now you're not. But you know I have to follow up on all leads. All leads Bill, and your coat was crying for attention."

Bill paused, slowly making his way towards the kitchen. He turned around. "What was the boy's name?"

Ralph hesitated. "Bobby Bates. He was a student at your school, Bill, a freshman."

Bill brought his hand to his mouth and backed against the wall divider separating the front room from the kitchen. "Oh, my God."

Ralph was surprised at the reaction. "You know the kid?"

"I just met him for the first time this afternoon." Bill shook his head in disbelief. "He mentioned maybe going ice skating."

"You knew where he was going to be?"

"No," Bill snapped, turning into the kitchen.

Ralph followed. "Then what gives, Bill?"

"I don't know what the fuck gives, man. I don't know how my coat got down there. I don't know how this kid was killed. I don't think I know anything any more." Bill glanced over to the kitchen table at the bottle of Jim Beam. Slowly he walked backwards to it, attempting to conceal it with his body before Ralph was able to see it.

"What do you think about the Snowman?"

Bill's face went blank, void of all expression. "Wh . . . what about him?"

"A witness says that the man that pushed him under called himself the Snowman."

"I knew it."

"Knew what?"

"He's back. The Snowman is back."

"From where, Bill? Where did this Snowman character come from, and where has he been all these years since killing Mary?"

Bill looked up as if he'd been bitten. He felt he had in a way. He didn't like what his brother was implying. *He still doesn't believe,* Bill thought.

After all the problems and all the years of suffering, he still doesn't believe me. The Snowman was and is real, dammit. Bill brought both of his arms out from behind his back, pointing his right hand at Ralph, his fingers clenched in a fist. He had forgotten about concealing the bottle on the table. "I don't know where he's back from, and I don't know why he's back. You remember this, Ralph. I don't know what you think I'm capable of doing, but whatever it is, you remember that I'm still your big brother. I don't appreciate these hidden accusations. You think I've done something illegal, you best come right out and say it. I don't care what kind of lofty position you have in the police department, there is something called respect, and that's something you better start showing me, little brother, or I'll show you the front door."

Ralph smiled. "The tide sure has turned over the years. It really has. Seems now that I am in control. I've got you by the balls. Do you like how that feels?"

"Regardless of your standards, I've turned my life around twice. I'm happy for me and my daughter, even if you aren't."

"I am, Bill. You *have* made a drastic change. You don't think I've noticed it? I may not say it, but I've noticed it. But I am also noticing something weird going on, and somehow you and the Snowman are being mentioned in the same breath again, and again it involves someone getting killed."

"You bastard." Spittle flew from Bill's mouth, but he refrained from throwing a punch. He turned slightly from the table, accidentally exposing the bottle.

"Bill, I didn't mean it like that, I—" he stopped, spotting the bottle of alcohol. Hastily, he grabbed the whiskey from the table behind Bill. "What the hell is this?"

"What's it look like?"

"Are you drinking again?"

"No."

"Drugs?" Ralph's voice was louder.

"No!" Bill shouted.

Ralph never let it be known, but he had developed respect for his big brother over the years. He had started to like him. He hated to see him drink, so seeing the bottle was tearing him up inside. He didn't want to see his brother go down again, and he hadn't intended for their conversation to come out like this.

Ralph raised the bottle above his head and brought it down hard against the edge of the table. It crashed against the wood, sending pieces of glass and sprinklings of alcohol all over the kitchen.

Bill covered his face with his arms and then lowered them. "Jesus, Ralph."

Ralph was furious. "I guess now the hallucinations and dreams are going to come back."

During their argument, the feather had fallen from the table. Bill picked it up and shoved it in Ralph's face. "They already have."

"What?"

"A feather. Just like the ones found in my house 20 years ago."

"You sure?"

"Yes, I'm sure." He pointed into the television room. "I had a vision over there by the window. I saw something out in the snow that I'd rather not talk to you about, but after it was over, this feather was sitting there in the snow."

Ralph released the neck of the broken bottle from his hand, and it fell to the floor with the rest of the mess. A sudden urge to leave the house swept over him. He felt like he was losing a grip on reality. For once, he was starting to believe his brother, feel his pain, but he was way too stubborn with their relationship to admit it. Staring at the feather in Bill's outstretched hand, Ralph backed away from the table and walked towards the front room. "I . . . I've got to go, Bill." He was allowing his emotions to override his reasons for coming here. This case was personal, very weird, and all of a sudden he didn't have the confidence talking to his brother that he had only minutes before. He needed time to think. He needed to get out before he said something to Bill that he would really regret. He felt bad enough for what he'd already said.

Ralph wasn't sure what it was, but after all the years of doubt, he was starting to believe in his brother's turmoil, and it scared him. He felt like the little brother again, and he wasn't so sure he liked it. He walked through the front room. "I've got to go."

Bill followed him, still holding onto the feather. "What is it, Ralph? Am I scaring you. Is it the alcohol? The feather?"

Ralph shook his head, grabbing for the front door.

"Do I scare you? You think I might kill you or something?"

"No, Bill, I don't." He walked out onto the porch. "I'm sorry. I need time to think. I'll check in with you tomorrow."

Bill walked to the threshold, propping the screen door open with his arm. The cold air and scattered flakes stung his face. "Time to think about what, Ralph?"

Ralph picked up his pace, now jogging to his car. In the distance, Bill heard him again say, "Tomorrow." His voice was muffled by the wind and snow.

The snow was picking up again, not heavily, but enough for accumulation.

Bill watched Ralph back out and drive the long winding driveway until the car's lights were no longer visible through the trees. He looked down. Gus was standing at his feet, rubbing his head against Bill's leg. Bill reached down and ran his hand under and around Gus's head. Gus licked him excitedly.

Just what I needed tonight, Bill thought. *He's adding stress to an already ugly situation.* Bill closed the door, turned around and looked at his house, into the kitchen and television room in the distance, over to the living room on his left, the stairs. Everything was empty and silent. He didn't want emptiness and silence. The argument with his brother was making him feel vulnerable, not only to the dangers outside the house, but to his fears and dangers within. He was glad now that the bottle was broken. It would not consume him tonight.

He was with Gus, but still felt alone, trapped in a recycled world of his memories and imagination. He was tired, but too afraid to go to sleep. He had too much on his mind, and his brother had only compounded his worries. He knew the night would be a long one. He dreaded it. He could talk to the dog, but Gus couldn't talk back. He had to keep his mind off of the Snowman. He had to keep busy, doing something to keep his brain occupied.

He did the dishes and vacuumed the floors. He cleaned the alcohol and broken glass from the kitchen floor and table. He straightened up and dusted the rest of the house.

This worked, but not very well. It kept him occupied until midnight, but then there was nothing else to clean. His body was worn down, his eyes were heavy; and he wanted nothing more than to rest his head on a pillow and sleep; but no, he was determined to stay awake, in fear of what might happen if his eyes were closed for too long. He had to stand guard, just in case something happened. He had to be ready. This was his battle he had to finish, and his alone.

His eyes were wet and dizzy. He drank some Mountain Dew from the refrigerator and then decided to set up the Christmas tree in the front room. He had intended to wait for Amy, but the tree gave him something to do while he yawned and waited.

I've got to stay awake.

At 3 a.m. Bill found himself draped across the small Victorian reading chair in the front room, staring blankly at the blinking, white lights on the eight-foot artificial tree. The lights were like stars in a clear black night. His eyes closed and then opened. He closed them again and he could still see the lights. The stars. He forced them open slowly, but he couldn't fight it any longer.

Bill yawned and then his eyes locked shut. His legs were hanging over the arm of the chair, and his head was bent in the top corner of the chair. His neck would most certainly ache in the morning.

Deep sleep came fast, and it was very welcome. He slept uninterrupted until morning.

Chapter 18

11:55 P.M. Dungeon, River City High School
5 Inches

Zoro approached the rat as silently as possible. Its huge black wings were ready to trap the prey in case it ran towards him. Hunkered down in the corner of the two corridors, the rat sensed something coming. It had a path to run down the east-west corridor, but hesitated because of the strange light coming from the far wall. It was bright and nearly blinding. The rat sniffed, turned away from the light, and faced the bird.

Zoro's red eyes locked in on the rat, extending its wings so the tips were scraping both sides of the corridor, leaving the rat nowhere to run except towards the light. The rat stepped back, cramming itself into the corner as far as it could.

Zoro came closer, never taking its eyes off of the rat. Its sharp, curved beak opened and closed like a machine. Now stuck, the rat decided to fight. It charged at Zoro and jumped towards the bird's beak.

Zoro leaped towards the airborne rat and pinned it against the wall with one of its wings. The last thing the rat ever saw was the inside of Zoro's beak. Zoro tore the head from the rat's limp body and flung it against the wall. It ripped open the rat's body with its sharp talons and dug in.

Within a few minutes, the only thing left of the rat was its bones and portions of the head. It had been devoured. Zoro stood in the corner, facing the light at the end of the east-west corridor, watching it like a television, waiting for its master to return. Its appetite now sated, Zoro waited for the Snowman.

The light started to change. First it got brighter and then it changed colors. The breakthrough point was filled with a pulsing, fluorescent green light, and it illuminated the entire corridor. Zoro covered its eyes with one of its wings and stumbled backwards as a strong burst of wind entered the corridor. The air was freezing cold.

The light from the breakthrough point cleared away, exposing a vast land of ice and snow behind it. A silhouette of a man with long, flowing hair emerged from the snowy background and stepped into the east-west corridor. Loose snow blew into the corridor from the other side, sticking in clumps to the floor and side walls next to the opening.

Zoro watched and waited with excitement. It hadn't seen its master in 20 years. It had waited mostly out of loyalty, but also out of fear of the consequences of non-cooperation. It was glad to be reunited and ready to help again when needed.

Outside the school, the snow was coming down again, and so was the temperature. Five inches had already fallen, and the accumulation was quickly growing. The Snowman could feel it in his bones, the storm would be here soon, and then the games would begin. It was almost time.

Halfway down the corridor, the Snowman looked at Zoro. "Come," he said in a deep, baritone voice, "we've got work to do."

The Snowman started to run. Zoro took to the air.

Part Two

December 15th
The Hell That Is Ice

Some say the world will end in fire,
Some say in ice.
From what I've tasted of desire,
I hold with those who favor fire.
But if it had to perish twice,
I think I know enough of hate
To say that for destruction ice
Is also great
And would suffice.

Robert Frost *Fire and Ice*

Chapter 19

1:47 A.M., New Cut Road
6 Inches

Just as the three Budweiser swimsuit models were getting into the hot tub with elderly Lewis Anderson, the phone started ringing and everything came to a halt. Lewis opened his eyes, his dream was over. The steam, hot water, foamy bubbles, and the Budweiser girls were gone.

He leaned up in bed and let out a long yawn, stretching his arms towards the ceiling. He knew what the call was about, more than likely the friendly coroner or hospital with some bad news. Well, that depends on how one looks at it. A sudden death for most people was bad news, but for Lewis Anderson it meant business. He had to look at his job that way to keep it from getting too depressing.

Lewis swung his bird-like legs out of the bed and picked up the phone. He rested his chin in his free hand. "Hello, Lewis Anderson speaking."

"Sorry to bother you like this, Lewis, this is Jerry from Audubon Hospital," the young man said nervously. He hated calling Lewis this late.

"Morning, Jerry. What do you have for me?"

"Well," Jerry said, glancing down at the paper work on his desk. "I've got a little boy down here who needs to be picked up. His name is Robert Bates. Twelve years old. His parents called a little while ago requesting that we call you to pick up the body."

"What was the cause of death?"

"He drowned, sir, under the ice on the Ohio."

"Christ," Lewis mumbled, jotting the information down on a notepad next to the phone. "Twelve years old," he said, shaking his head in disbelief.

"I can't really tell you all the details, that's if you really wanted to know them, but I heard the doctors who performed the autopsy say there was something real strange about the whole thing."

"Okay," Lewis said. He wasn't concerned about the details. That was his son's job to learn and understand the details of someone's death. Best not to know. That was Lewis's philosophy.

"The parents said to go ahead and embalm him, so don't worry about calling them tonight, or this morning, whatever time it is."

"I got it, Jerry." Lewis glanced at his alarm clock. "It's almost two now, and I still need to run over to the funeral home to get the van, so expect me there by three or before."

"Be careful out there, Lewis. I just drove here about an hour ago from downtown, and the roads are getting nasty. It's not snowing now, I don't think, but the roads are starting to freeze over. There have already been over a hundred accidents and fender benders since the snow started falling yesterday afternoon. Damn people don't know how to drive in this stuff."

"I'll be careful. Thanks, Jerry." Lewis hung up the phone and stood next to the bed. Every joint in his body cracked and popped as he stretched. "Here we go again."

Lewis, Ralph and Bill's father, lived alone in an apartment complex on New Cut Road, only a few miles away from his funeral home and also fairly close to where Bill worked as a janitor. His wife, Caroline, had passed away three years ago from brain cancer, ending a strong, 45-year marriage. Living in their house alone had been just too much for Lewis to handle; the memories were too strong. A few months after her death, Bill and Ralph had moved him into a small apartment, closer to work.

For now, work was life for Lewis Anderson. He didn't love being a mortician, but he was good at it, and it kept him very busy and active, even at age 70.

Lewis went into the bathroom to quickly clean up before going. Stepping on the cold, linoleum floor made his bare feet feel like ice. He turned the faucet on and splashed handfuls of water on his face. After toweling off, he stared at himself in the mirror. He was in great physical shape, but this morning he showed his age. For three days in a row business at

Anderson Funeral Home had been nearly nonstop, one funeral after another. He hardly had time to eat, breathe, and sleep, and this clearly showed in the mirror.

His hair was going from gray to white, even more so in the last couple of years, and the bags under his eyes were sagging onto his cheeks, adding to his many wrinkles.

He backed away from the mirror in disgust. "God, I look like shit." He parted his lips, checking out his teeth. They needed to be brushed. "Oh, well this kid isn't going to give a damn what I look like."

He dressed quickly. The chill of the apartment air sent goose bumps down his arms and legs. He couldn't get dressed fast enough. The apartment just didn't have the same warmth as his old house. He missed it, especially on the cold mornings of winter. He came out of his room wearing a heavy red-and-black checkered flannel shirt and an old, but warm pair of beige corduroy pants stretched tightly over his snow boots. On his way out the door he grabbed his gloves, his heavy winter coat, and his gray wool hat.

Lewis set out for the funeral home.

His red '92 Ford truck was weighted down in the back with blocks of cement to prevent sliding on the snow and ice. He definitely needed it tonight. Luckily, he was the only one on the road. Anderson Funeral Home was located at the southern end of New Cut, right next to a set of train tracks. The parking lot was a solid sheet of unmarked whiteness with a few stranded cars buried here and there. He parked his truck in back of the building next to the company van and quickly switched vehicles. He had done away with the hearse about five years ago and had been using the van ever since to pick up and transport the bodies. It was much more convenient and easier to drive, and with the tented windows, it still gave him the feeling of privacy that he thought a carrier of death should have. The interior of the van was divided into two sections. The driver and passenger seats were separated from the back by a large piece of Plexiglas. Lewis preferred to separate himself from the bodies.

The van wasn't as good on the ice and snow as his truck, but it didn't really snow that often in Louisville, and in the past hadn't been very much of a problem. Wheels spinning, he floored it up the slight incline of the parking lot and turned left on New Cut en route to Audubon Hospital. He looked at his watch. It was 2:30 A.M. and the hospital was only 20 minutes away.

Right on schedule, he thought.

When Lewis entered the morgue, he found Jerry with his feet propped up on his desk reading Stephen King's *The Dark Half.* The morgue was located in the basement of the hospital, positioned in the very back, secluded from normal traffic flow.

"Hey, not bad timing, Lewis," Jerry said, glancing at his watch. It was 10 minutes to 3.

"I'm a pro, Jerry, remember that."

"I forgot." Jerry laughed softly while handing Lewis a clipboard and pen. "Sign this, please."

Lewis scribbled his name on the release form and handed the paper back to Jerry. Jerry gave him some papers, and Lewis folded them up and shoved them in his coat pocket.

"What number?"

"Two."

Lewis walked over to the wall of coolers. He located cooler number two and grabbed the handle on the front. He opened the shiny metallic lid, slowly exposing the dead body to the temperature in the morgue. He pulled the cooler all the way out until the tray stopped.

Lewis had seen and dealt with just about every type of corpse, so the first sight of the kid's bloated body drew no shocking reaction. He had worked with drowning victims before, so he knew what to expect during the embalming process. The skin was blue and purple and stretched tightly due to the increase in moisture content in the tissues. He had expected to see a somewhat bloated and discolored corpse, but he hadn't expected to see strange bruises on the top of the boy's disfigured shoulders.

Large, dark purple splotches covered the deltoid muscles and anterior portion of the chest. His shoulders, severely bruised, also seemed to be crushed and separated under the skin. Major force and pressure had been exerted on his shoulders, this much Lewis could tell right away. *Don't read anything into this, old man,* Lewis thought, *and leave the detective work to Ralph.*

Lewis pulled a sheet over Bobby's body and backed away. Two men in white lab coats stood at his side, ready to load the body in the van. One of them asked, "Are you going to have to hurry and embalm this one? Don't the drowning ones decompose faster?"

"Normally with drowning victims, with the gastro-intestinal conditions, blood congestion, and moisture content in the tissues, yes, timing is critical." Lewis started walking towards the doors. The two men followed with the gurney. Lewis turned back towards them as they walked. "This body here, though, could have a little more time. The water in the Ohio was so cold, freezing actually, that most bacterial decomposition would be slowed considerably, if not stopped all together."

Lewis waved at Jerry, who was already back to his book and then followed the two men out to his van. After the body was loaded, the two men dashed back down the concrete ramp into the morgue. Lewis secured the body in the back, closed the doors, and ran for his seat. The cold wind stung his face like a whip as it curved around the corners of the hospital.

It was 3:05 when Lewis pulled out of Audubon's parking lot. His eyes were getting heavy; his lack of sleep was starting to catch up. He cracked his window to allow in some fresh air, turned the heater on full blast, and jammed the radio as loud as it could go. This was sure to keep him awake until he got back to the funeral home. Then he'd consider taking a half-hour nap.

Lewis slowed his speed to 20 miles an hour as he turned off of Eastern Parkway and onto Third Street. Everything was going smoothly until he heard the voice of a young boy through the music on the radio. At first it was muffled, and he paid it no attention, but when he heard the voice a second time a few minutes later, Lewis turned down the radio.

The young boy's voice called again. "Hey, Mr. Driving Man!"

Lewis thought he was hearing things. *Just your imagination*, he thought, now tightly gripping the steering wheel. He looked straight ahead, concentrating solely on the icy roads. Large flakes of snow pelted the windshield, but were quickly cleared away by the wipers. The snowfall was picking up again.

"Hey, Mr. Driving Man."

Lewis kept his eyes on the road. The voice was coming from behind, possibly from the back of the van itself. It seemed so close, but Lewis refused to give in to his imagination. *It's nothing*, he reminded himself, *it's only your imagination, nothing more. Just keep on driving to the funeral home, Lewis Anderson, and don't you turn around.* His adrenaline gave him a case of the lead foot, the speed of the van increased to 40 without Lewis even noticing.

"Hey, Mr. Driving Man!" This time the voice was even louder, now filled with rage and anger.

Lewis was starting to sweat. He was nervous, and his heart pounded in his chest. Leaving the morgue, he had forgotten to put his gloves back on. His knuckles were bone white from pressing so hard against the steering wheel. He bit his lower lip hard enough to draw blood, but kept his eyes on the road.

Why me? Lewis thought. He knew what was going on. He knew it was going to happen to him sooner or later. He was the transporter of the dead, and the dead was playing games with his mind. He wasn't about to give in and turn around because he knew what he'd see. The boy would be fastened to the cot in the back, dead as a doorknob, and everything would be hunky-dory.

"Mr. Driving Man," the voice screamed again. "I've got a message for you," the boy paused. "The snow isn't here yet, but the Snowman comes early. Seeee, look at meeee." The voice was high-pitched and drawn out, the voice of a crying and frightened child.

Lewis was never more tempted to turn around than right now, but he held strong against temptation. His speed was now close to 50.

Lewis then heard a thumping on the glass behind his seat.

The voice. "Seeee, look at meeee," the boy screamed, painfully. "Guard your family, Mr. Driving Man. The Snowman is here." The voice got louder, stronger and deeper, like that of a grown man, "now turn around and look at meeee!"

Lewis couldn't take it anymore. He glanced up at his rear-view mirror. He screamed.

He saw Bobby's dead and bloated body pressed up against the glass. His dislocated shoulders held lifeless arms that hung downward, swaying like pendulums, and Bobby was beating his mushy head against the glass.

"Look at meeee!"

Bobby's blue flesh smudged against the glass. Purple and red veins ran through the skin like tiny rivers. The glass was smeared with blood, and Bobby's eyes were yellow and bulging. The last smack against the glass had jarred the right eye loose. It hung by the muscles on the cheek, swinging. "Look at meeee!"

Bobby was laughing and crying at the same time.

Lewis lost control of the van. It fishtailed and then spun across the oncoming lane, crashing into the snowy embankment. He was shaking all over, trembling with fear and confusion. His heart raced. He pried his fingers loose of the steering wheel and took some deep breaths. No one was coming from the other lane, so he tried not to panic. He turned off the radio.

The van was quiet again. The only noise was the wind whistling outside the van. Lewis glanced in his rear-view mirror and saw the boy strapped down on the gurney. He turned around and looked through the glass just to make sure the boy was really dead, and indeed he was. There was no sign that Bobby had even moved at all.

Lewis Anderson, he thought, *you damn fool. Nearly got yourself killed.* He saw two bright lights coming from the other direction.

Lewis put the van in reverse and hit the gas. His tires squealed and spun quickly, but the van didn't move. The car in the oncoming lane was quickly approaching, honking its horn in warning.

"Come on, come on," Lewis hissed, grinding his teeth. He turned the wheel to the right and then to the left, loosening the snow around the tires, flooring the gas pedal at the same time, hoping that the snow would suddenly let go of him.

The car was one block away and it showed no signs of slowing down.

"Come on, come—" Just then the tires spun loose of the snow and the van slid backwards, the back end smashing into the curb on the other side of the road. The car flew past Lewis, the man's arm waving in the air, and he was yelling something muted by the rolled-up windows.

The van's back tires were resting on the curb, but at least now the coast was clear. Lewis checked the mirror one last time, and Bobby was still quite dead. Carefully, he drove to the funeral home.

The preparation room at Anderson Funeral Home was located in the basement directly under the chapel. The room itself was sound-proof, with square dimensions of 30 by 40 feet. The walls were apple green, and the ceiling was dark gray. Ugly colors for ugly work. The bottoms of the walls were surrounded by a shiny, black baseboard, and the terrazzo floor was a light shade of brown.

The three preparation tables were parallel to one another in the center of the room. Two additional tables, one for dressing and the other for embalming instruments, lined the far wall of the room. The wall next to the door was filled with other supplies, coats, and gloves. A large exhaust fan hung down over the middle of the preparation table for ventilation. Lewis made sure his staff kept the room spotless. Sanitation and cleanliness were essential to proper embalming.

Lewis was tired. His eyes were pushing him towards sleep, but the incident in the van had left him too high-strung. He was having a difficult time relaxing. He couldn't get his mind off of what he had seen, or what he thought he had seen and preparing Bobby's body wasn't going to make things any easier.

At 3:45 Lewis was ready. He cleaned and disinfected Bobby's body and then placed it on the center table so that it was facing the ceiling. He walked over to the cabinet and got out all of the embalming instruments he would need, along with the hydro-aspirator, pre-injection fluids, a few towels, and he placed them on the cart. After rolling the cart over to the operating table, he adjusted his germ mask over his nose and mouth. The motorized injection machine was ready, and the arterial, cavity, and formaldehyde fluids were prepared.

Lewis leaned over Bobby's body, scalpel in hand, ready to make the first incision, when he heard something strange coming from behind. He felt a breeze and heard the flapping of wings, large and powerful wings that created dark shadows on the table and over Bobby's naked body.

Lewis glanced over his right shoulder and saw a large black bird perched on the first operating table. He stumbled backwards into the rolling cart, catching himself on the corner of the operating table. His free hand grabbed hold of Bobby's leg to keep from falling. He nearly pulled the body off the table before regaining his balance. He held the scalpel out in front of him, but he was having trouble keeping the blade steady in his hands.

An intruder shot up from under the first operating table and walked towards Lewis. "Grandfather Anderson, I assume?" He extended his right hand for a greeting. Lewis saw the long, pale fingers and his stomach tightened. The strange man further extended his hand. "Snowman's the name. You must be Lewis."

"How'd you know my name? Who are you and what are you doing here?"

One of the fingers scraped at Lewis's nose. "Shut up, old man. Too many questions." He smacked Lewis hard on the back. Lewis cringed in pain.

"I have my way of doing things."

Now that his master had taken over, Zoro hopped off the table and crouched down in the far corner of the room.

"How'd you find me here?" Lewis asked, bumping into the table, trying like hell to move away from the Snowman and his creepy, light-blue eyes.

The Snowman followed him closely, now only a few feet away. He smacked Lewis on the forehead. "Like I said, I have my way of doing things." The Snowman smiled, tilting his head to the side. His hair swished like a rayon mop. "This is a bit different from what I'm used to, though. I'm not used to tracking people down. It's the randomness of my life that I thrive on. I go where it sends me, and I kill whatever is in my path." He looked Lewis in the eyes. His voice deepened. "But always during snowstorms, Lewis. It's got to be when it's snowing."

"Wh . . .what d . . do you want w . . with me?" Lewis stuttered.

The Snowman got right up in his face. His breath was foul and cold. Saliva ran down the corners of his pale, chapped and cracking lips, freezing there. "For once I'm on the hunt. There's an ultimate goal this time. This is no accident or coincidence. I didn't understand it then. I didn't know why I had to wait, but now I do."

Lewis, saying nothing, attempted to scoot away, but the Snowman grabbed him by the arm, squeezing tightly. Lewis squirmed like a little boy, now beginning to cry.

The Snowman turned his head. "Hungry, Zoro?" He grabbed Bobby Bates by the thigh, lifted him off the table, and hurled him against the side wall. Bobby's body smacked the wall with a loud thud, slumping down to the terrazzo floor. Zoro was on top of the body within seconds, nudging it with its beak, prodding it with its talons.

Lewis turned ghostly white, nearly as white and pale as the Snowman.

The Snowman lifted Lewis in the air, holding onto him by the neck with one hand. He slammed him down on the operating table and grabbed a knife from the cart.

Lewis wanted to scream, but couldn't. The Snowman's hands were freezing, squeezing and choking down on his neck.

"I saw the fear in your eyes when I told you my name. Bring back memories, did it? I am the memory man."

Lewis managed to spit out a few words. "Go to hell, you bastard."

"Oh, I will in due time. I'll go back home, don't you worry about that for a second. I've got some things to do here first."

The Snowman loosened his grip. Lewis started to get up, but the Snowman pinned both shoulders against the table. "Let me go!" Lewis demanded.

"Easy, Lewis. I'll be gone by Saturday at the latest. I promise. Too bad you won't be around to see me go."

Lewis spat in the Snowman's face. Spittle stuck in his stringy hair and oozed its way down the loose ends. The Snowman wiped it away and smiled.

"Going to have to kill you for that."

"Noooo!"

"It's Amy I want, Lewis." He watched the old man's eyes grow. "She's the one I'm back for. She's the one I want, and now is finally the time."

"Don't you—" The Snowman clamped his hand down on Lewis's mouth.

"Sssshhh. I'll do the talking." The Snowman showed the sharp knife to Lewis, slicing it through the air with swift swishes. "The snow is coming, Lewis. It will make everything just right for the picking."

Lewis said something that wasn't audible through the Snowman's hand.

"Shut up." The Snowman raised his hand from Lewis's mouth. Lewis gasped for air.

The Snowman laughed. "You're just going to be one of many. One more victim to my collection. They were all means to an end. Everything will end one day. My madness is random, and always has been, but I could get used to the hunt." He raised the knife high in the air. "Freeze in hell with the others. Live on in your soul, Lewis, and become one of ours."

Lewis pleaded, "I'm not ready to die, not yet!"

The Snowman grinned. "There's ssssnow time like the present, Lewis." He jammed the knife down, sticking it deep inside Lewis's neck, puncturing the windpipe. Blood sprayed out of the wound, some of it landing in the Snowman's hair and on his face. He enjoyed it. The rest of the blood flowed out over the metal table, quickly puddling around his body.

Lewis jerked and shook, but that was about it.

The Snowman switched on the motorized injector and rammed the tube into the dying man's belly button, pumping him full of formaldehyde.

Lewis stopped moving.

The Snowman backed away from the table and called Zoro away from the boy's body. Bobby's entire face was horribly mangled and disfigured. After leaving his mark, the Snowman licked the blood from his hands, and left the preparation room to the humming of the formaldehyde injector.

Chapter 20

4:35 A.M., Helen Newberry Hall

Amy had gone to sleep hoping that she would make it through the night without having a nightmare. She would not be so lucky. Her nightmare was weird and confusing.

She was frozen inside of a wall of ice. She could still see, her eyes being the only parts of her to go uncovered and untouched by the ice. Amy was a by-stander, a witness to an incredible and courageous rescue. A large man had fallen into some kind of hole or canyon and landed on a small ledge of ice directly in front of Amy's frozen body and watching eyes. She could see him clearly, but she wondered if he could see her. The man was hurt badly and could hardly move. She thought for sure that he was going to die or roll off the ledge and into the dark pit below. She was terrified for him, and also for herself. Where was she?

Then someone came to the man's rescue. The someone was a young man, strong and brave, and as far as Amy could see, handsome. He was a hero in more ways than one. He strapped the dying man to a harnessed rope and supported him while others from above pulled him up. He had saved the man's life, but unfortunately was not able to save himself. The small ledge in front of Amy broke away and the young man went down. Amy's heart dropped with him into the pit below. The hero fell quickly into the darkness, screaming and yelling, until Amy's eyes could follow him no longer.

She had seen something special in that young man. More than the rescue of the injured man, Amy truly felt that for a brief moment, when she had stared at him, that she had been rescued, too. She didn't understand why, but she felt that he was her hero, too, giving her a sense of freedom from the isolation of the cold wall that molded her. His face. There was something special about it. It made her feel good, and looking at his strength and courage gave her hope when she felt she had none, even though it had only lasted a matter of seconds. Then the hero, her hero and friend of her dreams, was gone, vanished into the bottomless pit. Gone forever. Amy was alone again, vulnerable, unprotected, and frozen in the wall of ice.

She could feel it coming, especially now that she was alone. She could feel his presence approaching, suffocating, slithering closer to her—the Snowman. He came upon her, pulling her from the wall of ice. A brief darkness surrounded her, and then, like all her other nightmares, she was surrounded by shifting walls. She was in the cold dark cave again, naked, trembling with a fear of the unknown. The four walls around her were like pictures, moving pictures with shadows dancing around them, highlighted by the sharp light shining through the small opening of the cave.

ICEVILLE.

She screamed, but nothing came out. She heard a voice. "All voices are mute in Iceville. Scream all you want." His eyes, bright and blue, froze her in place. His white hair was wild and growing longer as he knelt down beside her, straddling his legs over hers. Bracing his hands on her arms, he leaned towards her. His breath was a cold mist, showering down over her exposed flesh.

This is where her last dream had ended, but this one showed no signs of stopping. She was trapped and vulnerable. She was his. She closed her eyes.

The Snowman closed in on her, kissing her face, her ears, her neck. Her hair spread out on the ice in disarray. Its chaos excited him. He was aroused.

"You are so beautiful, Amy," he whispered, but to her ears it sounded like roaring thunder. "Just like…" he didn't finish. She moaned in discomfort.

Leaning off of her slightly, he ran his fingers down her chest, around her breasts and erect nipples, at the same time sliding his icy tongue down between them. He felt her belly. It showed tension, a sense of anticipation. She was so cold. It felt as if his tongue had cut into her. It seemed sharp. She was afraid to open her eyes.

His hands slid around her hips, her bottom, and back around her waist, stopping between her legs. His fingers danced in the triangle of hair between her legs and then slid back to her belly.

She hid her smile of pleasure, biting her lip.

She felt his breath on her face again. She tilted her head to the side. She felt something cold and hard between her legs. Her hips instinctively moved away.

He whispered, "Eliminate the righteous." He kissed her neck. "You have that power, Amy. Continue my purpose." He thrust. She couldn't avoid him. When he entered her, she was completely filled with a charge of pulsing ice through her veins. Her entire body went numb. She choked back the urge to join in the act as an uncontrollable passion swarmed over her. She pushed it away. There was no excitement on her part. It felt like she was being stabbed. No pleasure, only pain.

She not only heard the Snowman's heavy breathing, but also the distant cry of human voices. She could hear people screaming somewhere outside of the cave. The wind carried the voices into the cave, and one of them sounded familiar, as if she'd heard the cry before. She had. It was her mother's voice, or at least it sounded like her screaming, just as she had been doing before she was murdered. It got louder, closer, as if it were now coming from the ice, now inside the cave with them.

Amy opened her eyes. She was still moving on the bed, her hips sliding rhythmically as if the Snowman was still inside of her. She felt like a fool.

Sitting up in bed, she brought her legs close to her body and pulled the covers up to her neck, shivering. She was freezing. Her lips trembled. The room was dark. Kathy was still asleep.

She felt like she had been invaded, taken, abused. *Had she? Was it only a dream?*

It had seemed so real, she thought. *How could a dream be so real?* She had never been so scared, so nervous. His touch was electrical and so stimulating that it had to be real. She had felt him inside of her. Guilt overwhelmed her as she lay in bed, trying to shake away the memories. She felt guilty for not being able to stop him, for being embarrassed, for being a virgin, for being helpless in what was probably the most horrifying and most confusing instant of her life. Regardless of whether it was a dream, she would tell no one. This secret would stay with her until she died. She felt as if a part of her was dying already.

Amy buried her face in her covers and cried softly. She didn't want to wake Kathy. She was ashamed, confused, guilty, and upset. She would tell no one.

She needed help. She needed to be rescued. She needed a hero like the young man she had seen before the Snowman had entered her nightmare.

Chapter 21

6:25 A.M., Iroquois Park
7 Inches

Bill's head slowly rolled down until it hit the arm of the chair. His eyes popped open. *Where am I?*

The lights on the Christmas tree were still flashing. He felt like an old man getting to his feet. He carefully straightened out his back and loosened the crick in his neck. He looked out the front room window to see the early glimpses of the sun rising through the trees. It wasn't snowing outside, but by the looks of it, a few more inches had fallen during the three and a half hours he slept in the chair.

Bill yawned, and for a brief moment, felt calm. He had slept relatively free of turmoil, only dreaming once. He dreamt of a group of people skiing across a barren land of ice and snow, but couldn't remember anything specific about it, nor did he understand it. Regardless, it had been much more pleasant than anything the Snowman could have done to him. Looking away from the sun outside, reality came flashing back again. It was a new day, but as Bill distinctly remembered from yesterday, the Snowman was back, and there was nothing safe about that.

It was almost 6:30 in the morning, and Bill's drowsiness from the night before was fading. After starting a pot of coffee, Bill went upstairs to shower and dress. He slipped on a blue Michigan sweatshirt and an old pair of blue jeans. He brushed his hair, crammed his Cincinnati Reds cap on his damp head and laced his brown leather work boots. He was ready for breakfast. The fresh smell of coffee wafted up to his bedroom, calling him to come downstairs.

On his way down, Bill heard a rhythmic thumping. He stopped half way down the stairs, listening. Something was thumping against the door, not heavily but definitely there, like the ticking of a metronome.

"Who's there?"

The thumping got faster and a little louder.

Bill remembered last night; his conversation and argument with his brother, the death on the river, the Snowman. He no longer felt safe. His state of mind was deteriorating quickly, and with each thump, his heart pounded in his chest.

Bill descended the steps, closing in on the front room. The front door was just around the corner to his left. It sounded like the thumping noise was coming from there.

Thump thump thump thump.

Bill grabbed a stone bookend from a shelf. Clutching the piece of stone, he became aware of the sweatiness of his hands. *Why'd I pick up the knife? Shut up. Just shut the hell up. This is a stone, not a knife. Then why'd I pick up the stone?* Bill feared the answer. He was scared. Fear *was* the answer.

"Who's there?"

Thump thump thump thump.

The thumping came faster. He turned the corner, now facing the front room.

Gus was sitting, stiff as a board, on the welcome mat just inside the front door, tongue hanging out and panting, tail wagging frantically, thumping against the door.

Bill shook his head and put the stone bookend on the bottom step. *God, what is wrong with me? I'm so paranoid.* Bill felt nauseous. His adrenaline continued to pump.

Gus leaped up on all fours with his tail picking up speed. He barked loudly.

"Hold on, Gus," Bill said, rushing for the door as perspiration ran from his forehead. Bill pulled the front door open. His shirt was damp from getting out of the shower and from his nervous sweat, quickly absorbing the cold, morning air. He watched from the doorway as Gus leaped like a pup through the snow.

Bill laughed cynically. Even Gus frightened him.

The Snowman was gaining control again. Bill was angry and frustrated, but he wasn't going to let himself become self-destructive. Not now. Not ever. Those days were over.

He had to remain strong.

After sending Gus into the front room with two heaping bowls of dog food, Bill sat down at the kitchen table with his newspaper and breakfast. He was starving. His normal breakfast of coffee and toast was outvoted this morning by a glass of milk, a small glass of orange juice, two pieces of toast with grape jelly, three fried eggs, and six slices of bacon.

He finished off the entire plate while reading the sports section, washing it all down with a hot cup of coffee. After reading a story about Louisville's victory over Georgia Tech in basketball and checking the NBA box scores, he pushed his plate away and turned to the front page of the Courier Journal.

He saved the front page until last because it always contained all the depressing news. The cover was dominated by a picture of accused double-murderer O.J. Simpson walking into a courtroom surrounded by his team of lawyers, mobs of media, and security guards. Under O.J. was an article on the war in Bosnia. Both interested Bill, but the headline that grabbed his attention was on the bottom right-hand corner. It read: MYSTERIOUS SNOWMAN PLUNGES YOUNG BOY INTO OHIO RIVER. Bill covered his mouth. "Oh, my God."

Ralph had told him about this, but only after reading the article and seeing the picture did it now seem real, and final. He read the article twice. The memories of 20 years ago came flooding back. His aloneness, his fear, his confusion, and his anger all came back into focus. The memories of the ludicrous headlines, so untrue and crazy, filled with lies and made-up stories. The memories all came back.

Bill folded the paper neatly, stacking it on a pile at the end of the kitchen table. He stood, whispering, "How did I ever make it through that mess?" That ordeal was over, but it seemed as though another was beginning. He was scared, not only for himself, but also for Amy. He was tempted to call and tell her to stay in Michigan until this thing was over, but he didn't. He wondered if he was being selfish, possibly putting her life in danger. He honestly didn't know what to do but go on with his life. He refused to live his life in fear. He refused to let the Snowman win.

He placed his dishes in the sink and heard Gus's steps on the kitchen floor. He bent down and petted his head. "All done with your grub?"

Gus barked.

"I've got to go to work now, Gus. Won't be gone for long."

Bill walked into the front room and grabbed an old winter coat from the closet. His red one was still damp, and he would've felt uncomfortable wearing it anyway. He gave Gus one last pat on the head and left.

Gus ran into the front room and jumped up in the chair next to the window, nearly knocking over the Christmas tree. He watched as Bill drove through the trees and down the long gravel driveway.

Chapter 22

Except for Brice, team members slept two to a tent. Leroy shared with the Colonel, Loreda with Pam, Gabe with Dr. Moriarity, and Eric with Magnus. Brice, leader and odd man out, slept alone. It had its advantages and disadvantages. He loved the privacy that came with sleeping in his own tent. It was a way of isolating himself from the rest of the crew. On the other hand, the Antarctic nights often got lonely with no one to talk to while falling asleep. At night he had only his own thoughts to keep him occupied, and he'd often hear laughter and chatter from the other tents while he was alone listening to the wind, praying that they'd all make it back to the States in one piece. The tremors were starting to worry him. So far so good, but sleeping alone, Brice had a lot of time to worry about the safety of the crew. It was all riding on his shoulders, and now at the end of the journey, the pressure was building. He'd consider himself lucky to return home without an ulcer.

Well rested, the team was up and about early in the morning. The wind was strong, easily 30 miles per hour, at times shifting the frames of the tents to near collapse.

Leroy sat alone in his tent, thinking about the final two days of the trip. They would be long and grueling for sure. He was getting nervous, doubting his readiness for what was coming. He was dressed and set for the day to begin, and most importantly, he was alone. He pulled his small leather journal out of his bag and began to write.

THURSDAY, DECEMBER 15TH. (WE THINK)
The wind is strong and the temperature is cold! What else is new? I regret my argument last night with the gang, but regardless of what they think, I've got to hold strong to what I know. This place is bad, and it's not just the weather that makes it so. There is something about this place that they wouldn't understand, and they couldn't understand, because only I know what lives here. I feel guilty for not telling them. I need to, I know that, and really soon, but I fear telling them. I fear their reactions. Hell, I fear digging up the memories again. Talking about it scares me. They are not strangers anymore, and they need to know the facts before it is too late. I worry for their safety. I worry for my safety. I will tell them tonight. I am strong, but I can't face this alone.

I've waited so long for this moment. I'm old and tired, and I only hope I find the strength to do what is right. After all these years of painfully waiting, the opportunity has finally come. The time is now. I hope I'm ready. The others will find out soon, very soon, for only two days remain in our journey. Two more days until we find out what the Pole is really about. It's not what most would think, I know that much for a fact.

The tremor last night was sudden, and it frightened us all. I have a feeling there will be more to come. Dr. Moriarity gave his theory, and all of it was true, but …

"Leroy, you ready?"

Leroy was startled when Marvin poked his head through the opening of their tent. He dropped his pen in his sleeping bag and jerked his head up towards the Colonel, like a young boy in trouble. "Yeah, just let me finish this sentence."

"Okay. We're departing in about five minutes."

Leroy nodded. "I'll be out soon."

… I think there is more to it. I don't have the scientific back-up for my reasoning, but I know and understand the history of this place like the back of my hand. I know what I know, and I've seen what I've seen. I've got to go now. I think it is some time after seven, and we're ready to depart.

About 15 yards away from the tents, Brice, Gabe, Pamala, Marvin, and Mark stood in a cluster, waiting. Magnus was breaking down the food tent, while Eric was off to the side talking to Loreda.

Beneath his goggles and scarf, Brice was smiling at Loreda and Eric. He turned towards Gabe. "What do you make of them?"

Gabe chuckled. "They're definitely an item. I see the potential. Saw something sparking the minute they stepped off the plane." He paused, facing Brice. "They are only a year apart. Think we ought to leave them alone for a while?" Gabe asked, jokingly.

"For what?" Brice said, and then realized the answer. "Come on, Gabe. If Eric could get it up in a minus 30 wind-chill, I'd have sex with him."

"I don't think your wife would approve."

"Probably not."

Just then, Leroy stumbled out of the tent, wrapped from head to toe in his polar gear. He skied over to them, and five minutes later they were joined by Loreda. They set off, single file, in the direction of the Pole with Brice leading the way.

Eric and Magnus stayed behind to load the supplies and tear down the tents.

They had roughly 37 miles to go until they reached the bottom of the earth.

Chapter 23

10:10 A.M. River City High School
8 Inches

Bill's main job was to get the cafeteria ready for Friday night's Christmas party. He finished shortly after 10 o'clock. The tables were clean, the garbage cans were covered with fresh liners, the room was organized, and the floor was buffed to a perfect shine.

With the snow coming in, Bill doubted that they would even have the party. He wasn't going to take any chances though, just in case it blew over. Regardless of the weather, he knew the cafeteria had to be prepared. He was in charge of the cleaning, and the teachers would decorate later.

Everything was set except the heat. The school was much cooler than normal. Bill checked the radiators in the cafeteria. They were cold. Kneeling down, he reached under the radiator and turned the black valve. There was no hiss, not even a whisper coming from it. *What the hell? I know I turned the heat on before I left yesterday,* he thought. Hoping that nothing was broken, he locked the cafeteria doors and headed towards the boiler room.

Bill opened the door leading to the boiler room, walking past the wall stacked full of empty beer kegs, and down into the lower level of the room. He approached the boiler and nothing was clicking. He walked around the large tank and looked at the panel of gauges.

Well I'll be damned, he thought.

All the heat in the school had been turned off. All the heating switches were down. *Someone's been down here.* He reached for the panel, flipping the main switch to THERMO. There were five knobs to the side of the main switch, each accounting for the five sections to the school; NORTH, SOUTH, EAST, and WEST classrooms, and then the CAFETERIA. He flipped each knob to ON and closed the box above the boiler.

The clicking and the thumping inside the pipes soon followed, showing him that the heating system *was* working.

On his way up from the lower level he glanced over to the shop doors and saw two broken desks leaning against the wall. He walked over to put them inside the shop. Bill put his hand on the door, and it swung open. It wasn't locked. He remembered locking it yesterday, but then again he also remembered turning on the heat.

Flipping on the lights in the shop, he pulled the desks inside and set them next to the welding machine. The shop was freezing, much colder than the boiler room. Bill could see his breath. He looked around the room until his eyes locked on the doors to The Dungeon. They were cracked open, only about a foot, but open nevertheless, and he distinctly remembered closing them yesterday, just as he had locked the doors to the shop and had turned on the heating system.

Hesitantly, he walked up the stairs leading to The Dungeon and peeked inside. A frigid breeze whipped his face. Bill slammed the doors and locked them. *Something is wrong,* he thought, *something is definitely wrong here. Where could the wind be coming from? The Dungeon has no openings, no doors, or windows.* Bill wanted to know, but he wasn't about to enter The Dungeon and find out.

Stumbling down the steps, Bill glanced down and saw a large black feather resting on the bottom step. He backed away from The Dungeon, bumping into one of the sawing tables. He quickly turned around. His head was spinning, and he wanted nothing more than to be out of the school. *The Snowman has been here,* he thought. The school was now infested, not by rats, but with evil. *How does he do it? What does he want from me? And why?* The questions wouldn't go away.

Bill clutched the feather in his hand, stormed out of the shop and into the boiler room, leaving the doors wide open. The Snowman was going to go where the Snowman wanted to go. Bill saw no sense in locking them now.

Bill burst out of the boiler room and rested against the wall, breathing heavily. With one hand pressing against his heart and the other grasping the feather, he ran around the corner and up the cafeteria stairwell, taking two and three steps at a time.

Bill stopped at the top of the stairwell next to the entrance of the gym. The pipes were cranking and clanking loudly as the heat was turning on, forcing the resting water inside them to smack against the turns and angles as if someone was pounding the pipes with a hammer. It was a very normal sound, water hammering through the system, but now it was frightening. Everything to Bill was frightening.

He ran down the main hallway and out the front entrance to the school, nearly slipping on the ice on the front walkway. The snow was coming down hard again. He wondered why he had even come to school in the first place. There was no way they were going to have the party. Not with this storm.

Stomping his way through the snow in the parking lot, Bill hopped into his truck and started the engine. He was in a hurry. To go where, he didn't know. He was satisfied with simply being out of the school. He couldn't help to be frantic. The Snowman was back and much closer than he had imagined.

The back of Bill's truck was filled with snow, put there intentionally to add weight and keep the truck from sliding on the slick roadways. As Bill pulled out of the parking lot and onto Loftlin Avenue, the snow in his truck bed shifted, and it wasn't from the wind or the sharp turn. Something had moved within.

Chapter 24

10:27 A.M. Anderson Funeral Home, New Cut Road
8 Inches

Gerald Starks, Lewis Anderson's partner for the last 10 years, pulled into the back parking lot of the funeral home, parking between Lewis's truck and the company van. He turned off the engine and looked at the back of the brick building. He didn't feel like going in. His heart was still beating rapidly from the numerous wrecks he'd almost had on the way to work. A frenzy of light wind-blown snow bounced off the windshield and then swirled away into the grayness of the day. The snow depressed him.

Gerald got out of his '90 Escort and closed his coat tightly around his long, slender neck. The lot was slippery, so he took small steps towards the back door. At a gangling 6-foot 6-inches, Gerald was all arms and legs, barely tipping the scales at 170 pounds with his clothes on. His wild, blonde hair blew in the wind, covering his ears and eyebrows. Lewis often wondered if his friend even had ears; because in all their years of working together, he'd never seen them.

After stepping in the back door, Gerald took off his coat, shook the loose snow from it, and then hung it on the coat rack. He brushed the snow from his hair and then brought his hands down to feel his face. His tan, leathery skin was sprouting a light stubble. Waking up late, he had no time to shave. They were supposed to show Mr. Stevenson's body starting at 11:30, and he only had an hour to prepare. Gerald was relieved to see that Lewis was here early, getting everything ready. Gerald cursed himself for sleeping through his alarm. It was only his second late day in 10 years. A failed alarm clock wasn't a very good excuse, but it would work with Lewis.

Gerald walked into the front lobby, scanning it for Lewis. He didn't see him. He walked into the two display rooms, and Lewis was in neither.

"Lewis?"

No answer.

Gerald looked at the clock on the wall. They had 50 minutes until the Stevensons arrival, and nothing seemed to be ready. The body wasn't even in the coffin. *This isn't like Lewis to wait until the last minute,* Gerald thought, *I hope he's not just now embalming the guy.*

"Lewis?"

Nothing. Gerald walked into the chapel, and it too was empty.

He exited the chapel and walked into the elevator. He pressed the down arrow and crossed his arms against his chest, nervously tapping his skeletal fingers against his biceps.

The elevator door opened and Gerald stepped out.

"Lewis?"

He walked towards the embalming room. A strong whiff of formaldehyde stung his nose. His eyes started to water. Down at the bottom of the door, he saw the edge of a puddle oozing under the crack.

He reached for the knob, pushing the door open.

The room was a total mess. The formaldehyde machine was still pumping, and its contents nearly covered the entire floor with scattered puddles. Carts were overturned, tools stuck to the floor in drying spots of formaldehyde and what looked to Gerald like blood.

In the corner of the room, he saw the body of a young boy slumped against the wall like a bag of bones, blue, bloated, and smelling badly. Gerald covered his mouth and choked back the urge to vomit, inching his way closer.

Gerald quickly backed away from the mutilated body, slipping in a puddle. He caught himself on the edge of the first operating table, and when he pulled himself up he saw operating table #2, and his boss.

"Sweet Mary and Joseph," he whispered, "what the shit is going on here? Oh, Jesus, help me."

Lewis was dead. His right arm dangled over the side of the table. His throat had been cut. Gerald cautiously walked over to the table. Lewis was lying in a pool of drying blood and formaldehyde. His mouth was open, and his face was ghostly white. Gerald saw the bloody knife sticking to the edge of the table.

The machine was out of fluid, yet it continued pumping air into Lewis's mid-section. His stomach was bloated and expanding, as if ready to burst like an over-inflated balloon. His pores were enlarged and oozing with formaldehyde.

Gerald yanked the hose out of Lewis's belly before it had a chance to explode, and then he turned away from the table and vomited. Gerald went to the sink, wiped his face and lips, and on operating table #3 he saw written in blood: *SNOW DRIFTER BACK FROM ANTARCTICA.*

Trembling from head to toe, he ran out of the embalming room to the phone next to the elevator.

Andy Evans was the first to arrive at the funeral home. Gerald was waiting out in the parking lot. He quickly led Andy into the embalming room.

Andy covered his nose and mouth. The smell was suffocating.

"There's a message over here," Gerald said.

Andy followed him to the third operating table. He read the message slowly.

SNOW DRIFTER.

His attention was drawn to the murder last night on the river. He wondered if the two could be linked.

SNOW DRIFTER SNOWMAN.

The emphasis on snow frightened him.

BACK FROM ANTARCTICA.

My God, Ralph, what is happening here? He remembered Ralph's reaction last night to the name, Snowman, and now his father was dead.

"Do you want me to contact the family?" Gerald said, "I know them really well."

"That won't be necessary. I'll contact them. I think they should hear it from me."

BACK FROM ANTARCTICA.

Andy read the message over and over.

SNOW DRIFTER BACK FROM ANTARCTICA.

Andy surveyed the room, and then walked over to the body lying in the corner. Even though the face had been mutilated, Andy recognized the body. It was Bobby Bates, the young boy he had pulled out of the icy Ohio River less than 24 hours ago.

Andy noticed something sticking out from under Bobby's back. It was a black feather. Andy knelt down to get a closer look, unaware that the tail of his coat was dragging through a puddle of formaldehyde. He reached down to grab it and then stopped. He would wait until the crime scene investigators arrived before touching anything. He couldn't believe what he was seeing. The feather only added to his questions and confusion.

Just then, they heard a knock on the door. Louisville's homicide team walked into the embalming room and immediately started asking Andy questions, since he was the first officer at the scene. The forensics soon followed.

Chapter 25

10:35 A.M., Iroquois Park
8 Inches

Bill eased up on the steering wheel as he coasted along his driveway, trying to forget about what he had found at the school. In between the trees he saw two people standing on his front porch, knocking on his door. Bill slowed down to try and get a look at who they were because he wasn't expecting company.

Mike and Kathleen Greene heard the rumble of tires on gravel coming up behind them. They turned around to see Bill's truck flashing in and out of the naked, snow-covered trees.

Bill pulled up next to the Greene's car, now recognizing the two people. After shutting off the engine, Bill got out of his truck and met them on the front porch. He kept the feather in his pocket.

Bill offered Mike a handshake and gave Kathleen a hug. "This is a surprise. What brings you here?"

"Just wanted to run these by," Kathleen said, raising up a basket full of fruit.

"Ah, what's this for?"

"Christmas," Mike said. Kathleen finished the answer, "we know how tough of a time it is for you around Christmas. We're always thinking about you, Bill."

Bill hesitated and smiled. It was an awkward smile.

Kathy noticed the reaction. "Something wrong, Bill?"

"No," he shook his head. "Actually there is."

Mike put his hand on Bill's shoulder. "What is it?"

Bill slid his keys in the lock and opened the door. "Let's go inside first."

Both Kathleen and Mike were concerned. Something was definitely wrong, and Kathleen had an idea of what it might be. She had read the paper. She had seen the TV reports of "the Snowman", and by the look on Bill's face she knew that he had seen them too.

Gus shot out like a cannonball, salivating, barking wildly at Bill's truck.

"Gus!" Bill called. "Get back here!" He looked at Kathleen and Mike. "Sorry about this."

Gus smelled something bad. He was picking up the residue of something evil in the bed of the truck. The scent drew Gus closer.

"Gus!"

Gus didn't even turn towards his master.

Bill walked down the steps of the porch. "What's gotten into you, Gus?"

In, under, around, and within the snow, the Snowman could hear the dog barking and jumping against the side of the truck. He was surprised that the dog was able to pick up on his scent.

Before the Snowman emerged, the snow in the truck bed had been only substance. Now it was a substance with feeling, senses, and a mind. The snow could hear the dog barking. The snow could hear Bill yelling from the house. The snow could now feel and sense that all eyes were now focused on it. The snow felt the impact when the dog leaped into the bed of the truck.

It was a tough jump for an old dog, but Gus cleared the side of the truck with ease. His anxiety pushed him along, and the strange scent was driving him crazy. Gus landed with a thud, burying himself in the snow. Growling, Gus dug into the snow with his front paws, searching for the source of the scent. He found nothing.

The Snowman wanted badly to come out and rip the dog's head off, but he waited. He wanted them all dead, but it wasn't the right time, not yet. He would wait for Amy. She was the key to his goal, and together they would win the race. He couldn't expose himself now and still let them live. He had to wait until Bill brought her home, and then he would strike.

As Gus turned in another circle in the snow, he was quickly lifted out of the truck and smacked on the rump. He looked up towards Bill and then back towards the truck.

Bill pointed towards the house. "Go!" He looked inside the snow where Gus had been digging. He reached his hand inside, making the hole bigger, but saw and felt nothing.

Hesitantly, Gus walked up to the porch with his tail drooping between his legs, every few steps looking back at the truck and growling.

After hearing the front door close and the trio disappear inside, the Snowman emerged from the snow in full human form and turned to face the house. He saw the dog in the front window, barking and going crazy. "Doggy, try and mess with me," the Snowman laughed. "I'll give you something to chew on."

Slowly, the Snowman stepped out of the truck and then took off, laughing wildly, into the woods. Hunched over, he ran like a wild ape through a jungle.

He would wait in the woods, away from the dog. The Snowman was confused over the dog's actions. The Snowman controlled all animals. He spoke their different languages. He lived like an animal in a barren land of ice and snow; but there was something different, something very strange about this particular dog that worried him.

Gus hadn't been scared at all. He was old but hadn't been frightened. For the first time in a millennium of chaos, the Snowman had been hesitant, and the culprit had been a dog. The Snowman had felt the power of resistance, the power of the opposition. But in a dog? It was possible. The opposition could change mediums and persona at the drop of a hat, and the Snowman was well aware of it. But how long could it last in the dog? Something so small? Not long. He would kill the dog as soon as possible. The Snowman was ready. With the girl, he would continue his purpose.

His side would win.

Andy Evans walked into his cubicle at the police station and picked up the phone, dialing the Audubon Hospital morgue. A young man picked up on the fourth ring.

"Audubon morgue, this is Jerry."

"Jerry. Officer Andy Evans, Louisville Police Department."

"What can I do for you?"

"Well, hopefully answer a couple of questions."

"Shoot."

"How many pick-ups did you have last night?"

Jerry put his book down on the desk and grabbed his clip-board. "Just four, sir."

"Four? Was Lewis Anderson one of the morticians that came for the bodies?"

"Yeah, he picked up one of them last night. Came in about three o'clock, I believe."

"He just picked up one body?"

"Yeah, just one."

"Could you tell me anything about the body he picked up?"

Jerry shifted in his seat. The deep, serious tone in Andy's voice was making him nervous. "It was a young boy, 12 years old. Fished him out from under the ice on the Ohio yesterday evening."

"I know," Andy said, "I'm the one that took him out."

Jerry gulped. "Name was Robert Bates. Poor kid was as blue as the ocean."

Well, now his face has been chewed off, Andy thought, *and his mortician has been pumped full of formaldehyde. I don't think his coloring is important anymore. Was it a coincidence that the boy was found with the Snowman's second victim?* Andy certainly thought so. *A serial killer?* Andy knew it was a possibility. He'd learned a lot about them and even studied them in college. This one was hitting a little bit too close to home. At least two were dead because of the Snowman and possibly even more.

Andy gritted his teeth and squeezed the phone in his hand. "Thanks, Jerry."

"Officer, what's going on?"

"I'm not really sure."

"Is something wrong with Lewis?"

Andy grunted. "You can say that." He hung up and paced around the station. Now the toughest part of the job—telling his boss that his father was no longer alive.

Both Kathleen and Mike were floored by what Bill was telling them. Bill told them everything, starting with the missing coat on Wednesday, his dreams and visions, and finally, the feathers outside his window and next to The Dungeon doors.

"He's back in control again," Bill said, "and I don't know what to do. I don't know how and I don't know why, but he's back, and for some damn reason, he's got another bone to pick with me and my family. There's a blizzard coming this weekend, as you know, supposedly our worst one ever; and now he's back to welcome it in. Coincidence? I don't think so. As he said, he's the worldwide traveler, whatever the hell that means."

The Greenes stared.

"I believe that everything happens for a reason. He wants something in particular, but I don't have a clue as to what it might be." Bill banged his fist down on the coffee table. Coffee spilled from their mugs. "I'll be damned if I'm going to give him what he wants. I'm not playing his games anymore." Bill stood and placed his hands on his hips, shaking his head back and forth. "It's not just me though; it's Amy. She's who I'm worried about, not myself."

The crack of the rifle echoed through the woods. Birds scattered from the trees in pursuit of the safer sky, away from the winter hunter.

"Dammit!" Cletus grumbled. "Missed again." He reloaded his rifle, all the time keeping an eye on the deer as it darted in and out of the trees.

Wearing a fluorescent orange suit and an olive green hunting hat, Cletus stuck out like a sore thumb. The deer was able to see his every move.

Cletus squatted down on one knee, keying down on the deer who was half concealed by a large tree. He locked in on the head and squeezed the trigger. The deer ducked and took off running in the opposite direction, deeper into the woods.

"Damn, he's a fast one." Cletus kicked the bottom of a tree and stared into the distance, ready to give up. The deer was gone. He'd lost it again. He headed off towards the direction of the deer's escape, but stopped when he heard the crunching of snow and dead leaves from directly behind. He turned around and saw a strange-looking, pale man with long white hair, standing 10 feet away.

Cletus smiled and spat his chewing tobacco in the snow. "You gotchursef a starin' problem?"

The Snowman didn't say a word. He simply stared with his cold, blue eyes, stepping a few feet closer to the hunter.

Cletus didn't back away. "Cain't you talk?" He stared at the approaching stranger, his bushy, graying eyebrows, high cheek bones, and strong, box-like jaw that seemed to be shifting from side to side as if chewing on something. Cletus stared at the hair, the light-blue eyes, the chalky-colored skin. "You deaf'r somethin'?"

The Snowman took two more steps and then stopped. He reached out his hand. His voice bellowed like a burst of thunder. "Give me the weapon."

Cletus gripped his rifle and took a couple of steps backwards. "Who the fuck you think you are tellin' me what's doin'. I outta shoot you jus'fr bein' a wise ass."

"No hunting the animals, not in these woods," the Snowman said.

"I don't give a horny dog's pink pencil about no law. I do my hunt'n when and where I wanna do my hunt'n."

The Snowman stepped closer. "Want to live forever?"

Cletus squinted his eyes. "What?"

"For eternity. Eternal chaos. Feed my purpose."

Cletus backed away, shaking his head slowly.

"Don't spoil in the force of the opposition."

Cletus pointed the gun at the Snowman. "I ain't listenin' to no stranger, and sure as hell no one lookin' like yursef. No coat or nothin'. Yur one of those albinos? You are, ain't cha? I know cause I've seen'm before in magazines and stuff."

"Join the rest of them," the Snowman hissed, smiling.

Catching sight of the man's pointed teeth, Cletus's heart pounded. His finger touched the trigger, quivering. He couldn't hold it steady. "What are you?"

"I'm whatever you want me to be. I'm the bogeyman." He reached his arms out in an attempt to scare the hunter.

It worked. Cletus stumbled on the snow, fell back against a tree, and quickly raised the rifle back up at the Snowman. "T . . . take another step and I'll blow yur balls right outta yur jeans."

The Snowman lunged foreword. Cletus fired.

The bullet entered his chest and exited his back next to his shoulder blade. The Snowman stopped, moaned softly, and then covered his chest with his large hand.

Cletus shuffled backwards, watching the stranger, waiting for the blood to come spreading down over the white shirt. It never did. "I got'm," he mumbled, "I got'm good." He was proud for a second, and then he realized that he'd just shot a man. He'd never done anything like that before. Illegally shooting at the deer was at least reasonable to Cletus, but shooting another man had definitely not been in his plans for the day. He watched as the man removed his hand from his chest. There was a small bullet hole, roughly the size of the bullet, through the man's chest, but there seemed to be no major damage. The exit wound was the same size as the entrance, a perfect tunnel. There was no blood. Cletus stared right through the wound. A perfect hole had been blown through the man's chest, and there was no blood, no organs, no innards of any kind.

Cletus froze.

The Snowman laughed, pointing to the chest hole where his heart should have been. "Is this the only thing you've hit all day?"

Cletus tripped over an exposed root, falling down on his backside. He tried crawling backwards on his elbows. "S . . .stay away. I don't know where you came from, but'cha best go on back."

The hole in the Snowman's chest quickly filled itself in, although the hole in the shirt remained. Cletus watched in amazement. He felt something in his pants. His crotch turned wet. He tried to say something, but the only thing to come out was gibberish.

The Snowman stood over Cletus and ripped the rifle from his hands. Cletus screamed and then covered his eyes. He felt a cold breeze against his ear.

The Snowman whispered, "Preserve." He brought the butt end of the rifle down on the hunter's head, and the whimpering and screaming stopped. Cletus wasn't moving anymore. The Snowman threw the rifle to the ground and closed in.

For Cletus, the blow to the head had been instant death. He never felt that first cold bite into his neck. There was a lot of blood. It spread quickly into the snow that surrounded them.

"Where is Amy?" Kathleen asked.

"School. She's coming home this afternoon." Bill looked at his watch. "I'll pick her up in about an hour."

"Are you going to tell her?" Mike asked.

"I *have* to tell her something. She's coming home to a very abnormal situation. She's going to know that something is up."

"Do you think Amy might already know?"

"What do you mean?"

"She has never admitted it, but I've always been quite certain that she remembers something from that day."

"She was only two," Bill said. "What could she have remembered at that age?"

"I'd say a lot, Bill. It's amazing what goes on in the mind of a child. Believe me, children can remember, and I think Amy did, too."

"Why didn't you tell me this years ago. And why wouldn't she ever say anything to me?"

Mike leaned back in his chair, listening. Kathy went on. "What good would it have done, Bill? Every time I tried talking to her she'd clam up and insist that there was nothing to talk about. But I've always had my doubts. She was so young. I didn't want to pressure her into talking."

"You're saying that she could have had dreams like mine and never said anything about them?"

"I think it's very possible. You were constantly troubled by the dreams, and you weren't even in the house to witness any part of the killing. She was. Like I said, I could be wrong, and I hope that I am, but who knows what went on inside her head 20 years ago."

Bill stared past the Christmas tree and out the window. He could think of nothing other than his daughter. "She's always seemed like nothing bothered her. Never a word in all these years. She's always had questions, lots of them, but . . . could it have been that she also had some answers, and she was hiding, or . . . or afraid."

"Very possible."

"She was only two years old though." He looked at Kathleen, confused. "I've never seen any signs of trouble. She kept to herself a lot, but I guess that's normal for any teenager. She's always seemed so normal. Why would I even suspect that she was hiding something?"

"She's perfectly normal, Bill. That's not what I'm saying. You're perfectly normal too, but there is something about you that is psychologically connected with the Snowman. I kept quiet about Amy because she was so young. I didn't want to pressure her into talking. That was then, 20 years ago. The Snowman was gone when we'd met, at least physically. I didn't want to dwell on something that I wasn't even sure was there, for Amy's sake. I never thought the Snowman would be back; but, according to what you've told us, he is. I think it is possible that she has the same connection with him as you do."

Bill took a deep breath, rubbing his face with his hands.

"I'm sorry, Bill. I didn't want to worry you about this over the years, but if he really is back, I can't help but wonder what is going through her head right now."

"My God," Bill said, standing up, walking into the front room. "This is all crazy. All that you've said makes sense, Kathleen, but I've just got to talk to Amy. I'm so scared for her. This is all happening so fast." He rubbed his eyes. "I don't know what to do."

They followed him into the front room. "What about police protection? Or getting out of town, Bill?" Mike asked.

"It doesn't matter where we go. He's going to find us." Bill pointed to the side of his head. "He's right up here. Right here inside. He knows our every move. There is no place to run."

"What about police protection?"

Bill thought of Ralph. Police protection was an idea, but he didn't quite know how to approach it. As of now, he didn't know where he stood with his brother. Bill shook his head. "Maybe, I just don't know."

"But Ralph can—" Kathleen said.

"I don't know," Bill repeated. "I need time to think."

There was a brief silence, and then Mike placed his hand on Bill's shoulder. "You are not alone. You know that don't you?"

Bill nodded. "Thanks, both of you."

They were all startled by a knocking at the front door. Before Bill could ask who it was, Ralph entered. The greetings were warm between Ralph and the Greenes. Regardless of what Ralph believed of the Snowman, he knew of the Greene's support, and he knew how much they'd meant to his brother during his times of trouble. Ralph looked towards Bill. They nodded to each other, saying nothing. Bill was again surprised by his sudden visit.

Mike and Kathleen both sensed an urgency in Ralph's arrival, and decided they'd better go. "Look, Bill," Mike said, putting on his coat. "You can count on us."

"I will."

Bill closed the door behind them and turned towards his brother. They walked into the front room.

"What is it, Ralph? I don't want to get in a fight, not now."

"I agree."

In the front room, Gus was still on top of the chair, staring out the window. In the distance, he heard the crack of rifle fire. He ran whimpering into the other room, no longer feeling the courage and strength that had helped him to charge into the truck. He felt like an old dog again, helpless against any opposition. Something was out there in the woods.

The Snowman wiped his face clear of the blood and dripping flesh. He heard a noise from the trees and looked upward. Zoro flew down and perched on his outstretched arm. They walked into a tiny clearing where the snow was deep and falling. He sat down against the side of a tree. His eyes were tired. His face, hair, and shirt were matted down and tangled with drying blood.

He would wait for Amy. He could think of no one else.

He closed his eyes.

Chapter 26

11:45 A.M. Detroit Metropolitan Airport

The Continental Airlines desk clerk wrapped her pudgy hand around her microphone. "Flight 327 Continental to Louisville is now boarding passengers from rows 7 through 21. Any passengers sitting in rows 7 through 21 may now board at this time."

Walking down the extension tunnel, Amy turned to Kathy. "We'll be in Louisville before you know it. You look worried."

"So do you, Amy. You've been so distant this morning, almost like you're still hiding something. Remember, we're not keeping any more secrets."

"I know," she said, turning a corner, ducking into the plane. "I've just been thinking."

"About?"

"What do you think?"

Amy had been silent the entire morning. Ever since awakening from the horrible nightmare, she hadn't slept a wink. For four hours she had simply stared around her dark dorm room. She had tried to study for her final, but couldn't ever bring herself to concentrate. She was feeling dirty and ugly now, shying away from any conversation. What had happened during the night was still eating away at her inside, but she was determined to keep it a secret, even from Kathy.

Amy put their bags in the overhead compartment and sat in her seat. Kathy plopped down beside her, wasting no time in snapping on her seatbelt.

"Relax, Kathy. All the other passengers aren't even on board yet."

"I know, but the seat-belt makes me feel at ease." She leaned back and closed her eyes.

Amy stared out the small window. She couldn't wait to get home.

The 200 passenger plane filled up very quickly, and just before it started to taxi, Kathy's eyes opened. They both waited, eyes on the stewardess at the front of the plane, who was mumbling about all the airline procedures, devices, and important information about what to do in case of an emergency.

"Ladies and gentlemen, we now ask that you fasten your seat-belts while the seat-belt lights are on. We'll be taking off in another minute. Hope you enjoy your flight, and thank you for flying Continental." Two other women joined the stewardess, pacing up and down the aisle, making sure everyone's seat-belts were fastened and all carry-on luggage was securely sealed in the overhead storage compartments.

Kathy rotated her body towards Amy. "They don't look too enthusiastic about their job. I bet they wouldn't even care if our plane crashed into a mountain."

"Wouldn't you look bored if you had to do this all day, every day?"

"I guess so."

The plane jerked foreword and started down the runway. Amy watched out the window at the workers and landscape zipping by as the plane accelerated. "Here we go."

Kathy bit down hard on her bottom lip.

The lift-off pressed everyone against their seats. Kathy felt like her head was going to explode. She'd never felt this type of pressure before. It didn't feel safe. She would do her best to go to sleep.

The pilot then began to speak in his slow, deep voice. "Ladies and gentlemen, you may take off your seat-belts now. Feel free to use the restroom, although we encourage you to remain seated for the duration of the trip. Thank you and enjoy your flight."

Amy saw that Kathy was asleep, or at least she appeared to be. Closing her eyes, she tried to think of something pleasant, but couldn't. Nothing in her life seemed pleasant right now. She could only see the Snowman as he came down upon her. She could remember being totally defenseless. The walls, the moving walls, the air, the dirty feeling of being violated, raped. She could still picture it all.

Iceville.

She couldn't escape. She couldn't clear the image from her head. His hands had been so cold, rubbing her and touching her, feeling her in places she'd never been felt before. She hadn't been able to do anything. She hadn't been able to scream.

All voices are mute, Amy. I'm all you got. Now is the time, Amy.

Amy shivered in her seat, fighting back the tears. She was cold. Somehow though, she was able to find rest, and unlike her sleep last night, her short nap on the plane was uninterrupted by the Snowman.

"You come to arrest me?" Bill asked Ralph.

"No. That's not why I'm here."

"Then what is it, if it isn't a business visit? Somebody else die? Did you come back to rub the past in my face again?"

"Bill," Ralph held up his hand, "we got off on the wrong foot last night."

"As always. Did you come to apologize?"

"No."

"Then what?"

Ralph paused, scratching his head. "I came here to talk. I came here to listen. I'm not saying I believe everything from the past, but I think it's at least time that we talked about it. Me and you. A conversation, Bill, one where neither one of us is trying to outdo the other."

"You want to talk about this?"

"Yes."

"Why, after all these years? Why now?"

Ralph sighed. "I don't know. Maybe because it's time to sort things out."

"The real reason."

Ralph felt like the little brother again, drilled with questions he wasn't totally prepared to answer. Ralph had confidence when he was here last night until he saw the feather. "You want the real reason, Bill?"

"It'd be nice."

"It was the damn feather. I freaked out when I saw the feather. I don't know why, but when Mary was killed, that's the part of the entire tragedy that bothered me the most. Despite my thoughts on everything else, I could never get past the feathers."

"I found another one."

"You what?"

"I found another feather this morning in the school. It was resting on one of the steps in front of The Dungeon."

"Same kind?"

"Exactly. The Dungeon doors were wide open, and the air was freezing. It was colder in there than any place I'd ever been before."

"I'll get some guys in there to check it out."

"Tell them to be careful."

Ralph laughed. "They're cops, Bill. They'll be careful. Look. I know you're worried."

"That's an understatement."

"I'm getting you police protection."

"How?"

"I'm deputy chief of police. I can get protection for a family member if the situation calls for it."

"And you think it does?"

"I'm not sure if I do or not, but I know you'd feel better if someone was watching the house until this passes, especially with Amy coming home. Normally, I wouldn't be able to do this over the little evidence that we have. I'm basing this on your fears, a few feathers, and some dreams. There isn't anything concrete to go on here, but this once I'm going to take advantage of my position. I'd like someone to be here with you."

"Is this for my protection or do you just want someone watching me in case I want a drink, or maybe get the urge to kill?"

"Dammit, Bill. I'm here, aren't I? I'm throwing all my cards on the table."

"To help?"

Ralph hesitated. "Yes, to help."

"Well, what's the first move? Who's the cop gonna be?"

"Remember Andy Evans? I think you've met him before."

"Big black guy?"

"That's him. Of course there is more to him than that."

"Can he be here when I get back from the airport?"

"You go to the airport to get Amy. When the flight arrives, you call me at the office, and I'll send Andy to meet you there. He'll escort you back home and then wherever else you need to go."

Bill took a deep breath. "How am I going to explain to Amy about Evans being with us?"

"I'll leave that up to you."

"Great."

"What did the Greenes want earlier? You looked rattled when I came in."

"Something Kathleen told me."

"What was it?"

"You got a few minutes?"

Ralph checked his watch. "A few." He nodded.

"She's not even sure, but it sounds likely to me."

"What does?"

"That Amy remembers, and that Amy dreams, and that Amy may have been suffering through the same shit as me for the past 20 years without telling anyone about it."

The pilot came on again. "Ladies and gentlemen, we are currently cruising at 35,000 feet and are on schedule to arrive at the Louisville Airport at about 1:15. The current weather conditions in Louisville are: temperatures in the single digits, very overcast, about eight inches of snow on the ground, and it's still falling. We are actually a few minutes ahead of schedule, so I might use the extra time to go further east to avoid some possible turbulence. I hope you are enjoying your flight with Continental Airlines."

When the pilot finished, both of the girls were silent. The word—turbulence—was freaking Kathy out, so she was scared to speak. Amy was thinking to herself, *eight inches of snow.* She couldn't believe it. *Is it all happening again? The snow, the dreams, the timing. It is happening again.*

She turned to say something to Kathy, but she had her eyes closed and was biting down on her bottom lip again, probably trying to go back to sleep.

She could hear a voice in her head. *Amy, look at me out on the wing. I'm flying like a bird. Amy, check and see.*

Amy rubbed her lips together, grinding her teeth. She wanted desperately to look out the window, just give it a quick glance to prove to herself that nothing was out there. *It's silly*, she thought. *Come on, Amy. Ease your mind.*

That's exactly what she did, except when she turned to look at the wing, her mind was definitely not at ease.

She did a double-take, but it was there both times. She blinked, but when she opened her eyes it was still there.

She stared into those beaming red eyes as Zoro looked into her small window from the wing of Flight 327, beak open, talons clicking.

Ralph sat down on one of the stools in the kitchen, pulled a pack of cigarettes from his coat pocket and lit one up.

"Thought you quit?"

Ralph inhaled and then blew two spikes of smoke through his nostrils. "Almost. Given that everything happened as you say, Amy could have remembered something from back then?"

Bill was tempted to ask his brother to put it out. He didn't like smoking in his house. After not smoking for so many years, his eyes burned at the slightest hint of it. "That's what Kathleen picked up on, and I believe her. She said she sensed something many years ago, but never said anything about it."

Ralph took a long drag. "Why not?"

"Kathleen didn't want to drill a little girl with questions. Amy didn't want to talk, so she didn't force her."

"You going to ask Amy when she gets here?"

"Yes. I can't have her suffering alone any longer."

"Good luck." Ralph put his cigarette out and checked his watch. "I've got to get back to the office. You better go ahead and leave for the airport. The roads are getting slick, especially the side roads."

Bill grabbed his coat out of the front room closet and slipped it on. "I had another dream last night."

Ralph stared at his older brother. He was trying so hard to believe, but it just wasn't happening, not yet. After all of their history together, stories of the Snowman coming back, seeing the bottle of alcohol on the kitchen table, Ralph still wasn't sure what to think or what to believe. "Was it about the Snowman?"

"Well, I don't think so, it . . . it was just really weird. Didn't make sense at all."

They stopped before opening the front door. "Go on," Ralph said.

"I remember being in a far-away desert, a very cold place. It went on and on forever, like a frozen, snow-filled Sahara. It was all ice and snow. The weather was miserable, and the wind," he paused, shaking his head at the thought of it, "my God, the wind was horrible. I couldn't see how they could stand it, traveling through that icy wilderness."

"Did you say they? Who is they?"

"I'm not sure why, or who, but eight or nine people, dressed all in winter gear, were skiing."

"Skiing?"

"Yeah, and they were tired, very tired. Almost as if they were lost, or stranded. The land never ended."

Ralph opened the door.

"I wish I knew what it all meant," Bill said, closing the door behind them. The snow was falling much heavier now than in the morning.

Ralph ran to his car and just before he got inside, Bill called his name. Ralph sat down in the car with the door open. "Yeah?"

There was a short silence.

"Thanks," Bill said.

Ralph held up his hand and then closed the door. Bill watched him drive away, and then he ran to his truck.

In Bill's bedroom upstairs, Gus twitched and shook in his sleep. Something was bothering him. His eyes moved rapidly behind his closed lids.

Dogs can dream, too.

"The Twilight Zone." Amy remembered watching the movie. John Lithgow was the only passenger on the plane to see the hellish creature on the wing. The other passengers thought he was crazy. Amy felt the same way. She tried to remain calm, not wanting the others to look strangely at her. They'd for sure think she was nuts if she started screaming, *Bird on the wing. Everybody look, little birdie on the wing.*

This bird wasn't little, and in a blink of the eyes, he owned her again. Just like last night with the alarm clock, he owned her. She couldn't hear or see anything around her. Everything was blocked out in ultimate blackness, except for what she saw out on the wing.

Zoro extended his wings, maintaining his balance on the wing with little trouble. He was dancing and hopping around as if Flight 327 was cruising inside of a wind-free bubble. Clouds flew by, flashing like lightning, shaking the plane, but Zoro kept his equilibrium.

Red eyes glowing, Zoro approached her window, flapping his wings with each step.

Amy whispered, "This is not real, this is not real, this is not real," clutching the arms of her seat.

Zoro was bobbing his head as if saying, *Yes, yes it is my darling, this is all very real. Now, let's have us some fun.*

Suddenly, the wing dropped out of sight and everything around Zoro turned black. Zoro hovered in mid-air. Amy looked at her feet; she was doing the same. She was no longer sitting in the plane next to Kathy but was surrounded by stars and darkness. It was just the two of them, Amy and Zoro, floating in some kind of dark space.

Zoro's black body blended into the darkness. The contour of his wings was not visible. She only knew where he was by those eyes. Those red eyes would never go away.

Amy was afraid to move. Afraid that if she stepped an inch to either side that she would go plummeting to her death down below.

Zoro's beak opened wide, revealing strange bird teeth. The wide-open beak shielded the rest of Zoro's bald head from Amy's line of vision. Even the eyes were temporarily blocked out.

Amy saw the inside of the bird's beak and then screamed, or at least tried to scream, but nothing came out.

All voices are mute in Iceville, Amy.

A red halo formed around Zoro's head, and then the beak closed. It was no longer a beak, but now a mouth; and the head was no longer a bird's head, but the head of a human. It was the head of the Snowman. His long white hair cascaded down over his bird-like body, wings continuously flapping.

The Snowman's eyes popped open, his pupils were light-blue and glittering brightly. A neon-green halo surrounded his head. The Snowman smiled and winked. His rough, baritone voice filled the air with a thunder-like explosion.

"Hello Amy. Give me what I need," he hissed.

Amy couldn't speak. She couldn't move. She couldn't do anything but float and watch.

"Nice of you to hang around," the Snowman said, laughing, pointing downward with his thick wings. "Follow me to your new home. I hope you'll like it. I sure do." He took off flying directly towards Amy, approaching her as if shot from a cannon.

A foot away from Amy's body, he crashed into thousands of tiny pieces, crumbled like brittle glass, quickly disintegrating into space. Something had been blocking her from the Snowman-Zoro creature, and it was starting to come into focus. She could now see that she was surrounded by an invisible glass tube. It had a small crack in it, and the crack was getting longer, growing downward, splitting. She watched it as it splintered down the glass tube that surrounded her, and then she felt herself falling. Something was sucking her down like a vacuum, and she watched the crack splinter down the tube in front of her as she fell. The crack was following her, or she was following it. She couldn't tell. The color was also changing. What once was black space sprinkled with stars was changing into a beautiful dark blue. She looked down below and saw a white landscape.

The sky around her was changing from blue to a yellowish-green, glistened by the hovering sun. The white ground was painfully bright, and getting larger and closer very quickly. The air was getting much colder. She prayed, reminding herself that it wasn't real, hoping that it was all a dream or vision because the impact with the icy white ground below would instantly kill her at the speed she was traveling. About 20 feet above ground level her speed declined rapidly, halting to a jerking stop like a roller coaster at the end of a ride, until she landed softly on the beautiful white landscape.

It was freezing, and the wind was whistling around her body. She shivered. Her feet hurt, and her shoes were sticking to the ice. She lifted them and then turned in a circle. The scenery was the same on every side. *Where am I?* she thought. North, south, east, and west, the only thing she could see was snow and ice. It was Iceville. She was in her dreamworld. The wind blew drifts of loose snow in every direction, stinging her eyes. She shielded them with her arms, at the same time trying to peer off in the distance. About 20 yards away she saw something about a foot-and-a-half tall, black and white, walking towards her. The tiny creature wobbled as it approached. It was a penguin. She'd seen pictures of them before and knew what they looked like, but never had she seen this strange-looking creature in person. It stared with shocked eyes up at Amy.

Just as Amy reached down to the penguin, it opened its mouth. "Go ahead and touch, Amy. Down here I'm all you got." It was the Snowman's voice. The penguin quickly shape-shifted into Zoro, jumped up, and then disappeared into the sky. Amy stumbled backwards, falling clumsily to the hard ice. She was alone again. From the same place the penguin had come, she saw something else moving towards her. Skiers. They passed directly in front of her, kicking mists of snow in her face and hair as they skied along, completely unaware of her presence. They were no more than five feet away from her, but none of them had seen her. She called out to them for help, but none of them could hear her, either.

Voices are mute down here.

She waved, but they didn't turn around.

I'm all you got.

Within seconds, the main body of skiers was gone, and all she could see of them was their skis kicking up puffs of snow in the distance. Amy noticed that one person remained, but this one wasn't skiing like the others. It was a man, and he was now directly in front of her. He looked familiar to Amy, and he was crawling along the ice, very slowly and carefully. He looked tired, seemingly fighting for his life; not so much crawling across the ice, but rather, it appeared as if he were climbing a horizontal surface. Amy thought, *What is he doing? It seems like he's climbing up something. Maybe in his world he is vertical, and he's climbing some sort of wall. He needs help.* The man had an ice axe in each hand and spikes on the bottoms and tips of his boots. The man was using all the energy he could gather to climb the surface of ice. She could hear his thoughts as he took turns plunging the ice axes into the ground, following it with large steps, digging into the ice with each boot, scaling the ice like a soldier. *Ice axe, ice axe, and then an upward step with each boot. Ice axe, ice axe, boot, boot.* The pattern was hypnotic.

Then the man stopped to catch his breath.

Amy recognized the face. He looked towards her. It was the man in her dream. The good man. Her hero. He was climbing from the hole into which he had fallen in her dream last night.

"Help me," Amy whispered.

The man nodded.

Amy couldn't believe that he'd reacted to her. He had heard her, she was sure of it. Someone had heard her in Iceville.

"Help me," she said again, louder this time.

Again the man nodded, and then continued down the ice. Or was it up the ice? Amy didn't care. She didn't feel alone. Her hero had come for her again. Someone had heard her speak while she was in Iceville. Amy looked down at her arm and noticed that it was shaking, and she wasn't making it do so. She heard someone calling her name in a whisper.

"Amy."

The voice grew louder.

"Amy!" Kathy said, shaking Amy's arm. "Amy, what's wrong?"

Amy opened her eyes. Her head snapped back against her seat. She brought her hands to her mouth to muffle her scream. She looked all around her, and everything was safe. The passengers were all there again, and so was Kathy. Everything was back to normal, inside of the plane at least.

No more Snowman, no more Zoro, no more penguin, and no more ice and snow. The skiers were gone, too, and so was her hero, the only person to ever hear her cry for help.

Kathy grabbed Amy's hands. "Everything is okay."

The plane took a dip, tilting from side to side.

"Ladies and gentlemen, we ask that you now fasten your seat-belts to prepare for landing. We should be touching down in about 10 minutes. It may get a little bumpy going through these clouds, but that's normal. No reason to be alarmed."

The plane took another dip and dropped a few hundred feet. Kathy tightened her grip on Amy's hands, trying to keep her eyes closed.

The plane rocked to the right, silencing the passengers, and then it rocked back to the left, dropping even more.

Amy glanced at her side window and noticed that it was cracked, just as she had seen the crack in the glass tube from her vision. But it wasn't the only thing that she saw. On the wing sat a long black feather, unaffected by the wind.

Amy freed her right hand from Kathy's grip and closed the shade on her window; something she wished she had done long ago. She swore never to have a window seat again. Like Kathy, Amy closed her eyes until the plane was safely on the ground.

Minutes later, the wheels thudded to the pavement as Flight 327 bounced and touched down on Standiford Field's runway. As soon as it came to a stop and all was apparently safe, both Kathy and Amy opened their eyes.

Chapter 27

Eric and Magnus had just pulled up when the rest of the crew was finishing their 15 minute snack break. The temperature was dropping, now close to 50-degrees below zero. The wind was strong, and despite the thick Everest screen with which they coated their faces, it still cut into the exposed areas. They were eager to get going again. The sooner they reached the Research Station the better.

Gabe skied away from the pack to where Brice was busy with the radio. Brice had his coat unzipped, holding one loose side over the radio to protect it from the wind. He turned around as he heard someone approaching from behind.

Gabe squatted down and pointed towards Brice's coat. "Don't think that's working." He had to raise his voice to be heard over the wind.

Brice smiled underneath his gear and then nodded. When he spoke, it was muffled by his wool scarf. "I can't get anything to work in this wind."

The only sounds coming from the radio transmitter were scattered beeps and bursts of static. Brice's hands shook as his frozen fingers fumbled with the knobs and buttons.

"No word from the station I assume?" Gabe yelled.

"Static and more static. That's it." He zipped his coat back up and then switched off the radio. "What's the reading on the wind?"

Gabe adjusted his goggles. "Marvin got a reading of 42 miles per hour, and it feels like it's increasing."

"No wonder it's so hard to stand up." Brice shook his head. An icy film covered the edges of his goggles. He stared into the hovering sun, squinting. "We better get going."

"Yeah, I think—" Gabe stopped abruptly, his face stiffened. "Did you feel that?"

"Feel what?"

Gabe looked around in every direction. "It's happening again."

Another rumble from below sent them all off balance. Frightened by the sudden disturbance, the team members looked around, frantically seeking a place for shelter. There was nowhere to go. In a panic they separated, skiing off into different directions as if they knew where to go to avoid a tremor. They had no place to hide. They were too far out in the open.

The shaking stopped, as did the skiers, and for the moment everything was silent. Eerily, the wind had stopped, too. Colonel Marvin broke the silence. "I think it's over."

Another tremor struck the ice from below. The blast was much more violent and lasted twice as long as the one the night before. The ice shook and knocked them around as if they were dice on a craps table. The snowmobiles slid, bounced, and banged together, knocking one of them on its side. Tiny cracks opened in different parts of the icy surface. Everyone tried to stay on steady ground, but it was difficult to maintain any kind of equilibrium. The wind was picking up, and with the rapid movement of the earth beneath them, visibility was near zero. It was like being caught in the middle of a tornado and earthquake at the same time, as the blustery wind sent the loose surface snow into wild spirals and thick cloud-like mists. They yelled and screamed, but no voice was able to carry through the wind and rumbling ice.

Eric held onto the end of his snowmobile as it bounced off the other one. He lost his balance and tripped. The ice roared and crashed as a loud splitting sound echoed all around them. Eric felt something pulling against the snowmobile until he could hold onto it no longer. Something was sucking it into the ice, pulling Eric along with it. He couldn't see a thing, as specks of ice and snow smacked against his goggles. His heart pounded as his entire body trembled against the ice. It was painful. He was starting to slide again and could find nothing on which to brace himself. His skis made any kind of movement very awkward. He tried clawing into the ice but it was too unstable. He was at the ice's mercy. They all were, it seemed.

What only lasted 20 seconds seemed like 20 minutes, but finally the ground settled and the wind died down. No one was left standing. All were pressed against the ice, shaking, frightened, afraid to move in fear of the earthquake picking up again. They waited for a few minutes, all of them breathing heavily, looking around the broken surface of the ice towards one another.

Brice was the first to get to his feet, and then one by one the rest of the team slowly made it to their knees and then eventually stood on their skis. The ground all around them seemed as if it had been hit by a bomb, now broken, cracked, and uneven. An eight-foot-wide crevasse separated the members of the team. Well over 200 yards deep, the newly-formed crevasse extended as far as they could see in both directions, like a never-ending highway in the ice. It was an awesome sight, but its existence separated the team in two, with both sides staring across the crevasse at the other, wondering how they were going to get across.

Eric was the only one still lying down. Slowly, he made it to his knees. Realizing that he was only inches away from the edge of the crevasse, he quickly rolled away. The mouth that had eaten his snowmobile was only inches away from taking him with it. If the quake had lasted a few more seconds, he probably would have fallen down into the abyss with his machine.

Brice immediately counted heads.

One, two, three, four, five, six, seven, eight . . .

He panicked, turning around in a quick circle, counting, and again he stopped at eight.

He watched as everyone looked around, seemingly unharmed. One snowmobile was gone and the other had been turned on its side.

Who is missing? he thought. And then it dawned on him. Dropping his scarf below his chin, he cupped his hands around his mouth. "Mark!" he yelled. He took off his skis and carefully walked towards the crevasse. Gabe followed.

"Help!" A strained voice echoed off the walls of the crevasse and out through the top. "Help meeee!"

Gabe and Brice hurried to the edge and knelt down, peering over the sharp lip. "There he is," Gabe pointed.

"Oh, God." Brice took a deep breath. Looking down into the pit made him dizzy.

The crevasse was dark, and they could barely make out what appeared to be the bottom of it about 200 yards or more down into the ice. Mark had been lucky. His body rested safely on a three-foot-wide ledge, about 30 feet from the edge of the crevasse. The ledge was about two feet longer than the length of his body; a perfect landing pad for a deadly fall. It was miraculous.

Gabe stared down into the crevasse, amazed and shocked at what he was seeing. *He should have died*, he thought. *This is a miracle.* "It wasn't his time," he whispered.

Brice looked back down into the crevasse. He saw that Mark wasn't moving. "It might be his time if we don't hurry up and get him out of there."

Gabe closed his eyes. He crossed himself, touching first his forehead, then his chest, and then both shoulders. He felt strong. A growing sense of power swirled within him.

"Help!"

Gabe yelled down into the crevasse, "Mark, just stay still. I'm coming down."

Brice looked at Gabe. "Gabe, wait a second. Don't you think we should think this out for a second."

"I know what I'm doing. I've mastered some of the toughest mountains this world has to offer." He yelled across the crevasse. "Eric. Throw me the rope." He looked back at Brice. "I'm going down, and I'll need your help." Marvin and Pam walked up next to them. "I'll need everyone's help."

Eric threw everything across the crevasse that Gabe would need. All Eric, Loreda, Magnus, and Leroy could do was watch, wait, and pray. The action would be coming from the other side of the crevasse.

On the other side, about ten yards away from the edge of the crevasse, Gabe and Brice had tied four skis together, driving them down about three feet into the ice. They tied one end of the 180-foot rope around the four skis and the other end around Gabe's waist. Loaded with a pair of crampon climbing boot straps inside his coat and two ice axes strapped to his back, Gabe backed his way to the edge of the crevasse and lowered himself into the opening. In fear of the rope tearing on the sharp edge of the crevasse, they placed a ski horizontally on the ground to act as a cushion.

After digging small grooves into the ice for footing, Brice, Marvin, and Pam pulled on the rope, watching and feeling the weight of Gabe's body going down into the hole. They slowly lowered him into the hole. They wanted to take as much pressure as possible off of the four skis sticking from the ground in fear of a sudden shift or break in the make-shift brace. Fortunately for the three holding the rope, the wind had died down considerably, and the grooves they made in the ice were holding their boots securely in place. They were able to support Gabe's weight fairly easily as he descended down to the ledge.

Every five or six feet, Gabe kicked off the side of the wall, allowing the rope to slide freely through his gloved hands. He moved quickly but cautiously, quite aware of the long drop down if their pulley system was to collapse. His decline was a little faster than the rope holders would have liked. For a second, they thought he had fallen, and then they felt three short tugs on the rope. He was safely on the ledge with Mark now. Feeling the signal, they let go of the rope, taking the time to rest their arms and legs. Magnus was busy working on the snowmobile. Leroy was off to the side, not even watching what was going on. Eric and Loreda stood next to the edge, watching over the side as Gabe tied a rope around Mark's waist. They gave the thumbs-up signal across the crevasse and then returned their focus down on the ledge below.

Mark's eyes remained open the entire time he spent lying down on the ledge. Gabe had landed about a foot and a half away from his face. It was difficult for him to move at all, but Mark shifted closer to the wall to make more room for Gabe. The pain in his legs was like nothing he'd ever felt before. His right leg was surely broken. He could feel the bone splitting through the skin directly under his knee, and he could feel the wetness of blood coating his pants and the ledge of ice underneath him.

Mark slowly shifted to his side, grimacing in pain. "Legs broken," he hissed.

"Bad?"

"Very."

"You just sit tight and try to think of something other than your leg."

"Oh, like the bottomless pit we're about to fall into," Mark said.

"Always joking, Dr. Moriarity. I'll have you out of here in a few minutes."

Mark grabbed his arm. "I'm losing feeling in my thigh. So cold." His head dropped back down to the ice. He could no longer hold it up. "I think I'm dying."

"Stay with me, Mark. Stay strong."

"I'm dizzy . . . and nauseous."

Gabe tied the rope around Mark's waist again and then his shoulders, securing it near his back in four tight slip-knots. "Almost ready."

"Dying."

"Easy, Mark."

"Don't leave me here, Gabe."

"I'm not leaving you. This might hurt when they pull you up, but believe me it's the only way." Gabe tugged on the rope three times. He waited, watching the rope until it tightened from their pull on it.

Then Gabe heard something crack. The ledge shifted, lowered, and then stopped. It was now slanting down towards the pit. A foot of ice had chipped away from the ledge, falling down to the bottom of the crevasse. Quickly, Gabe looked upward and yelled, "Pull! Pull!"

Eric and Loreda joined him. Their hearts sunk as another portion of the ledge gave way, plummeting down into the dark shadows below. They yelled across the crevasse at their friends holding the rope. "Pull!" they screamed.

Instead of panicking, the trio pulled. The pressure on the rope was incredible now; Mark weighed twice as much as Gabe.

Gabe waited until Mark's body was completely off the ledge before he even thought of saving himself. It had happened so suddenly and without warning, just like the emergence of the tremors. The ledge was quickly crumbling beneath him, lowering into the icy abyss, separating itself from the wall of ice.

"Pull!" Gabe yelled, staring up at Mark as he was being raised away from the ledge.

"Save yourself," Mark yelled. "Hurry!"

"I'm right behind you," he said, thinking, *but without a rope.*

The ledge cracked in half. Gabe jumped to the remaining side and watched as the rest of the ice dropped. He reached inside his coat and strapped the crampons to the bottoms of both boots. Each boot now had four inch-long metal spikes in the front and eight more on the bottom.

What was left of the ledge shifted again, cracked loudly, snapped like giant twigs from a tree, and then lowered another inch. Just as he removed the two ice axes from the straps on his back, the rest of the ledge ripped away from the wall and dropped. With nothing left to support him, he fell down along with the broken ledge of ice. He was scared, but not near panicking, confidently thinking of the only way out alive. He swung both of his arms towards the wall, hoping that one, if not both, of the ice axes would grab hold.

One did. The axe in his right hand barely clung to a small groove in the wall, but as soon as it was forced to support his weight he felt himself falling again. The sharp point of the axe crunched out of the ice, scraping down the side of the wall as he fell. He jabbed the ice axe in his left hand at the wall but it didn't catch hold. He tried the right again, then the left, but everything was moving too fast. The light from the opening of the crevasse was quickly shrinking into a sliver of whiteness. He continued falling. The wall flew past him, but it was like he was moving in slow motion. He thought for sure that he would already have hit the bottom by now, if indeed it did have a bottom. He never gave up hope the entire way down. His axes would not penetrate deeply enough to hold his weight, not at the speed at which he was traveling, but the scraping of them did slow his descent, even as it painfully jarred his arms and shoulders.

Peering over the edge of the crevasse, Loreda screamed as Gabe fell. Eric grabbed her, pulling her against his chest so that she could see it no longer. She buried her head in his arms, crying. Eric raised his head and looked across the crevasse. Marvin, Pam, and Brice were struggling to pull Mark out of the hole. Eric cupped his gloved hands around his mouth and yelled across, "He's almost out. Just another five feet to go."

Brice was the first in line, and his boots were starting to slide. Mark was heavier than they'd thought. From the straining pressure of his dead weight, the ski under the rope and on the edge of the crevasse snapped in two and fell into the pit, both pieces bouncing on top of Mark before falling the rest of the way. With the rope now grinding against the sharp edge, it tightened even more, cutting into the fibers one by one.

"Keep pulling," Pam screamed, leaning backwards as far as she could go, face oddly contorted with tension. She turned her head. "More, Marvin, more."

"I'm pulling," Marvin screamed ahead and then slipped on the ice, crashing down on his back, accidentally letting go of his grip on the rope. Both Pam and Brice were jerked forward now that the extra weight was on their shoulders. Mark's body dropped a few feet further down into the hole. The skis in the ground behind Marvin bent, slanting towards the crevasse, but held.

"We need help!" Brice bellowed, although he knew they would not get any. They were the only ones on this side of the thin crevasse. There was no way for the others to get across. He leaned back, closed his eyes and pulled, using strength that he had no idea that he possessed. "Get back up, Marvin! We need you."

Marvin struggled to his feet again, grabbing the rope back by the brace of skis in the ice, digging his boots once again into the protective grooves. Mark's body was lifted slightly, but it didn't look like they were going to be able to get the footing or leverage to hoist him up and over the edge. Fiber by thin fiber, tiny strands of the rope snapped from the pressure and sharp razor-like edge; it was now half its normal thickness. They would have to hurry. They would have to think fast.

Magnus did just that. He grabbed two skis off of the snowmobile, and without giving it a second thought he stretched them across the opening of the crevasse, hoping like hell that they would reach. And they did, barely, with less than an inch to spare on each side. Eric didn't try to stop him. The jump itself was probably possible wearing normal summer clothing, but the bulky polar gear made the leap out of the question. He watched as Magnus positioned the skis side by side and set out to walk across them, totally unaware of whether or not the skis would hold his weight. He would have to take that chance. They needed someone on the other side or there was no way that they would pull Mark onto the ice. He would surely die. For this, Magnus thought his stupid, daring, and brave act was justified.

The wind continued to swirl around them, lowering down into the crevasse, reaching up to grab them and force them down inside, still blowing close to 20 miles per hour. Magnus's legs shook, not only from the freezing temperatures and fierce wind, but also from his nerves. He had never done anything this dangerous before. He grabbed two ski poles, screwed them together so he could use them as a balance stick, and cautiously took his first step out over the crevasse.

About 20 feet from the bottom of the crevasse, the walls curved inward towards the center and the axes and boot spikes slowed his fall. Gabe plunged both ice axes into the wall and hung there, amazed that he was still alive. When one of the ice axes had grabbed hold of the wall, jarring his shoulders, catching him safely in what could have and probably should have been the last few seconds of his life, he believed he'd witnessed another miracle. First, Mark falling directly on the small ledge, and now this. But Gabe had actually been part of this one. Fate? He didn't know. Luck? More than likely. He was simply glad to be alive, now deep into the heart of the crevasse, regardless of the reasons. *It wasn't my time*, he thought. *I can feel it. God is on my side.*

The temperature down near the bottom, several hundred yards down into the ice, was much warmer than the outer surface. He was also protected from the wind. This didn't mean that he wanted to stay down here though, and now, rested as he was going to get, hanging like a human decoration on the wall of the crevasse, he started his climb upward. His tired limbs moved, digging into the ice in the repeated pattern: ice axe, ice axe, and then he'd dig in with each boot, pushing himself up the wall. Ice axe, ice axe, boot, boot. He would think of nothing else until he was safely out of the hole.

Eric held Loreda tightly as they watched Magnus cross the crevasse, inching across the skis like on a tightrope, except Magnus was no acrobat. He looked clumsy and slightly off balance. He tilted slowly to the left, but quickly regained his balance against the wind, using the long pole to maintain his equilibrium. He could see the other three struggling to keep Mark's body afloat. He could feel the skis bending in the middle, but he couldn't do anything about that right now. If they cracked they cracked, then he'd be dead. He'd join Gabe down in the darkness. He refused to look down. *Magnus, think light,* he told himself. *You're as light as a feather. Keep walking straight ahead. Don't look down. Light as feather. Light as a feather.* He took another couple of steps and then stopped, focusing straight ahead towards the other three holding the rope. The wind continued to whip against his vulnerable position. Would it blow him away like a feather?

Brice couldn't believe what he was seeing. Magnus was being brave, but also stupid. He had already apparently lost Gabe to the crevasse, and Mark was not yet out in the clear; he couldn't bare the thought of possibly losing another, especially if that other should have been waiting on the other side of the crevasse with Eric, Loreda, and Leroy. Brice didn't know whether or not to be angry or relieved. He was leaning towards the latter. They did need the extra help, and he was already half way across. Brice was starting to lose his footing again, his grip was slipping too. He would delay his anger until later, given that they all got out of this alive. "Come on, Magnus," he grunted, clenching his teeth. "Just a few more steps."

He'd survived the dreaded middle and was now only a few feet away from the other side. Gaining confidence with each small step taken, Magnus took the last two feet of the skis with one leap. He cleared the edge with less than a foot to spare, knocking one of the skis lose and down into the crevasse, and then ran straight for the front of the rope. His extra added strength was all they needed to boost Mark over the top. With the rope only fibers away from snapping completely in half, Magnus grabbed hold of Mark's arms and pulled him over the edge. Brice, Pam, and Marvin let go of the rope and ran over to them. Together they pulled Mark into the clearing, not stopping until they were a good ten yards away from the edge. Still trying to cope with the fact that they had just lost their second in command, they sighed in relief that they had been able to at least save Dr. Moriarity's life. Now they had to work on saving his leg.

Brice looked up and across the crevasse at Eric, who appeared to be contemplating the balance act that Magnus had just accomplished. Brice shook his head. "Don't even think about it, Red. Stay there," he yelled, pointing towards the end of the long highway of crevasse. "We'll find the end of this thing. Don't do anything stupid." Eric lifted the remaining ski from the crevasse, pulling it back to his side, and then got to work on the damaged snowmobile, all the time thinking of Gabe plummeting down into the deep, dark hole. Loreda moved closer to him so that she could help. Leroy was still off on his own, probably unaware of what had just happened.

Mark was conscious but unable to speak or feel their hands touching him. The pain was subsiding; the numbness was quickly setting in. Brice looked Mark's leg up and down, softly feeling for anything abnormal. He wasn't a doctor, but he was able to diagnose something as serious as the injury Mark had just below his right knee.

Brice could feel the bulge of a compound fracture.

Sitting on the ice next to Mark's body, Marvin leaned towards Brice. "What do you think?"

"Feel that," he touched the bulge.

Marvin felt it, quickly pulling his hand away in disgust.

"It feels like the tibia, or part of it anyway, has cracked and ripped through the skin just under the knee."

Magnus and Pam moved around the body. "What about frostbite?" Magnus asked, heart still thumping from his jaunt over the crevasse.

Brice lifted his arms. "That's why I'm afraid to remove or cut away the pants. I don't want to expose the wound to the wind or the temperatures."

"I think it'd be worse if we left it as is though," Pam said. "I mean, the frostbite would set in faster if we left the bone jutting out and exposed. The pants may work in holding in a bit of warmth, but I don't know if it'd be enough to keep out the frostbite. We need to set it somehow."

They looked at each other for volunteers.

Pam made the move. The right pants leg was ripped near the wound so she reached her hands under the thick material and made the opening larger. She sat there for a brief moment, staring at the exposed bone. "This looks bad."

Ice axe, ice axe, boot, boot. Gabe methodically continued his climb, now only 30 yards or so from the top. He was making incredible time, as if something was pulling him and helping him along the impossible climb, now close to the spot on the wall where the miraculous ledge had been. He couldn't rid himself of the process of fatigue. His shoulders ached, his legs were starting to cramp, his muscles were sore and wearing down, and his vision was blurry, partly from the slivers of ice falling down on his goggles from every time his axes hit the wall, but also from being extremely tired. He made it his goal to finish the rest of the climb without stopping, but that was before he saw something very unusual inside the wall of ice on which he was climbing.

Or maybe he thought he saw it. It could have very well been his eyes playing tricks on him, swimming in and out of focus on the wall, although he'd never experienced any problems with his eyes before this. A pair of eyes hovered, staring, frozen inside of the wall. Gabe stopped moving, mesmerized by the sight. He saw a face, a nose, cheek bones, and a chin, all molded and covered by the ice. The girl's face was frozen inside of the wall. The eyes were a beautiful blue. They were clear, glittering, almost perfect, but he could see the tiny signs of trouble in them. This girl needed his help. He stared at the eyes, following the lines and spindles of green and blue that raced around her dark pupils. His vision no longer seemed blurry. The eyes enslaved him. They blinked.

Gabe jerked back, nearly tearing himself from his grip on the wall, but he never took his line of vision away from the eyes. He shook his head and then blinked trying to get rid of them. They were beautiful, but at the same time very frightening. They shouldn't have been there. He wanted to continue up the wall, but couldn't bring himself to leave the frozen beauty, especially in her time of need. *What is going on?* he thought. *I'm seeing things, going crazy. I'm hallucinating. This face can not be inside the wall. Had it been here when I was on the ledge earlier with Mark?* He didn't remember seeing them, but they very well could have been. The excitement of the time had been enough to overlook them. Or had it? He thought, *they are not there. These eyes are not—*

The thin layer of ice that covered the girl's mouth cracked, crumbled, and then dropped away, exposing two lovely shaped, red lips. His heart pounded, awaiting the possible words. The lips struggled open, slightly parted. The frozen face hissed, expressing words that sounded much less beautiful than Gabe had expected. "Help meee."

Gabe was speechless. His body was tired, but his spirit now felt strong. *He* was strong, but he didn't know what to say. He had something to give, but didn't know how to go about giving it.

"Soooo cold!" the lips whispered, now quivering.

He felt her pain.

"Help meeeee!"

He kept his eyes on hers as they continued to blink. Her voice faded. He could feel his vision going blurry again, and then the girl's face vanished. The eyes were gone, and the wall had returned to normal. He no longer doubted what he had seen. He was sure that it had really happened.

He wanted so badly to help her, to pull her from the wall and hold her in his arms, but he didn't know how. He felt the need and the obligation to help the girl, as if it was his duty. But why? And How? He wanted to know. He would never forget this experience. It was a message; a message that would have surely freaked out the common human being, but Gabe was no longer rattled. He felt more than human. He was strong and very confident. He would help the young woman in the wall. He would pull her away from her frozen captivity. He would do his part to help her, whoever she was.

Feeling stronger than ever, Gabe continued up the wall.

The leg below the knee was matted down with blood, frozen and clotting around the exposed ligaments and separated tibia bone that stuck out of the middle of his shin. Pulling from the heel with one hand and pushing the bone back into the leg with the other, Pam wrapped the wound with a towel from her bag. Mark shifted and shivered during the process, but never came out of his nauseous stupor to feel her poking and prodding inside his leg. She did the best that she could.

Eric threw two ice axes across the crevasse, and Pam used both of them to brace the leg, one on each side; positioning the pick near the front of the boot and the adze next to the heel. She then wrapped the leg with rope until it was tight enough for a make-shift cast. It would have to do until they reached the research station.

The next obstacle for Brice was getting the rest of the crew on this side of the crevasse. Their only option was to ski around it until they found where it ended. While Pam continued to work on Mark's leg, Loreda and Leroy started skiing the length of the crevasse in search for the ending. Eric stayed behind to work on the snowmobile.

It seemed much longer, but luckily the end of the crevasse was only about 400 yards away. Where the end of the crevasse cornered into a point, they screwed two ski pole handles together, pulled the baskets off of both of them, and then hammered the pole into the ice. Acting as an avalanche probe, the poles together were long enough to ensure them that the ground around the crevasse's end was solid enough to ski on. It was. They skied around it and headed for the rest of the team.

Marvin yelled across the crevasse. "Eric. How's it coming on that thing?"

Eric gave him the thumbs up. "Almost there. You all get going. One of you can stay with Mark, and I'll be around to pick him up as soon as I'm . . ," he paused, staring in amazement down into the crevasse. "Holy shit!" He saw an ice axe dig into the wall about six feet from the top edge. He stood, pointing, stepping closer to the crevasse, "Look! It's Gabe. He's alive. Someone help him."

Everyone turned around as Gabe dropped one of his axes on the ice and draped his right arm over the edge. Marvin and Magnus ran to help him, frantically pulling him out.

Gabe laid down beside the crevasse and rolled onto his back. He stared up into the blue sky and whispered, "Finally."

Pam stayed with Mark, but still watched what was going on near the edge.

Brice said, "You're alive." He couldn't contain his excitement, kneeling down to the ice, touching Gabe's shoulders, lifting him up, hugging him. "How? I mean, we thought you were . . ."

"Dead?"

"Yeah. They saw you fall."

"Oh, I fell. Call it a wild stroke of luck, or maybe it was something else all together, but I was able to catch myself with those axes just before hitting rock bottom."

"Unbelievable," Brice said. "You climbed all the way out? How? You must be exhausted."

Gabe leaned on his elbows and then started to his feet. They grabbed his arms, helping him up as if he was a fragile, old man. His knees were shaking. "I'm fine," he insisted, looking around. Loreda and Leroy were just arriving from the other side. "We better get going."

"You sure?" Brice asked. "You don't need a few minutes?" He smiled, overjoyed. His entire crew was still amongst the living. "I mean, it's almost like you've risen from the dead."

"I'm fine, let's go." He thought, *I've got someone to help.*

When Loreda and Leroy arrived, they were as shocked as everyone else. Leroy smiled, saying nothing, but Loreda immediately skied over to embrace Gabe.

Growing up in a home of strict Catholic parents, Gabe was a weekly church-goer. He, too, was quite religious, but his initial decision to join the priesthood was based more on curiosity than faith. He had always wondered if the priests really had that special connection with God. He wondered if they could really change the bread into the body, and the wine into the blood, and so for many years he planned on becoming one of them. He had never doubted that there was a God watching over them, but he wondered if he believed for the right reasons. When he was young, he went to church because he had to. He didn't hate going, or even dislike it for that matter, but he just wasn't totally sure why he was there, Sunday after Sunday, year after year. He went to worship because his parents went to worship. He believed because his parents believed. His faith was based on his family's faith, as if passed on from generation to generation. He was afraid to believe anything different, partly because his parents would have looked down on him, and partly because he knew that God was listening and watching, whoever he or she was.

Despite all the questions and possible doubts as a kid, he always felt better coming out of church, even if he had paid no attention to the actual mass or slept through the sermon. His mood was always better when mass was over, and it wasn't because it meant that it was time to go out for lunch and a chocolate sundae afterwards, as was their family ritual. It was because something was there. Whether it was in the priests or deacons, the music, or the gathering of friendly people, something was obviously there for him. For Gabe as a child, church meant feeling better afterwards. Along with his family's beliefs, he had his own. He had his faith in God. Even though he didn't always understand it, he always felt the presence. He was convinced that it was this presence that made him feel better. God's presence made everyone in church feel better afterwards. That was faith to Gabe Mulloy.

Gabe had that feeling again, that same wonderful feeling he always had coming out of church, when the sun always seemed to be shining, as it was here in Antarctica. Despite the tremor and near death of a friend, Gabe felt better now than he had before all of the chaos had started. He could feel the presence, not only around him, but also inside of him. Why? He didn't know for sure, and he didn't really want to know. Or maybe he did, and this is why he was chosen to save this mysterious young woman from the trouble that endangered her. Maybe he had seen a miracle, a concrete and physical reason for having faith.

As everyone prepared to leave, Leroy stood apart from the group.

Loreda said to Brice, "He's been acting strange. I know what we just went through was quite an ordeal, but he's scaring me. He was mumbling to himself the entire time we were skiing over here."

Brice looked at Leroy, who was standing about 10 yards away with his arms folded, facing the wind, his body rocking from side to side, swaying. "I'll check on him."

"Leroy?" he called.

Leroy didn't even turn to look, still staring off into the distance, mumbling.

Brice was close enough to hear what he was saying.

Leroy was wearing an awkward grin. His scarf was pushed down loosely around his neck. "He's used it too often, the Pole. It's falling apart from within, over-extended internal heat that he doesn't know about, but I do. It's crumbling down, just like the tremors, and it's bringing us down with it. Something is wrong, Millennium quickly approaching, dying away. Time is almost up. He . . . he . ."

Suddenly Leroy stopped mumbling and started skiing away. *He's insane,* Brice thought. *He's gone crazy.* He motioned for the others to get going. Magnus stayed with Mark, waiting for Eric to arrive with the snow-mobile.

Brice would have to wait to confront Leroy. In a way he was afraid to find out what was on the old man's mind, but he couldn't just let him go through it alone. If someone was struggling emotionally on this team, it had to be dealt with. He and the others followed Leroy's path. It didn't take them long to catch up. Leroy was not a sprinter, and his skiing was slow and steady.

Chapter 28

Louisville Police Department
10 Inches

Ralph lifted his head up from his folded arms on his desk. Moisture stained his sleeves. His eyes were red and blurry; he struggled to hold back the tears. "Should I have seen it coming?" he asked, peering over Andy's head towards the back wall of his office. It had been close to an hour since they'd left the crime scene at the funeral home, but the sights and smells of the embalming room were still planted firmly in Ralph's mind. He could still see Bobby's body slumped in the corner, face chewed away. He could see his father lying on the table with his life puddled around him. He could still picture the black feather, the killer's signature message that had been left from his father's blood, the suffocating smell of the formaldehyde. He would remember it all for a very long time.

Andy closed the glass door to the office, blocking off the chattering and ringing phones of the busy police station. "How could you have seen it coming?"

Ralph stood up from his desk, weak-kneed and internally still trembling from the trauma he'd already experienced throughout the morning, folded his arms, and began pacing around his office.

"For all these years," Ralph paused, staring at the ceiling, "I've been so close minded. So God damn close minded."

"You had your reasons not to believe."

"No, I didn't really. I spent so much time and energy convincing myself that my brother was the bad guy, that he was the weird one, the one that was always high, drunk, and in trouble. I spent so many years stubbornly trying not to believe my brother, and I finally got blind-sided. We all did. When he first mentioned that the Snowman was back, whoever the hell he is, I blew it off." He sighed, waving his arms in the air, and then dropped them back down to his side. "I just blew it off. All I had to do was listen. Just listen. Why couldn't I do that?"

"Don't blame yourself, boss. We all know that some weird things happened in the past with your brother, but they were unpredictable. How in the world could you have known where this guy was going to strike next, if he was going to strike at all? You could not have stopped him."

Ralph pounded his fist on his desk. "My father is dead. My eyes and ears were closed to the entire thing. Believe me, Andy, my eyes and ears are open now. I'm going to find him, and I'm going to kill him."

Ralph stared out the window. The words written in his father's blood slid down his tongue like a melting cube of ice. "Snow drifter. Back from Antarctica."

"That message. I can't stop thinking about it," he repeated, "Snow drifter. Back from Antarctica."

"Any ideas?"

"Possibly."

"Serial killer?"

"Yes, but I think it's more than that. You know it's funny."

"What?"

"For years I was so determined not to believe my brother, but now," he snapped his fingers, "just like that, I'm coming up with theories about this man's existence. These are cases that could take a long time to solve and explain, but it seems like ideas are just popping in, as if . . . as if someone is putting them there for me, like something is helping me along."

"Like what?"

"I'm not sure, but I know I wasn't thinking this way before. I'm usually very conservative, but the ideas that are running through my head right now are . . . are crazy, wild and purely imaginative. Andy, he's more than just a signature serial killer, and he has killed a lot more than two people."

Someone knocked on the door.

"Come in."

The door opened slowly, and a 22-year-old rookie, Adam Hofmann, timidly stepped inside the office.

"What is it?" Ralph said.

"Sir," Adam said, holding up a small white envelope. "This must have been dropped in our mail early this morning. It's got your name on it."

"Okay, just put it on my desk if you can find a spot."

Ralph looked at the envelope. The return address was Anderson Funeral Home. *What could this be? I'll check it out in a minute.* "Andy. I suddenly have this crazy theory about all of this. It's about a cycle of time when the deaths increase during winter months and especially during heavy snowfall. I'm basing most of it on my experiences and on things I've read."

"Like what?"

"My sister-in-law was killed in 1974 during the worst snowfall in Louisville's history."

"And you're relating that to the blizzard we're expecting this weekend, and to the fact that the Snowman seems to be back in town?"

"Exactly."

"I can see where you're coming from, but that is only two instances separated by 20 years of nothing. Where has this guy been all these years?"

Ralph snapped his fingers. "That's where you may be wrong. There could be something historical about this killer, something very unusual, and I'm going to find out what it is. I saw something on the news last night that startled me. It startled me then because it was already on my mind from my argument with Bill, but now I'm starting to see things more clearly. I'm focused. I'm sorting things out of this terrible state of confusion."

"Was it about the Snowman?" Andy asked.

"Yeah, well . . . I guess it was in a way. I was watching the late news, the national news, and it was something that one of the guys mentioned as a prelude to a later story. The news man had said, 'Snowman kills a little girl in Sweden today' "

"What?"

"Lisa thought I'd seen a ghost. It turns out this little seven-year-old was playing in the snow with a few of her friends, and they built this extremely large snowman. You know, I figure, how big could a group of little girls build a snowman, but I guess it was large enough. The damn snowman they built toppled over on the poor girl and suffocated her."

"That's terrible."

"It was, but in hearing it now it is impossible not to think of the Snowman that seems to be terrorizing Bill and our family."

"You thinking that he had something to do with this death in Sweden?" Andy asked.

"That's what I'm thinking. What if it could have been this same Snowman? He's bound to have been in more places in the world than Louisville, right?"

"Yeah, but not two places at once. If he's here, he can't possibly be in Sweden."

"I'm not saying this incident in Sweden happened because of the Snowman. I'm merely suggesting that the Snowman, hypothetically speaking, could do something like that, or like he's done to us here in Louisville. I bet he's done things like this all over the world, and he does them during major snowstorms, and he's been at it for a very long time. Bill mentioned that in one of his dreams, the Snowman referred to himself as the worldwide traveler." Ralph paused, waiting for an answer.

"And?"

"And what do you think he's been doing the past 20 years? Where do you think he's been?"

"I don't think we'd have any way of knowing unless we were to ask him for an interview, and if I do come into contact with him, I'm not going to waste time striking up a conversation."

"Twenty years he was gone, Andy. I find it hard to believe that a man as evil as this would spend those years sitting around. He's a killer. That's what he does, and I can guarantee that he has been hard at work somewhere ever since. He's back from Antarctica, or so he has written. Maybe he lives there."

"He may have been to Antarctica, but there is no way that he lives there. Nobody, at least no normal human being, could live there for an extended period of time," Andy responded.

"This Snowman character isn't exactly what I'd call normal. He's running around the city in a T-shirt, for Christ's sake. He must love the cold weather; probably thrives on it as his source of power and strength. I don't know how he does it, how he gets from here to there, but what if he rides the wave of snowstorms all over the world? Think about it, a serial killer that strikes only when it's snowing. That's his purpose, that's his calling. He's probably killed many, and what he has done to our family is like a grain of sand in a beach. It sounds crazy and unbelievable, but I don't think this Snowman is human."

Andy shook his head. "What else could he be?"

"I don't know. I'm not ruling anything out as of yet. I hope I'm wrong, and we're dealing with a regular man, but in light of everything that has happened, I can't help but wonder. He could be a monster of some kind, an evil monster, or a link between the living and the dead. Maybe he's even the Antichrist himself."

"You believe in that stuff?"

"I believe in Hell, and I believe in evil, pure evil that is innate, and in some way or another this Snowman is a product of that environment. The way the Snowman is able to get into my brothers head, it's . . .it's almost like possession, as if he's possessed by the devil."

They were interrupted by the phone.

Ralph picked it up on the second ring. "Chief Anderson."

"Ralph. It's Bill. I'm at the airport. The plane just landed about 10 minutes ago, right on schedule."

"Considering the weather, that's pretty amazing."

"We're waiting for the luggage to come through, and then we'll be ready."

Ralph moved the receiver away from his mouth long enough to whisper to Andy that Bill was ready to be picked up. Andy got the message, grabbed his trench coat, and left.

"Bill, you still there?"

"Yeah."

"Andy just left for the airport. How are the girls?"

"Okay. Amy is a bit more distant than usual, so I'm anxious to find out what that's about, although I think I may already know. Here they come, Ralph. I better go. I'll talk to you tonight."

"Okay. I've got some things I need to do, and then I'll be over." He would wait until then to tell Bill about their father's death. Now wasn't the time. "Good luck."

Ralph hung up, put his black coat on and started to walk out of his office, and then his eyes caught sight of the envelope. He checked it on the outside. It hadn't been sealed, the flap was tucked inside. He unfolded a white piece of paper, and like the envelope, it too was from his father's funeral home. It read:

ANDERSON FUNERAL HOME
1256 NEW CUT ROAD
LOUISVILLE, KENTUCKY
40214

Sorry about your father. He was a real lively one at the end. My time here on earth is coming to an end, and I think my anxiety is getting the best of me. The snow has been slow in its arrival, and Lewis and the little boy were simply, unfortunate as you may see it, the results of my extreme boredom. My ancestors ruled from the Hell that is Fire. So many paid the price. I come to you now from the Hell that is Ice. Hell has two dimensions, and this one is mine. Come feel the icy realness with us. Mary and Lewis feel it. The little boy, Bobby, feels it now. There are millions that feel it. All dead to the physical world, they are trapped forever in the ice. All frozen. On cold, clear nights when the wind is soft and the air is light, I can hear them screaming. All of them screaming for help. The immortal souls of Hell. It's always winter some-where. Remember that. Ask Amy if she enjoyed what little she saw of her new home. She will know of what I mean. Research me well and good luck.

The letter was unsigned. "You son-of-a-bitch," he mumbled, storming out of his office.

He had some research to do.

Chapter 29

1:50 P.M. Standiford Field Airport
11 Inches

Although Amy was aware of the background, in the airport her father told her and Kathy everything, starting with the death of her mother and ending with the most recent events of the last two days. He explained why they were waiting for officer Evans and why they could be in danger. All the while, Kathy sat silently, listening, not knowing what to say, or if she even had the right to say anything at all. She felt it was very much a family matter.

Amy asked a few fearful questions about what had already taken place and about the dreams her father was having, but mostly she listened. She had expected that it was all happening again to her father, so she wasn't too surprised. Just before Amy was ready to reveal some of her secrets, Andy Evans walked into the airport. It had been hard enough telling her best friend about her dreams. It would be even harder to tell her father.

Andy's size immediately made them all feel safe. His voice was strong and deep. "Ready to go?"

They got up and followed him out of the terminal. Outside, the snow was continuing to fall at a rapid rate. Cars in the parking lot were buried, including Bill's truck.

Bill said, "I think my truck is out there somewhere."

"Leave it," Andy said. "It'll be safe here for a couple of days. I'd rather have you all in one car anyway. Mine is right there." He pointed to his unmarked white Crown Victoria.

Amy and Kathy got into the back seat while Andy and Bill placed the luggage in the trunk. "Roads are getting nasty," Andy said. "Road crews are doing what they can, but there is no way they can keep up with this pace. I think we're in for something big. I imagine the airport will close down soon."

Bill noticed the chains on Andy's tires. "Those work well?"

"To an extent. I can already tell you that at some point, we'll have to go back to the station and get one of the 4-wheel-drive vehicles." Andy could see the worry and fear in Bill's eyes of what was yet to come. "How you holding up?"

"Okay, I guess. The girls are hungry though. Can we stop for something on the way back?"

"Sure, if there are still some places open."

Ralph sat alone at a table on the second floor of Louisville's downtown public library, flipping through book after book on snowfall. The only other people in the building were the security guards and the librarians.

He read about the Arctic and the North Pole and even more about the Antarctic and the South Pole, including its earliest explorers. Captain James Cook in the late 1700s, Fabian Gottlieb von Bellinghausen in the 1800s, and Shackleton, Scott, and Amundsen in the early 1900s were all lucky enough to cross the mysterious Antarctic circle and live to tell and write about what they saw and experienced. Many unfortunate explorers were not so lucky and were never heard from again.

Then Ralph remembered Bill's dream about the desert of ice and snow. *Could he have been dreaming about this place? Antarctica? The people he saw skiing and exploring. What could it all mean? What roles do they have in all of this?* Ralph saw a possible connection, but couldn't quite make anything fit, not yet. He wondered if those people in Bill's dream were real, because if they were, they too were in danger. *The Pole?* Ralph thought. *Why did that just snap into my head? Why is it of any importance? Is it dangerous? Does it stand for something?* Ralph was curious about why he would even think of it standing for anything other than the geographical marker for the bottom of the earth. *It's the South Pole. Nothing more, nothing less.*

These thoughts were coming to him way too easily, and it seemed as if everything he'd read out of the books was of importance and relevant to what he needed to learn. He thought it unlikely that he would strike gold on every page, research didn't work that way. He had gathered stacks of books, but so far, everything he'd grabbed and flipped through had significance, and in some way may have had something to do with the mysterious history of this Snowman.

Ralph closed the book on Antarctica and grabbed another one, a book on the history of worldwide snowfall written by a man named Leroy McCalister.

Worldwide traveler. Ralph couldn't get the message out of his head. He opened to the middle of the book, and the first paragraph on the page read:

"Plot thirty years of snowfall depth in a certain region and compare it with the consensus numbers of its population, and the two charted lines should have about the same highs and lows offsetting one another. The lows in population will coincide with the highs in snowfall, and it . . ."

Ralph closed the book. His head was filled with snow storms, blizzards, avalanches, snow squalls, whiteout conditions, and what little he'd read on Eskimos. He was tired, but had to keep on reading. Bill and Amy were depending on him, and he still had a lot more to learn.

Amy sat quietly in a booth at Shoney's, running her fork through her mashed potatoes and gravy, thinking of what to say and how to say it. Kathy was the first one to speak. "In case you'll are wondering about me, I'm going to stick with this. I'm staying right here with Amy."

"Think about what you're saying," Amy said. "Our lives are in danger. There is a psychopath out there killing people, and more than likely we are his main target. You still want to be around this family?"

"I've already come this far."

"You could get killed."

"I could get killed in a car accident tomorrow, too. I understand the danger involved, but I've got nowhere else to go. I have no parents or home to go to, or even any relatives for that matter. This is better than sitting alone in my dorm during Christmas doing nothing. At least this is going to be interesting."

"If you want to stay, okay," Bill said. "Just know, Kathy, that if you want to go at any time, please tell us. I'd hate to see something happen to you, especially if it could have and probably should have been avoided."

"Thanks, Mr. Anderson, but I feel safe with Andy watching us, and I've been supporting Amy through her troubles with the dreams and flashbacks she's been experiencing. She's been—"

Bill cut her off. "So Kathleen was right."

Kathy slumped down in her seat, now remembering that Bill didn't know about Amy's dreams. "Sorry, Amy."

"It's okay. Dad, what are you talking about, Kathleen being right about what?"

"I spoke to her earlier this morning, and she told me it was possible that you also have been haunted by these dreams throughout your life. Is it true?"

Amy looked down at the table, tearing up.

"Amy. How long have you had them?"

"Off and on. For about 10 years I didn't have any, but recently they've started again."

"Same here," Bill whispered, shaking his head. He felt like a fool for not being able to recognize her childhood problems, given that they were so similar to his own. "Why didn't you tell me, Amy?"

"Are you angry?"

"Absolutely not. How could I be angry with you? I just wish that you would have told me. I wish I could have helped you. I'm feeling a lot of guilt and responsibility for what you've gone through."

"I didn't want to bring back all of your memories and pain. For a while I was scared to tell anyone, but when I got older it was more focused on you."

"What do you mean?"

"You struggled for so long, and when you started to turn your life around I didn't want to disrupt things by dredging up old memories. I was young, but not naive. I figured that I was old enough at the time to handle things on my own, and for a while things went my way. I guess I was wrong. Things are never going to go away, are they?"

"I wish I knew, honey," he said.

"How did Kathleen find out?"

"She'd had her suspicions for a long time, but never said anything to me. She thought you were doing fine, coping fairly well to what happened to your mother and didn't see the need to go digging around in your head at your young age. She figured that if you were having them too, yours probably ended just as mine had. But, as none of us expected, the Snowman is back, and so are our dreams. That is why she told me now, because she thought you might be in trouble with them again just as I am. What do you remember? Tell me about your dreams."

And so she did, starting with yesterday afternoon.

Reading through the articles, fiche documents, government documents, and books, it was all the same, tragedy after tragedy, death and turmoil, all caused by snow. Ranging from simple car accidents to tragedies in war, snow had been and continued throughout history to be a major cause of tragedy and death all over the world.

In 330 B.C., Alexander the Great's conquest into India was stopped because of the snow-filled mountains in the East. Hannibal and his troops, a century earlier, suffered incredible losses because of the snow in the Alps. The "white enemy" had been an extreme force of fear for all travelers.

Because of the snow, the Moors in the thirteenth century were unable to enter France from Spain. For some, snow was the enemy, and for others it was a friend and important ally.

Thousands of soldiers were killed during the first World War when Austrian and Italian forces released avalanches for defense purposes in the southern Tyrol. It was estimated that over 60,000 deaths were attributed to avalanches during the war.

In World War II, the severely overmatched Finns nearly defeated the Russians in the "winter war" of '39-'40 because of the massive snowfall. All around the world, from Europe to the United States, the results all led to the same conclusion—large amounts of snowfall often lead directly to an increase in the amount of deaths.

Ralph flipped through more pages, not sure where to stop and start reading again. He figured something in his head would trigger him to stop and read when the time was right.

He stopped near the end of the book and read on:

"**PURGA BLIZZARD:** One of the most devastating blizzards of the world is the purga that arrives over northern Siberia down to the Kamchatka Peninsula usually every winter. This blizzard is so violent that people caught inside of it can't even open their eyes and have difficulty breathing and standing upright. Many have frozen to death only a few yards away from their houses, completely losing their direction and orientation in the suffocating snowfall.

"**THE BURAN:** A devastating snowstorm that sweeps from the northeast over southern Russia and central Siberia, filling the frigid air with blinding snow. This storm is very similar in nature to the purga of northern Russia. Extremely violent winds make the coldness unbearable. Many men and animals have become lost in the storm's blindness, ultimately resulting in death. . . .

"**TRAGEDY AT DONNER PASS:** October, 1846, a wagon train of 87 pioneers traveling from Illinois to California led by a man named George Donner, ran into severe difficulties crossing the Rocky Mountains. Snow began to fall over the Sierra Nevada mountain range in northern California, trapping the entire crew.

"Driving their wagons through the Truckee mountain pass, a few miles north of Lake Tahoe, they encountered snow up to five feet deep and drifts up to 40 feet high. They set up camp and tried to survive the winter storms. With a quickly shrinking food supply and absolutely no outside help, in desperation they began to eat their own dead. Months later, a small group of pioneers rescued them, but it was far too late, only 47 of the original 87 pioneers remained.

"According to the survivors, the inclement weather was not the only cause of death during that winter. Some of these pioneers fell prey to a mysterious crazy man they called Piektuk. Frightened survivors claimed that this man alone roamed the mountains for days and nights, feasting on the trapped pioneers, killing everyone in his path. The memories of his long white hair and ghostly appearance prompted survivors to label him the *snow phantom*, and, true or not, the legend of this killing machine would deeply embed fear into the hearts and minds of all future pioneers of the Truckee Mountain Range. The fear still lingers today, although nothing has occurred there since the tragedy of the Donner party. As one survivor put it, 'The ultimate death in those snowy mountains was not falling victim to the wind, cold temperatures, avalanches, and snow drifts, but falling into the violent path of the snow phantom, Piektuk.'

"Details of the tragedy are vague and somewhat controversial, and much has been lost over the years to support what might have happened during that winter. Sightings of the snow phantom were scattered, and denied by some survivors, which only added to the mystery and validity of the legendary story. Further research into the name Piektuk, shows it translates into an Eskimo name for drifting of snow, or snow drifter. With the validity of the story in question, it is difficult to . . ."

Snow drifter.

"It was him," Ralph said. "Unbelievable. It was him."

Back from Antarctica.

How old is he? Ralph thought, reaching for his legal pad. He scratched down the event and name, Piektuk. *It's got to be the same man. Regular as clock work. You name the major snowstorm, no matter the place or the time, and he's probably been there. He's the snow drifter, the worldwide traveler. He is the Snowman. How does the author know about it?*

Ralph resumed reading.

"**BLIZZARD OF 1888:** Sunday evening, March 11, two snowstorms crashed the East coast from Washington D.C. to Maine, and from New York to Pittsburgh. Reported snow drifts were 40 to 50 feet high, isolating towns and cities, burying houses, stranding trains. From Chesapeake Bay to Nantucket, 200 ships were blown ashore, or sunk into the Atlantic Ocean. More than 400 people were killed . . .

"**COLORADO:** Just over 75 inches of snow accumulated at Silver Lake, Colorado, on April 14 and 15, 1921, in a single 24-hour period. The total devastation of the city sent citizens into a panic and state of chaos.

"**PERU AVALANCHE:** January 10, 1962, a huge ice mass weighing 3 million tons broke from a glacier on the Nevada Huascaran Mountain in Peru. The massive avalanche rolled over and destroyed six villages. More than 4000 people were crushed, and an estimated 10,000 animals were also killed.

"**BLIZZARD OF 1966:** This storm lasted four days in February over the eastern part of the country. In South Dakota alone, 96,000 cattle were found dead. The main portion of the blizzard hit central New York, dropping 53 inches of snow on Syracuse and 28 on Rochester. Over 200 people were killed . . .

"**HAMBURG:** 51 inches of snow and ice fell on the city of Hamburg, Germany on January 7, 1968, paralyzing the city for nearly two weeks. Snow drifts up to 30 feet were recorded, smothering houses and buildings, capturing everyone left inside. Sixty-three people were killed by the storm. One of the most unexplained and unusual incidents of the city's history occurred over the course of those two weeks, or so they say. Different dates were given, but during the first week when most of the snow was still falling an eerie green light pulsated for days from the windows and doorways of the city's main bank. It was out of this light that the Snowman emerged and started his killing spree. Twenty people were said to have been killed by this mysterious creature. The local townspeople called him the Snowman because he killed in the snow, he lived in the snow, and as quickly as the storm had dumped its supply, he'd appear. Randomly killing from home to home, he left his mark. From victim to victim, he'd left his messages in their blood—the white enemy, the snow drifter, the worldwide traveler—and the list went on as he roamed and pillaged, feeding his evil purpose. After three days, the green light coming from the bank had disappeared and so had the man that had come out of it. The basis of this legend had been questioned by many, but who really knows what the frightened citizens of Hamburg witnessed in that devastating winter."

Green light. Ralph wrote it down, along with the date and details of the event. He wrote down the messages that had been left—the white enemy, snow drifter, worldwide traveler. They all pointed towards the same man. Ralph thought, *All of them occurred in different parts of the world and in different times in history, but everything points towards this Snowman. He travels the world, randomly killing, and he's using the snowstorms as his mode of transportation. How old is he? How does he do it? How does he get from here to there? And what does he have to do with Antarctica? The Pole?* Ralph was confused. What he was reading was coming too easily. He was suspicious of his own thinking process. He wondered if the Snowman wasn't yanking his chain, filling these pages with words and information simply to play with his mind, just as he'd done with his brother for so many years. In one book, and only a few different pages, he had read about legends of the same man. *But why would the Snowman want me to know about him? Why would he want me to learn about his past? He wouldn't want to give it away so easily, or would he? Or maybe it's something else. Maybe it's a different force all together that's helping me with this research, some kind of force of opposition.* Ralph didn't know. The possibility scared him. *Maybe he is a demon, or devil with supernatural powers, and that's how he does what he does. But if that is the case, there is no need for me to go on with this. There would be no explanation for how he survives, because supernatural beings can do anything. Supernatural beings can not be stopped. That is how he's been inside Bill's head. That is the reason he's always had the visions and flashbacks. It has nothing to do with Bill not being able to forget, but everything to do with the Snowman's ability to do anything he wants.*

Ralph banged his fist down on the table, quickly closing the book. "He's got to have a weakness. There has got to be a way to stop him."

Ralph was frustrated but determined to learn more. He re-opened the book to the middle and read on.

The page focused on the northern plains blizzard of 1887, and it was half filled with a black-and-white picture from the storm. It showed one of the first rotary plows being tested on the front of a train. The train had been stopped in its tracks over a bridge, and everything around it was covered with snow. The accumulation had piled up to five and six feet high on the ground, and in the distant hills, only the tops of trees were visible.

Seven men stood on, in, and around the plowing train, posing for the photograph. Ralph was drawn into the life of the picture. He felt as if he were actually there with the men, standing knee-deep in the snow. Each one of the men had a long handlebar mustache and a hat, and all were obviously freezing from the snow and wind, although the smirks on their dirty faces didn't show it.

The words—The Rotary—were written across the side of the train in large white letters. One man leaned against the 'R' with his arms folded and a shovel resting against his side. Three more men stood in front of the plow, arms folded, staring straight at the photographer. Two more were kneeling on the top of the train, one waving and the other laughing. The last man sat inside the train, waving his arm out of the open window.

Ralph concentrated on the picture. He was focused and staring into those coal black eyes and cold faces, wondering what those men were thinking. All seven men looked the same, all frozen inside the picture, but far from lifeless.

And then something inside the photograph started to change. It was the man inside the train. His arm was waving. He had suddenly come to life, even though the rest of the crew were frozen in time. The man seemed to be waving at Ralph as if Ralph was the one taking the picture.

Ralph closed his eyes. When he opened them again, the man inside the train was still waving, now with both arms. The man's mustache was gone, and as he peeled his raggedy hat from the top of his head, a bundle of long white hair cascaded down over his shoulders. The man in the train was alive.

He jumped out of the train, landing thigh-deep in the snow. Instead of the heavy winter coat he'd had on earlier, he was now wearing a white T-shirt and blue jeans.

Ralph stared in disbelief. The man was trying to say something, but Ralph couldn't make out what it was. And then the man began running towards the photographer, knees kicking high to avoid the surface, within seconds getting so close to the camera that only his torso could be seen. His shirt blocked out the plowing train, the snow, and the other men in the background. Something was written across the man's chest, the letters wet, red, and running. It spelled *chaos*.

Ralph's hands clutched the table like vice grips. He tried to tear himself away from the picture, but couldn't. He couldn't move. He couldn't take his eyes away from the scene in the photograph, not yet.

The man backed away from the camera until his entire body was in view. His white hair was growing, unraveling like rolling spools of yarn. He moved to the side, pointing to the plow train behind him. The other men were all dead now, and the snow around them was quickly turning red with their spilled blood.

The man spoke. Ralph could hear him clearly. He wasn't sure if the voice was actually coming from the page, or if it was only in his head, but he could hear what the man was saying. "Doing some research, Ralph? I don't appreciate you sneaking behind my back like this. I think you've learned enough." Still pointing towards the men, he said, "I killed them all."

The man walked up to the camera again. Ralph could only see the shirt again. The man's arm was out, stretching for something behind the photographer. When he backed away again, he had his arm resting around the shoulders of a pretty young woman. It was Amy. She was wearing a white nightgown, but nothing else.

"Take a picture of the One, Ralph. Now is the time."

Ralph slammed the book shut. He felt nauseous. Not bothering to put anything back on the shelves, Ralph grabbed his coat and stormed towards the elevator.

The librarian pushed her horn-rimmed bifocals up on her nose and watched Ralph run out the front doors. "And I thought the kids were bad," she mumbled, stamping another book on her pile.

Amy didn't tell them everything while they were eating, but she did tell her father about what she remembered from the day her mother had been killed—the black bird. It was the black bird that haunted her dreams over the years. It wasn't until this week that the Snowman had entered, and Iceville had opened up. She was too scared to tell them about the Snowman and what he'd done to her last night. She didn't want to tell anyone about that.

Bill held both of her hands. A single tear rolled down his cheek. "I'm sorry, Amy."

Amy nodded. *I remember the screams, Dad,* she thought. *I remember mom screaming for help and I was too young to do anything about it. I was too young to remember anything, right? I remember all right, and now I'm paying for it again. Nobody can hear me screaming. When his cold hands are touching me and feeling me, why can't anyone hear me screaming for help. Nobody can hear me. All voices are mute in Iceville, Dad. I scream and scream, but no one can hear but him. I can hear others screaming, although I do not know who they are or where they come from. When the wind is soft and the air is light, I can hear them all, and Mom is one of them.*

Amy looked into her father's eyes and whispered, "Help me, Dad. Help me."

As they stood up from the booth, Bill was holding his daughter, never wanting to let go. "Let's go, Amy." Kathy and Andy followed them to the car.

It was after 4:00 P.M., and the snow was picking up again.

Chapter 30

4:45 P.M., Iroquois Park
12 Inches

The trip home was a difficult one. With the snow continuously falling and the day drifting into twilight, visibility was quickly dwindling. The packed down ice and snow was settling in layers on most of the roads, and the road crews simply couldn't keep up. In a few hours, 4-wheel-drive would be the only mode of transportation possible.

Bill unlocked the front door to his house. Andy entered first, pulling his revolver from his belt. "Stay behind me. You can never be too safe."

They waited just inside until Andy returned from checking all of the first floor rooms. "Looks okay down here," he said, heading for the stair-well to the second floor.

"Dad. Will you show Kathy to my room. I've got to go to the bath-room."

"Sure. This way."

At the top of the stairs, Andy asked, "Which room is it?"

"The one on the right."

Immediately, Andy noticed something strange. The closer he got to Amy's room, the colder the air got, and he felt a slight draft swirling around his ankles. The door to her room rocked slightly.

Andy pushed the door open. "What the hell?"

"What is it?" Bill asked.

Kathy stopped on the top step.

"Someone has been in here." Andy flipped on the lights. "Look at the window."

Without saying a word, Bill walked past the bed and over to the window. His breath was visible in the chilling night air, and flakes of snow were entering through the cracked window. His boots crunched on the scattered pieces of broken glass that littered the floor.

"How did anyone get in through this window?" Bill asked. He looked out the opening and down towards the snow below. "It's got to be 15 feet down, and there is absolutely nothing to climb on. It's so cold in here."

Just then Amy screamed.

Andy ran out of the room, darting past Kathy, flying down the stairs.

Bill slipped on the glass, planting his hand down on the carpet to brace his fall. He was so concerned with checking on Amy that he didn't even notice the shard of glass sticking deeply into his palm. "Amy," he called. He couldn't get down the stairs fast enough, taking four and five at a time. His left hand was dripping blood, smearing against the wood railing, but he didn't care. He had to see Amy.

Amy screamed again.

Lisa was getting some milk from the refrigerator when Ralph hurried through the back door. He was breathing heavily and his hands were trembling.

"What's wrong, Ralph?"

"Honey, get some clothes packed. I'm taking you over to your parents' house."

"May I ask why?"

"Trust me, please. We have to hurry."

"Something wrong? I've never seen you this worked up before. Does this have something to do with your father's murder?"

"Yes, it does. Something is very wrong. I've never acted this way before because I've never felt this way before. I'm frightened and confused. I'll explain everything later."

"Have you told Bill about your father?"

"Not yet. I will when I see him tonight. Lets go. Please. I'll call and tell them you're coming."

They found Amy in the bathroom, sobbing. She pointed towards the shower. Bill looked to the shower curtain and then back at Andy. The shower curtain was closed, and the bottom of the shower was wet and red. Gun ready, Andy jerked the curtain aside. Gus hung from the shower nozzle. A thick piece of rope was around his neck, and his head lolled limply to the side. He'd been gutted, and his insides strung down to the floor of the shower.

"Gus," Bill whispered. His dog and most loyal friend was dead, murdered, gutted.

Amy stumbled out of the bathroom. Kathy helped her over to the couch.

Bill and Andy saw something sticking out of the hair on Gus's back, just below the neck. At first they thought it was a knife, but then they noticed it was shiny, wet, and dripping, and it was holding a small piece of paper in place.

"What is it?" Bill asked.

Andy reached for it, pulling it from the dog's back, catching the note as it fell. "It's an icicle. This was underneath it." He handed Bill the piece of paper.

"Sorry I missed you. I didn't like what was inside your dog. He'll fear me now. We have the upper hand. More sinners will die.

"Snowman," Bill said, crumbling the note. "Andy, we aren't safe here."

Andy looked at the hanging dog. "Grab what you need, Bill. We're leaving."

"What about Gus?"

"Don't have time."

Bill ran his hand over the dog's back, patting him gently, and then closed the curtain.

Ralph pulled halfway into his mother-in-law's driveway at 5:30. It was as far as the snow would allow his car to travel. The sky was already dark, and the snow was coming down hard. It wouldn't be long until the entire city was snowbound.

Ralph hadn't gone into all of the details on the way over, but he'd told Lisa as much as he could, enough so that her questions had ceased.

With the rear end of the car sticking halfway out into what was left of the street, Ralph kept the car running. The windshield wipers thumped loudly from side to side, clearing the snow away as soon as it hit the glass.

"What reason am I going to give my parents for crashing in on them in the middle of a snowstorm?" Lisa asked. "I don't want to scare them. They're already upset about your father's murder."

"Just tell them that I want you and the baby to be safe. I don't want you to be alone for the next few days."

"A few days?"

"Yes, I'm sorry, but it might take that long to get this mess cleared up. Tell them I'm going to be working around the clock, and with the blizzard coming in this weekend, you didn't want to be home by yourself, snowed in with our baby being so close to being born."

"When are you going to quit this job, Ralph? It's too dangerous. You'll be a father very soon, remember that. We need you. Your family will need you more than your job."

"I know, Lisa," he whispered softly. "I know. This is more than just doing my job, and this is very much a family matter. My family needs me right now."

"So you're finally considering Bill as part of your family again?"

"I have to do this to protect our family. Everything is going to be fine." Ralph kissed her softly, holding her in his arms.

She whispered in his ear. "I love you."

"I love you too."

"Be careful."

"I will." Pointing to her stomach, he said, "Take care of our little boy."

"You mean, girl." Lisa gave a weak smile and then closed the door.

Lisa's father helped her up the stairs to the front porch. Ralph waited until they were safely inside the house before pulling away. He dreaded the evil he was about to confront; and, as he watched his pregnant wife walk into the house, he wondered if it was the last time he would ever see and talk to her again.

Amy was leaning against the sink, staring out the window above the table at the falling snow. Andy passed by her, meeting Kathy in the front room. "How is she?"

"Terrified. Until now it was all in her head. She'd thought she was losing her mind these last couple of days. Now she knows she can lose her life, and her father's as well. I can't get anything out of her. She just doesn't seem herself."

"Who would?" Andy mumbled, staring at his watch. It was ten minutes until six, and twilight had already given way to nightfall. The house was dark, with only the kitchen light still on.

Something slammed against the front door of Bill's house, and the kitchen light flickered off. They all froze. Andy removed his revolver again.

A second impact against the door sprung it loose of its hinges, knocking it to the floor just inside the front room.

A strong burst of light shone through it, reaching all the way into the kitchen.

Ralph pointed his gun at the open doorway, but couldn't see anything because of the light. It was yellow-green, no wider than the doorway itself, and it was radiating and pulsating. Blocking his eyes with one arm, Andy tried to get closer to the doorway. The smoky air that hung around the light source was freezing cold, much colder than the air outside the house.

Amy turned towards the light which then engulfed her. As if being pulled forward in a trance, she took a step deeper into the light that surrounded her. Her eyes were wide open, unblinking, and her face was ghostly white, almost transparent. The pulsating light made her look like an apparition, weightless and floating towards the front door.

Andy saw her coming into the front room. "Amy, stop."

She didn't even look his way.

Aware that something was happening, Bill shot down the stairs, stopping on the bottom step as he saw the light coming through his front door. Amy was not yet in his line of sight.

Amy reached her hands out in front of her, smiling. The light did not frighten her. It welcomed her.

"Amy," Andy said. "Freeze right where you are."

She kept walking.

"Amy," Bill screamed. He started to run towards her, but froze when Amy looked his way. "Get away from that door," he said.

"Sorry, Daddy." The light was shining through her now. She was a phantom inside of the glowing source of light, not only walking into it, but also becoming part of it.

Andy fired a bullet at the open doorway, but nothing happened. Amy neared the doorway, now only five feet away from the opening. A voice inside the light began laughing. Amy turned towards her father. "It's so cold, Daddy." She sounded like a little girl. "He's so cold."

Suddenly a shadow flashed across the light, knocking Amy out of the light and onto the floor. Kathy quickly rose to her knees, crouching over Amy. She sobbed in relief of what she'd done and in fear of what could happen, because the light was still shining inside the room. Her quick actions had scared her. Amy's eyes were closed and she wasn't moving.

Andy felt for a pulse. It was weak, but she was still alive. He saw Bill approaching the light from the other side of the room. "Bill," Andy yelled, "Stay there."

Bill didn't listen. He had to check on Amy.

Andy charged towards Bill. He would try and pass through the light as quickly as possible, fearing what it could do to him if he were to remain in it as Amy had done. Penetrating the light, he suddenly felt numb and weak. His speed decreased, so when he tackled Bill it was with restricted force. Bill gave no resistance. Together they tumbled, rolling into the wall.

The light started dimming.

Carefully Andy inched his way closer to the light and the doorway. Seeing the outline of someone standing on the front porch, he fired two shots out through the door. As Andy moved closer, the light continued to dim, and the bursts and pulses were less frequent and not as strong.

It hurt his eyes to do so, but Andy looked into the heart of the light source. He saw the silhouette of a man against the background of the green light and dark woods. He could only make out the contour of the body. It was a large man with a long mane of hair. The black silhouette raised its hand, waving to Andy, and then everything vanished. The light was gone, the dark man was gone, the cold air gone, and the house was silent again.

Andy felt a hand on his shoulder.

It was Kathy. "Is it gone?" she asked.

Andy touched her trembling hand. "I think so." He stared back out the doorway. "For now. I think this was our warning. He's coming."

Ralph's visibility was down to twenty yards. The wipers were on high speed, but he still had trouble keeping the windshield clear. His windows were fogging and his defroster had stopped working. The car was slipping and sliding into the oncoming lanes.

With two more miles to Bill's house, Ralph glanced at his watch. "Damn. It's taking too long."

Then he saw the image of the Snowman from the picture in the book. That evil grin and long ratty hair. His arm around his niece. Ralph gripped the steering wheel and clenched his teeth, wishing the memory from his head. It wouldn't go away.

The roads were treacherous, but still Ralph increased his speed.

He couldn't waste anymore time.

Andy grabbed Bill by the elbow, helping him to his feet. "What happened?" Bill asked.

"I tackled you to keep you from walking into the light."

"Where's Amy?"

"In the car with Kathy."

"How is she?"

"She's alive and breathing, but unconscious."

"I want to see her."

Amy was leaning with her head against the window in the back seat of Andy's car. Kathy got out and let Bill sit with her. She sat up front with Andy. The car was already running, so Andy switched the gear to reverse and pulled out of the driveway.

Ralph pulled all the way up Bill's driveway and stopped. There were no other cars. *Either they never made it or they were chased out of the house by something,* he thought. Looking at the house which no longer had a front door, he assumed the latter. Something had happened. He was too late.

With his gun in hand, Ralph ran through the blinding snow and up the front porch. He stepped inside the front room and stood on the fallen door. Every light in the house was off, and the air was freezing, colder than the air outside. Ralph flipped the switch by the door, but no light turned on. Then the light in the stairwell flickered, and stayed on. "Amy? Bill? That you?"

No answer.

Walking through the living room, he stopped at the foot of the stairs. "Andy?"

No answer.

Slowly, he started up the stairs. He heard the pecking keys of a typewriter. Amy's typewriter. He recognized the sound, because it had once been his years ago.

peck peck peck…ding…peck peck peck peck…ding…peck peck peck … of the worn-out keys smacking letters on the pages.

The typing became faster and louder.

PECK PECK PECK…DING …PECK PECK PECK PECK PECK…DING…

"Amy," Ralph called.

No answer.

PECKPECKPECKPECKPECKPECK…DING… PECKPECKPECKPECKPECK…

Ralph reached the top of the stairs, cocking his gun. He felt a breeze coming through the cracked open door to her room. He kicked Amy's bedroom door open, sending it crashing into the wall. The unexpected wind from the broken window stung his exposed face. The air was bitterly cold.

PECKPECKPECKPECKPECKPECKPECKDINGPECKPECKPECKPECKDING

The typewriter was on the table next to her bed, violently vibrating and bouncing up and down. A huge black bird with an incredible wing span was pouncing on top of it as it rocked and bounced.

"Get out of here you bastard," Ralph shouted, firing two shots at the bird, one of them clipping its wing, puncturing it with an inch wide hole. It had no effect on the bird.

Zoro lowered his head and flew straight at Ralph, his red eyes beaming like lasers through the dark room. Its talons ripped across Ralph's forehead, sending him stumbling backwards into the door. He turned again and fired at the devilish creature as it flew down the stairs and out of his sight.

The bird was gone. Ralph felt something running down the sides of his face, and when he raised his hands up to feel it, they came back red.

A piece of typing paper was sticking out of the typewriter. With his eyes watering and his head pounding, Ralph picked up the paper, trying to read it. Words were written diagonally across the page—"child, eternal, hell, birth, sinners, new reign." Some words were written backwards—"winter, wind, Antarctica, ice, Armageddon, preservation, Zoro." Some words were written straight up and down—"storm, successor, not satisfied, home, white enemy, immortal, Piektuk, snow drifter, lost souls." And at the bottom of the paper, these words were written straight across the page—"I am back. She is the one. Now is the time."

"Amy?" Ralph whispered, looking out the broken window, confused. "What does he want from her? Why Amy? He studied the jumbled words, remembering the end of the letter he'd gotten in his office. "Ask Amy if she enjoyed what she saw of her new home."

"What new home?"

And then words came to him from the page.

"Antarctica."

What does he want?

"Successor. Child."

Why Amy? he thought, searching for the words on the page.

"She is the one. Now is the time."

For what?

"New reign."

Amy was the target, he was sure of it. He ran quickly down the stairs to his car, not noticing the black feather that was now on the fallen front door. He prayed that the Snowman hadn't gotten to her first. He took off into the snow and icy roads again in pursuit of his niece and brother. *Andy, don't let me down*, he thought. His teeth were grinding together again, his hands glued to the wheel. He was driving fast, much too fast. *Don't let me down, Andy. Don't let me down.*

Chapter 31

Brice tried to radio the research station again, but he heard nothing but static. The wind was decreasing, and by Antarctic standards, the weather was quite reasonable. Brice walked around the camp as the rest of the crew finished setting up the tents. Ever since the incident with the crevasse, he could think of nothing other than getting everyone back to the States safely. He was still amazed that they'd escaped the latest earthquake and crevasse scare without tragedy. It had been a miracle that Mark wasn't killed, and that Gabe had somehow managed to make it back up the crevasse's wall. Brice was not a religious man, but he could find no other way to explain their luck other than calling it a miracle. They'd lost one snowmobile, but they still had another. Mark's leg was a setback, but not a total disaster. He was in severe pain, but the cold weather kept it numb. The fight against gangrene and frostbite would be the next obstacle to overcome.

As Brice passed Gabe's tent, he heard Mark straining in obvious pain. He saw Gabe working on the wound. "Pretty bad?" Brice asked.

Mark nodded.

"Just do what you can to hold it together for another day," Brice said. "Hang in there just one more day."

A lot of their food had fallen into the crevasse along with the second snowmobile, so they'd have to survive the final day with what they had, mostly oatmeal.

Magnus and Eric were outside sawing blocks of snow and ice to build small walls on the south side of each tent to protect them from the wind during the night. They only had two more walls to make before joining the others.

Amy was out cold the entire drive to the Louisville Police Station. Bill tried waking her up by talking to her and gently shaking her shoulders, but nothing seemed to be working. He wrapped his arms around her and held on.

Pulling into the parking lot, Andy radioed for assistance. When he parked against the back wall of the main building, two more officers joined him to stand guard. Andy turned to Bill in the back seat. "I'll get the 4-wheel-drive Ford Explorer, and I'll be back here in a minute. These officers will watch you until I get back."

Bill nodded, smoothing the top of Amy's head with his palm, lightly touching her hair with his frozen fingers.

Kathy watched out the window as the snow continued to pelt the car like hard rain. She watched Andy run inside the three-story stone building, nearly slipping twice on the icy concrete. Despite the craziness, she was feeling comfortable with their bodyguard. She knew that they were vulnerable to anything, that was obvious seeing what had happened to them at the house; but at least with Andy watching them, she felt somewhat safe and secure. Now the two strangers standing outside the car were giving her a different feeling; they weren't very reassuring. She could tell that by the looks on their faces and their frequent chuckles of laughter, that they weren't taking any of this seriously. They weren't in the house when the lights went off. They didn't see the dog hanging from the nozzle in the shower. They didn't see the supernatural presence enter the house, rattling the windows, blowing out the door, bringing with it the Arctic air and wind. They didn't see her best friend nearly kill herself by wandering into the tunnel of light. Kathy knew that the two guys simply didn't understand her fears. She couldn't wait until Andy returned with the Explorer.

Kathy tried her best to keep her mind from thinking about the snow, but it was difficult, as it was constantly falling and sticking to the windshield, matting down against the glass, quickly darkening the inside of the car. It was like being buried live, and suffocating, as if they'd been trapped inside the car and the snow was closing in on all sides, with strangers who didn't care lurking out on the other side, and the car was getting darker and darker, colder and colder. She quickly reached over and turned the keys in the ignition. The radio turned on, and the windshield wipers cleared away the heavy accumulation. She could see again, and the car wasn't as dark anymore. The two men outside the car were startled, snapping to attention when the wipers had turned on, and inside, Kathy laughed at them.

Andy grabbed the keys to the Explorer and was on his way out when an officer said, "A 911 call came in about an hour ago. We've had another murder, well more than one actually."

"What happened? Quick, I'm in a hurry."

"The guy broke into Smith's Hardware store over on Palatka and slaughtered everyone inside. He smeared their blood all over the walls, spelling "Snowman" on the counter."

"How many are dead?"

"He got Mr. Smith and his son, and I think two customers."

"Customers? What in the hell were they doing shopping in this storm?"

"Probably getting shovels."

"The store shouldn't have been open in the first place. The whole damn city should be closed down by now, and hiding."

"Are you going to check it out?"

"I can't. Send someone else."

"You can't?"

"I'm more concerned about saving some lives, not checking on some that are already dead. Send Hofmann, or Thomas. I've got to go." Andy hurried out of the office and ran into Ralph, who was also in a hurry.

"Andy, what's happening?"

"Come with me."

"Where is Amy?"

"She's in the car with Kathy and Bill."

"You left them?"

"No, I've got two men standing guard right next to the car. I've only been inside for a few minutes." He held up the set of keys. "Had to switch vehicles."

"I was about ready to do the same."

"Well now we just need one."

Andy unlocked the doors to an Explorer in the garage and they jumped inside. Andy backed out of the garage, drove up a ramp and out.

"Let's go to protection house number four," Ralph said.

"That one in the Highlands?" Andy asked.

"That's it. It ought to be safe for the night, or at least until we can figure out another plan. We'll move around as much as we have to." Several houses around the city were owned by the Louisville Police Department, used primarily for citizens needing protection. Use ranged from abused wives on the run from their husbands to anyone thought to be in harm's way, and the entire Anderson family was definitely in harm's way.

Andy could feel the tires gripping the ice as he turned around the back corner of the building. "He killed some more tonight."

"What?"

"Smith's Hardware. He killed four. Blood was smeared over the walls and he left his name again."

"Which one?"

"Snowman."

Ralph punched the door. "Damn." His thoughts quickly returned to Amy. He had to make sure she was safe. He had to see her to convince his mind that the girl in the photograph with the Snowman had not been his niece.

"We're sending someone else to take care of it," Andy said. He stopped the Explorer next to his car, and they got out. Ralph saw that Bill was with Amy in the back seat, and Amy wasn't moving.

Andy opened the back door of the car so that Bill could step out, holding Amy in his arms.

"What's wrong with her?" Ralph said to Andy.

"Something very strange happened in the house. I don't know exactly what it was, something supernatural, but she's been unconscious ever since."

"Did the Snowman get to her?"

"Ralph, I don't know what happened in that house. He didn't touch her because I don't think he was actually there, but something sure as hell was and the Snowman was probably behind it. Poltergeists. Ghosts."

"Let's get her to the house quickly."

Throughout the calm and silent Antarctic night, the members of the team rested. The oatmeal was gone, and everyone was full. Although everyone was thinking about what could have happened to them, no one wanted to talk about it.

Gabe thought about how close he'd come to dying in that crevasse. He felt the pressure of something he had to do, the pressure of saving that young lady with the beautiful blue eyes in the ice. He would have to help her, but from what?

"I've got something to tell everyone," Leroy said. They could tell that he was nervous about something. They could see the worry and fear in his aged eyes. His skin was pale, almost white and powdery, and crows feet wrinkled the outside of his eyes just above his cheek bones. His gray hair was in disarray, his eyebrows were pointing inward towards his nose as he stared at them in deep thought.

"What is it, Leroy?" Brice asked, concerned but also curious.

Leroy paused, looking them all in the eyes, one by one.

"If you don't think I'm crazy from the way I've been acting of late, you probably will after you hear what I've got to tell you."

"Does this have something to do with what you were mumbling about earlier, or this morning when you said that only you know what lives here?" Mark asked.

Leroy nodded. "I have an ulterior motive for being here. I'm here for revenge."

"For what?" Brice asked.

"My daughter's life. She was murdered 32 years ago during a terrible Colorado snowstorm. She was three years old. I believe the thing that killed her lives here on Antarctica."

"Nobody could live here, Leroy," Marvin said, "It'd be impossible. You know that."

"It is possible. This guy isn't human. He can do anything he wants."

"Is this the guy that is heating this place up, this increased global warming theory of yours?" Marvin asked.

Leroy shook his head. "Global warming is a very gradual process. Normally it isn't something you could live through and watch, but in this case we can. There is something here that accelerates the rate, and nobody knows what it is exactly. It's something underneath the ice. A presence of some kind." He saw some of them smile "Make jokes if you want, it won't change my mind."

"I'm sorry to hear about your daughter, but some of this is a little hard to imagine," Marvin said.

"It gets harder, believe me."

"Go on," Brice said.

"This is a dangerous place, and it isn't only because of the weather. The earliest explorers found that out. They saw some things, evil and frightening things, and many of them went to their graves still holding on to what they'd witnessed. Some were lucky enough to live through their expeditions when the supplies and equipment were nowhere near as good as ours, and many of their stories were similar in a very bizarre way. On more than one occasion, the fortunate survivors spoke of an Antarctic snow phantom, a ghost that ravaged everything in its path. It's been recorded on tapes, in journals, with interviews. Our government has an idea of what lives here, but yet, year after year they put more scientists in the line of fire, covering up whenever and whatever they need to. This phantom, this evil monster that killed my girl is called the Snowman, or at least that's what the newspapers had called him, and that's what had been written in blood on the walls of my house 32 years ago." Leroy fought back tears. "I still have dreams and nightmares of that day. I don't think they'll ever go away, not until he's dead and gone. The memories are so painful."

"Then why dig them up?" Brice asked.

"I have to. The year was 1962, and it was a snowy Sunday afternoon. I was shoveling the front sidewalk and porch when I heard my daughter screaming from one of the rooms inside the house. I ran in the house and he was still there. He didn't see me at first, but I saw him running towards the back doorway. He was a fairly large guy with long white hair. I took off after him, but he got away."

"What happened?" Brice asked.

"The snow in our back yard was at least three to four feet high, up to ten in some spots because of the drifts, but he had no trouble running through it. It was too deep for me. I was trapped, and I could do nothing but watch him run away.

"We had an old storage shed about 30 yards from the house. While this Snowman was approaching the shed, the door slid open on its own, and a weird, pulsing green light shone through it and all the way to the back of my house. It lit up everything around it: the snow, the trees, my house. The crazy bastard turned around just before entering the shed and hissed at me, like a serpent or a cat. Then out of nowhere, this huge black bird flew down, circled around the Snowman, flew through the branches in the trees, circled around me and the house, and then flew off again. The Snowman smiled at me. It was an evil smile.

"Once he walked into that shed, the light started changing, and everything went back to white again. The back wall of the storage shed wasn't a wall anymore; what was there instead was a scene of ice and snow from some other land far away. The brightness of the land hurt my eyes but I continued to gaze at it. It was hypnotic. Then the Snowman whispered something."

"What did he say?" someone asked.

"He said, 'Times almost up. Got to get back to the Pole.' He was pointing to the back wall of the shed when he'd said it. After that, he stepped through and into the land of ice. In the distance, he turned and waved, and then ran off. After a few minutes, the wall closed up, and it was again the back of my shed."

"I've written books on the subject, if you can call it that," Leroy continued. "Most consider it fiction though, but I don't. It isn't like I've been wallowing in revenge for the past three decades, because I haven't. I've been actively researching and studying these types of killings, and I've learned that my daughter's death was not an isolated event. The government knows about it, too. They've been searching for this creature for years, and even now, they're searching for it under a secret operation called WHITE OUT. It's being run out of a program called SCARE. Strategic Center for Antarctic Research and Exploration. The government developed it in the early 70s. I found out about this project early in its development. In 1976 I was set to testify in a trial in Louisville, Kentucky, that had something to do with the Snowman. A young man was accused of killing his wife and was only days away from being wrongfully convicted. The Snowman was the real killer. I was ready to present evidence that the Snowman was a real entity, and then the government officials from SCARE heard about it and immediately stepped in. They wanted to keep the Snowman's identity covered, so they gave me a large sum of money not to testify, and not to go public with what I knew, and what I'd learned over the years."

"You took the money?" Pam asked.

"I didn't have much of a choice. They never came out and said it, but I knew that my life was going to be in danger if I didn't cooperate. I put a lot of this information in my books, but they were able to censor what was in those, too."

"What happened with the trial?" Brice asked.

"SCARE officials had it fixed. That was the deal. I didn't testify. I didn't mention certain things in my writings. I collected the money, and the young man was found not guilty. SCARE was then free to pursue their research. England, China, Japan, the Soviet Union, India, they all were in the game too, but SCARE was eventually able to quiet them. This is why only Americans are around here now. All significant biological research has just about stopped here on Antarctica. The National Science Foundation and nearly all remnants of our research committees have all but vanished. Everything has been pushed aside by the greed and curiosity of a group of bureaucrats that don't have a clue what they're dealing with. They still allow expeditions such as this to go on because we're harmless to them. By the time we get close to the research station, I'm sure they'll be covering everything up, acting as if they're carrying on with what the NSF has been doing for years, but it will all be a facade.

"This land right here. This land of ice and snow was in my backyard 32 years ago in the back of my shed. There is some kind of passageway or energy field at the South pole, a portal, you might say, that allows him to go where he wants to go. It may even be this that our government is trying to control and researching so secretly. Could you imagine what they could do with a special doorway that allows you to travel around the world in only a few seconds."

Leroy felt as if a great burden had been lifted from his shoulders and realized that the load had now been dispersed equally amongst the others. Even if they didn't believe him, he wasn't in this alone anymore.

Without saying more, and to the surprise of the others, Leroy walked out of the tent. Tomorrow would be the day, the final day, and it would also be the longest. Time was drawing near. His time was finally coming. Leroy's time for revenge.

Chapter 32

8:50 P.M. Dungeon
14 Inches

Halfway down the east-west corridor, frigid air engulfed the Snowman's body as he neared the green light. The cold air refreshed him. The air was home. The portal was at the end of the corridor. Like a scene in a picture frame, the landscape on the other side was nothing but ice and snow. Wind gathered loose snow from the ice and swirled it in frantic circles, some of it landing on the floor inside the corridor.

The Snowman walked deeper into the light, breathing in his source of life. The sensation was electric, yet soothing and calming at the same time. He felt aroused. He'd been away for too long, allowing his defenses to be lowered. The job at the hardware store had not gone smoothly, and he began to tire. Icy beads of sweat trickled down his wrinkled, pale face, slowing, freezing before reaching his chin. His hands and legs trembled, and his eyes danced from wall to wall, blurry, as the landscape of his home drew him in. His time must be near.

Breathing in the air, the Snowman's chest expanded. The Antarctic wind was energizing, but he needed more. He needed to feel and breathe what was home, what was his domain. He needed to feel the ice and become one with it again.

Ten feet away from the breakthrough point, he inhaled deeply and strongly the drug he craved. His eyes shone brightly with a light-blue luster, like diamonds, and his limbs were suddenly calmed, his hands no longer shaking. The polluted Kentucky air was quickly released. Out with the old, in with the cold. Inhaling through both his mouth and nose, his body was slowly regaining its power. With the breakthrough point directly overhead, he stepped across the threshold, covering thousands and thousands of miles in only a few steps. His boot crunched on the Antarctic ice, and the wind sent his hair reeling. Looking over his shoulder, The Dungeon's corridor was dark and musty. He would wait until the morning to return.

The breakthrough point was a paper-thin wall in the middle of the land, marking the location of the geographical South Pole and the southernmost region of the entire planet. It was his doorway to the rest of the world, and only he had the key to open it.

As the Snowman walked away from the breakthrough point, The Dungeon fell behind him in the distance, becoming smaller and smaller. Something was wrong, the Snowman could smell it in the air. The air was infected with the encroachment of visitors. He sensed someone coming. He'd felt something even after killing off all the scientists, but now it was much stronger and closer.

The Snowman stopped suddenly and closed his eyes. He could sense them. It was blurry. Some of them were on skis, and one was on a snowmobile, and they were quickly approaching. The Snowman focused on the front skier, an older man with some white hair of his own, but much shorter. The man's face appeared frozen in the wind, and the Snowman mentally focused in on it. He raised his hands in the air, bellowing out in laughter, as the image swept away as quickly as it had appeared. The explorers were gone, but the Snowman's smile remained. He remembered the face, the face of the front skier, the old man. "Been a long time, Leroy McCalister." The Snowman turned slowly in a circle, surveying the landscape in every direction. "Listen closely. I think I can still hear your daughter screaming."

The Snowman hunkered down to the ice and sat down cross-legged. "Feel the power of the Pole," he whispered. "Need guidance with its union." The Snowman pressed his bare hands down on the ice between his legs and slowly rubbed the surface in slow circles. He could immediately feel the energy and power growing beneath the ice. A tingling sensation started from his fingertips and surged throughout his body. He closed his eyes, lowered his head, dropped his shoulders. "Need the power of the Pole," he whispered, moaning softly as a green glow of light began to surface from the ice between his folded legs. The light then began to pulsate, beating like a heart. The Snowman took a deep breath and then inhaled strongly through his nose, drowning himself with its power. Suddenly, a pole shot up between his legs, cracking the ice, and the Snowman grabbed hold of it with both hands. He felt nothing around him except the pulsating heart of hell. The glowing green pole extended from the ice on up into the sky, seemingly without ending. The Snowman was bathed in its brilliant glow, reveling in its beautiful presence. His hands rubbed up and down on the Pole until he was lost in its activity. He felt friction. The connection had been made. A final burst of light flashed through the Pole, stinging him like an electrical current. The Snowman's eyes popped open. He focused on the Pole and smiled. "Oh, God."

The Pole listened.

The safe house was old but well kept. Located near Seneca Park, on the outskirts of the Highlands, it was well hidden by trees and set far enough back from the street so that it was secluded. On only one floor, it had two bedrooms, a bathroom, a kitchen, a den, and a living room. In one bedroom, Amy was lying across the bed still unconscious. Bill had stayed in the room with her since they'd arrived, and the constant worrying was driving him crazy. She was showing no signs of improvement. Kathy and Andy now sat with her while Bill and Ralph talked in the living room.

Ralph sat on the edge of the sofa, staring at Bill, who was sitting in a recliner across from him. A small coffee table separated them. "Bill."

Bill looked up, sitting on the edge of the seat. His eyes were red and his face was rough with stubble. He needed sleep. "Yeah?"

"I've got some bad news about Dad."

Bill paused, showing no change of emotion. He felt as if he had no more emotion to show. "I heard."

"Who told you?"

"The radio, the news, Andy. We talked about it earlier."

"I'm sorry."

"About what?"

"Finding out like that."

"Me, too."

"I wanted to be the one to tell you, but I didn't want to tell you over the phone, and this was the first chance I've had to sit down and tell you. Everything has been so crazy. Did Andy tell you everything?"

"He did. I made him. I wanted to know all the details, and in a way I feel guilty because of the way I reacted. I wasn't really surprised or shocked, or anything like that. I was scared, sad, and downright pissed, but it was almost as if I had expected it to happen. I was numb."

"Me, too," Ralph said, rubbing his chin and mouth with his hand.

"You mind if we don't talk about this anymore?"

Ralph nodded. "That's fine."

Bill looked into the bedroom. He could see Amy's legs and feet on the bed. There was no movement in them. Bill looked back towards his brother. His eyes were wet. "About yesterday."

"What?"

Bill bit his quivering lip. His hands were shaking. "When you saw the bottle."

Ralph started to say something but didn't.

"It's so hard, Ralph. I don't think you understand how hard it is." He paused to wipe his eyes. "Do you know how much I want a drink right now? How much I need a drink right now?"

"Bill, I—"

Bill cut him off. "But I won't do it. I'm going to be strong. I'm going to be strong like I was yesterday, strong like I've been for the past 18 years, Ralph. I'm going to resist, just like I would have yesterday."

"I think I may have over-reacted on that, I'm—"

"Don't apologize. You had your reasons for how you reacted. We can't control our feelings."

"But we can control our emotions."

"Maybe so. It was probably a combination of the fear, anger, and resentment you've had pinned up on me over the years. Seeing the bottle gave you a chance to let it all out, to say I told you so."

"No, Bill."

"It's okay. It's tough, and this is all making it tougher, but it's very important to me."

"What's very important?"

"That you don't believe I was really going to open that bottle of alcohol."

"Why now?" Ralph stood up.

"I was not going to take a drink, Ralph." Bill's voice grew louder, desperately trying to convey the truth to his brother. "And I want to know that my little brother has faith in me."

Ralph stared Bill in the eyes and nodded. Gently, he pressed his hand on Bill's left shoulder. "Bill, everything is going to be okay."

Bill looked up. "I wish I had faith in that."

Ralph let go and turned towards the bedroom.

Kathy stood in the doorway, excited about something. She waved for them to come. "Amy's moving. She's trying to talk."

They hurried into the bedroom.

Clutching the glowing Pole with both hands, the Snowman began to speak. His voice was low, a whisper, a prayer. "I believe in the one God, the one and only soul of creation, manifested in two physical forms, of which I am in union. I remember the work of my Father during the first thousand years, the souls of fire that burned in hell, the melting pain. I believe in His ancestors. I believe. My frozen souls feel no pain. They feel nothing. They're numb. My millennium soon will end. The dualism of your two arms will rise in the war against the opposition that is Armageddon. The elimination of the opposition. Elimination of the righteous. I believe in my purpose. Chaos, random chaos. Amy is the one and the time is now upon us. The upper hand will be ours at the beginning of the coming millennium. The beginning and the end." The Snowman squeezed on the Pole. A burst of electricity surged like frozen ice through his veins. "The force of opposition works against us. I can feel the tension. It draws near, but I will do my work. The power will be passed. The final union will be made. The union of fire and ice."

Just then, a burst of green light flashed up through the Pole, giving its approval. The Snowman's arms jerked away as a spasm of energy stormed through his body. It was painful, but he again held on. He heard the voice signaling up from the ice, through the Pole, into his arms, rhythmically beating through and with his heart. The powerful voice rumbled like thunder in his ears.

"Snowman," it called.

"Yes." The Snowman looked down into the ice.

"Eliminate the righteous, the sinners, but remain strong to your ultimate goal and purpose. Our goal and purpose. Amy is the one. Now is the time for the final union. It is she. Only she has the power to produce the ultimate evil or ultimate good. The forces of opposition are strong, so you must lead the way and get to her first. The winner will depend on your actions."

"Tonight?"

"Timing is critical. Strike when your power is at its greatest. Strike when the snow is strongest. You own her mind, now all you need is the body."

The Snowman rubbed the Pole, stroking it with both hands, smiling. "And tonight?"

"Rest. The snow will be stronger tomorrow. Rest."

The Snowman closed his eyes, whispering what the Pole had just told him. "Rest, rest, rest, rest." The thundering in his heart decreased. The words he now heard were his own. "Rest, rest." When he opened his eyes again, the Pole was gone. His arms were reaching out, but the Pole was no longer there. The small crack in the ice from where it had emerged was gone. As the last living minion of Satan, the Snowman was aware of the importance of his job. He stood up, inhaling deeply the frigid air around him. Filled with the power and wisdom, he focused in on Amy's mind.

Bill sat down on the edge of the bed, holding one of Amy's cold hands. She shifted slightly on the bed, grasping the covers with her free hand, squirming with discomfort, moaning with an unnatural pleasure. Bill couldn't read her mixed signals. Her inability to control herself frightened him. Then, for the first time since the incident at the house, she opened her eyes. They were glossy and opaque. Her lids fluttered, trying to stay open.

Bill leaned towards her, gently touching her shoulder. "Amy?"

She didn't answer. Instead, she hunched into a fetal position, shivering all over. Her lips were cold and blue, and her teeth were chattering, although sweat dotted her forehead and damp hairline as if she were hot. Bill turned around. "Someone turn the heat up, quick, she's freezing."

Andy immediately left the room to adjust the thermostat. He was back in the room in less than a minute. Amy had yet to say a word.

"Amy," Bill whispered, lifting her chin up so that her face was pointing towards his. "Can you hear me?"

No response. Her eyes were wet, swelling with tears, but none came out. They too were trapped, frozen.

"Please, Amy. It's your father. Say something. If you can hear me at least try and blink."

They all waited. Andy looked in and out of the room nervously, his heart racing with every little sound that the house was making. He was ready for anything.

Suddenly, Amy blinked. And then her mouth moved, trying to produce words.

Bill leaned closer, gazing into her cold eyes of stone. "What is it, Amy?"

"Co . . . c . ."

"Take your time, honey."

She blinked again, struggling to choke out the words.

Bill's anxiety was leading to impatience. He needed proof that his daughter was going to make it. He needed proof that she wasn't dying or slipping into a coma.

"C . . . cold." Amy breathed rapidly, moving her head from side to side, her chest expanding, inhaling, exhaling. Her skin was cold and clammy.

"I know," Bill whispered, trying to pull the covers over her. She resisted, tearing them away with her free hand, throwing them off the other side of the bed.

"So cold."

Bill looked up and around, not knowing what to do or say. "Amy, do you know where you are?"

Amy paused, taking another deep breath before answering. "In between."

"In between where?"

"In between here and there."

"Where is there?"

"Iceville, Daddy." Her voice sounded like a young girl's voice.

"What is Iceville?"

"My dreamworld. He touches me there, and nobody can hear me. All of our voices are mute, but he can hear them. Sometimes I can hear them, too. Sometimes when the wind is soft and the air is light, I can hear Mommy screaming, too."

"Where is Mom? How can you hear her?"

"I don't know."

"Where is she?"

"In the ice."

"Where?"

"He pulls them there."

"Where, Amy? Where is Mom?"

"My new home. Not the place for exploration, but—"

"Where is home?"

"Not for exploration, but for preservation."

"What are you saying?"

"Preservation of the souls."

"Amy, where is home?"

"They are all dead to the physical world." Amy blinked, holding her eyes closed for a few seconds before opening them again. "He's cold when he touches me."

"Who?"

"The Snowman, and he's bringing me home."

"Where is home?"

Softly and very slowly, Amy said, "I don't know." She closed her eyes again, but this time they stayed closed for the rest of the night.

About 30 yards away from the wall and breakthrough point was a tiny crevasse in the ice, nearly 10 feet deep and 20 yards long. It would be his bed for the night so that he could get the rest his ancient body required. Above him, the wind was increasing, brushing across the ice, whistling and moaning, singing and blowing. The sound was soothing, relaxing the Snowman as his eyes grew weary. He stared at the picture he'd stolen from their house, a framed picture of Amy, taken only one year ago at Easter. She looked lovely in her peach, flower-covered, silky dress that hung down just above her knees. Her long and curly hair cascaded down over her shoulders. The Snowman rubbed his right thumb gently over the glass, smudging a path free of dust. She was beautiful, and she would be his. He studied the picture with joy and lust. He focused in on the red, pink, purple and blue flowers on her dress; they were connected by branches and green vines that wrapped her shoulders and breasts, the curves of her hips, her legs. He could smell her, and it soothed him as much as the wind and cold air.

Her beauty was strikingly familiar. When looking at Amy, he was seeing his mother again. Their looks were the same, the same eyes, hair, lips, cheeks, smile. It was more than her looks that claimed her as the special one. It was her soul, and the Snowman had felt that in the winter of 1974. As he was told it would happen then, his randomness had finally brought them together. The connection had been sudden and strong then, but even more so now that it was the time. She would give him the successor, the final element, the final piece in their puzzle.

The Snowman closed his eyes, leaning his head against the bottom corner of the crevasse, holding the picture close, pressing it against his chest. He could still see the image in his head. He could still see the blooming flowers on her dress. He could smell her flesh. He dreamed. He dreamed of Amy, all the time drawing her closer to him, bringing her closer and closer to home. Mentally, the Snowman controlled her, and when he awoke he would claim her.

Yes, Amy was the one. And now was finally the time.

None of Bill's questions had been answered by Amy's sudden outburst, and now she was unconscious again. *He touches me there.* Bill couldn't get the words out of his head. Increasingly, as he thought of it he was filled with fear, anger, and rage. Ralph told them about what had happened to him at the library, and hearing it only made Bill's emotional state worse. It made him sick to think of Amy with that monster, but he was tired, and by 11 he was asleep on the bed next to Amy. Kathy was using the other bedroom.

It was now midnight, and Ralph was asleep on the couch in the front room, scheduled for guard duty at two a.m.. He and Andy would watch the house in shifts throughout the night. Andy sat in a wooden rocking chair with his feet propped up on the large bay window ledge, staring through the two-foot-wide opening between the curtains, watching the heavy snowfall. He could see some trees outside the window, but the snow was falling so hard, sight of the road in the distance was impossible.

Before these last couple of days, Andy had loved the snow, but now he wasn't so sure anymore. He was tired. His mind wandered back and forth, from the beauty and cottony whiteness of the snow to the ultimate death and destruction it now camouflaged. His views were split, and his thoughts and imagination were running wild through a tired mind that wanted nothing more than to sleep. But he couldn't sleep, not yet. He would wait it out, and his defenses would not be lowered.

A few hours passed, and a few more inches had fallen. It was two o'clock in the morning. Andy looked over his shoulder at the couch. Ralph was exhausted, sleeping like a baby but snoring like a lion. That is what kept Andy awake during his shift. Andy didn't wake him though. Instead, he continued to wait and watch.

PART THREE

DECEMBER 16TH
ANTARCTICA

And now there came both mist and snow,
And it grew wondrous cold:
And ice, mast-high, came floating by,
As green as emerald.

And through the drifts the snowy clifts
Did send a dismal sheen:
Nor shapes of men nor beasts we ken—
The ice was all between.

The ice was here, the ice was there,
The ice was all around:
It crack'd and growl'd, and roar'd and howl'd,
Like noises in a swound!

Samuel Taylor Coleridge, from *The Rime of the Ancient Mariner*

Chapter 33

7:25 A.M. Antarctica

Despite the tremors, freezing temperatures, and wind, the injury to Mark's leg, the near tragedy in the crevasse, and the fact that she was physically and mentally worn out, Loreda Cranfield grinned as she lifted her head from her pillow. Outside her sleeping bag, her breath crystallized in mini-rainbows as it mixed with the frigid air. It was her last day on the skis, and time was running out on her if she still planned on asking *the* question. She was shy, always has been, and day after day she'd given herself excuses to wait, allowing her nerves to get the best of her.

For Loreda, the trip had gone very well, and she planned on making it even better if only she could gather up the nerves to ask him. She couldn't understand why it was so difficult for her to ask Eric the Red out on a date. They'd already become good friends throughout the trip, and they'd talked every day. She knew that it shouldn't be any different from any of their normal conversations, but still she dreaded doing it. Ever since the time in high school when she'd been turned down twice in one month for her Junior dance, she's always been reluctant to go for it again with anyone. She had come to consider herself a late bloomer, and she was content with that role. Getting married and starting a family had not been her number one priority throughout high school and college. Instead, she'd always planned to become one of the elite in her field, making a name for herself, and that she had done. But now she wanted more. She could fool herself no longer. She was 38 years old, and she'd been alone, waiting and passively searching for years for Mr. Right to come along and sweep her away. So far it hadn't happened.

Financially, Loreda was set, having firmly established herself with, at least, minor popularity in the fiction world. On the trip, she'd already gathered more than enough notes and ideas to get a solid start on her next adventure novel. All her expectations for coming along on the journey had been fulfilled and then some. What she certainly didn't expect was to fall in love. It only complicated things for her, but at the same time she'd been reveling in that special feeling for weeks now, dreaming of a bright future with a man she truly loved.

Pam eased her head out from her sleeping bag, leaning up on one elbow. She saw the grin on Loreda's face and wondered how she could be so happy this early in the morning. "Loreda?"

Loreda didn't say a word. She stared through the crack at the bottom of the tent's door, watching tiny rays of the morning's light glisten off the ice outside.

"Earth to Loreda."

She turned towards Pam. "Yeah?"

"What had you so spaced out?"

"Oh, nothing really," she said, her grin now turning into a broad smile.

"Sorry, I don't buy it. What's on your mind?"

Loreda hesitated, but then decided to reveal her feelings. She couldn't hold them inside any longer. "Okay, but you can't speak a word to the others."

Pam leaned up. "This sounds good."

"Promise?"

"Promise what?"

"Not to tell." Loreda felt like a high school girl again, but this time it felt good. She was having fun with it, and for once she'd forgotten her age, allowing her emotions to come spilling out.

"I promise. What is it?"

"I think I'm in love."

"Anyone I know?"

"Yep."

"Well?"

"Eric."

"Red?" Pam's eyes grew to the size of quarters. Her hunch had been correct. She knew there was something between them, or at least the potential for something, but working to their disadvantage, he was less assertive than she. They were sure to get absolutely nowhere with this. But still she acted surprised. "Our snowmobile man?"

"Yes," Loreda said confidently.

Pam was 11 years younger than Loreda and was engaged to be married next summer. At first, she felt awkward giving an older woman tips on relationships, but that's what she did, and they chattered away like two young girls. Suddenly the ice started moving again.

The tremor was short, only lasting for a few seconds, but it was enough to remind them of what had happened yesterday. It was also a warning of what they could expect during the day to come.

The tremor had occurred only minutes before the team was ready to depart for the day. After the ice stopped rumbling, one by one they emerged from their tents, checking the surroundings for damage or fresh crevasse slivers. They found that nothing had changed. Seven of them stood in a circle, locking their skis in place, fastening every article of clothing. Marvin and Leroy were the only ones still in their tents.

Leroy had been the early morning topic of conversation for several of them, as they were still shocked with what he'd told them and still unconvinced that any of it could be true, except the fact that he'd lost his daughter to a crazed killer. They had questions, lots of them, and if what Leroy had told them was true, they deserved answers. They allowed him to leave them hanging last night, but the time would come when they would insist on knowing everything, and that time would be very soon. This was their last day, and if they were to confront this Snowman character, they wanted to be totally prepared.

All eyes were on their tent, watching and waiting for them to come out. They were all anxious to get their final day started. Then Marvin came out, walking slowly, and Leroy was not following behind him. As the Colonel approached the group, he held up a piece of paper. His goggles were propped up on the top of his hood; the fear in his eyes was painfully visible. "I've got bad news."

Before finally falling asleep last night, Bill could think of nothing but Amy and her safety. What she'd said during her brief and strange awakening had frightened him. He was angry and worried, willing to do anything to snap her out of her trance. He couldn't believe it was happening to *his* daughter. *Why Amy?* he thought, repeatedly asking the question in his mind for hours before he'd fallen asleep. Nothing made sense, and the possibilities he'd come up with only added to his confusion, reminding him that they had no control over anything anymore. He was now more afraid of the snow than ever. His worst fears had surfaced; the Snowman was in control again, and was mentally controlling Bill's daughter. He knew that they were going to have to think of something, some kind of plan to tip the scales in their favor. But what? He'd hoped the ideas would come to them in the morning because they were running out of time, and Amy's health was declining rapidly.

He'd suggested calling Kathleen Greene, possibly getting her to the house to see if she could do anything for Amy. Even if it meant putting another life in danger, Bill was willing to go through with it. He was desperate and didn't look at it as selfishness. The Snowman had already taken his wife and father. He looked at it as a last ditch effort to save the most important person left in his life. He couldn't go on living if the Snowman were to take her too.

By 8:30 Ralph was the only one in the house who was awake. He read the front page of the paper, amazed that any paper boy had been able to deliver it, and the headlines immediately jumped out at him: LOUIS-VILLE GET READY ! THE SNOW IS COMING. He read no further.

Ralph stared out the bay window at a sea of white. The snow was still falling heavily, with clumps the size of cotton balls flying against the window, bouncing and spiraling off until finally landing silently to the pristine white surface. The sky was gray, and the sun seemed to be gone forever. He'd read yesterday that the sun in Antarctica this time of year never leaves the sky. He wondered if that would be a better place for them. Probably not. It was more dangerous there than here. Ralph couldn't stand to watch out the window any longer.

He called the police station. Surprisingly, the Greenes had been there all night looking for him. Ralph spoke to Kathleen briefly.

Andy was asleep on the couch. Ralph nudged him. "Andy."

Andy snapped his eyes open, jerking his arm towards his gun.

"Relax," Ralph said. "We aren't under attack. Not yet, at least."

Andy yawned. "What time is it?"

"Nine. I just called the station. Kathleen and Mike Greene are waiting there now."

"How?"

"They must have gotten there before the snow was too bad. They tried to contact us, but once they'd been there for a few hours, it was much too dangerous for them to try and get back home that late at night."

"They spent the night at the station?"

Ralph nodded. "I talked to Kathleen, and I told her about Amy's condition."

"And?"

"I'm going over to pick them up."

"You're bringing them here?"

"That's what Bill wanted."

"But, Ralph, that's putting two more lives on the line."

"Kathleen was the one that suggested it. She seems to think she can help Amy, possibly get through to her, and right now we don't have many choices."

"I guess we don't," Andy agreed, strapping his holster over and around his bulky shoulders. "Be careful out there."

"I will." Ralph closed the door, running out into the deep snow.

Even in the 4-wheel-drive, Ralph had difficulty handling the snow. The city was buried, and according to the latest news flash, the heart of the storm was still hours away.

In the house, Andy watched and waited, ready and alert.

Brice walked towards Marvin. "What is it?" His first thought was suicide.

"He's gone." Marvin handed Brice the note.

Brice stared at it, looked around the group, and then read it aloud: "Please do not think of my actions as irrational, and as difficult as it may be to believe what I told you last night, you've got to trust me. Stay aware. My dreams are happening again. I know I'm getting close, and I also know he senses that I'm coming. He knows now that I'm here. The internal heat is increasing. We'll be lucky to make it out alive. I wanted to be the first to confront him, and possibly spare you the turmoil. I've been waiting and preparing for this day. Be ready, for it is not assured that I will win. It is nearly impossible to fully understand the power that stands in front of us. Revenge is all I want, so I hope the Snowman is prepared to die. I am. The time has come, and by the end of the day I will know. We will all know what really lies at the Pole." Brice looked up from the paper.

"He signed it, 'sorry, Leroy'." Brice folded the letter and put it in his coat pocket.

Sitting on the back of the snowmobile with his leg elevated and braced with two ski-poles, Mark asked, "What do we do now?"

Gabe pushed his goggles down over his eyes. "We ski. We ski and we find him."

Marvin grunted. "There's no telling how much of a head start he has on us."

"We don't have much of a choice. Given that Leroy isn't living a life of illusion and this thing is real, we can't let him face it alone no matter how crazy it sounds," Brice said.

Gabe plunged his ski poles into the ice and pushed off. "We will find him," he lowered his voice to a whisper, "And I will also find the young woman. They both need my help." Gabe skied off in the direction of the South Pole. The others followed.

Chapter 34

11:35 A.M. Highlands
17 Inches

Bill knew it was a nightmare, but there was no way for him to pull himself out of it. He'd have to endure the horror until the Snowman was finished with him. An early exit was not likely. He was in the middle of nowhere, naked, standing in a freshly snow-plowed road; his knees knocked together as his entire body shivered.

The sky was black and without stars, not because of low clouds or pollution, but simply because there were no stars in the sky. The only light was coming from what little the crescent moon offered. Bill's bare feet pressed against the icy pavement of the road. He felt stuck, frozen to the street like a tongue freezes against metal at sub-zero temperatures.

As far as Bill could see, both sides of the road were stacked high with snow, and the pavement seemingly had no ending in either direction. Walls of hard-packed snow, close to 10 feet high, surrounded him as if he were inside of a tunnel, and the walls were growing higher. He was standing there, frozen and nearly convulsing, watching the walls of snow and ice grow upward to the point where he couldn't tell if they were really growing or if he was shrinking. The thought of either frightened him.

He heard movement, a slushing and scraping sound coming from above. He craned his neck upward, peering towards the top of the wall to his left, and through a faint light-green glow he was able to see several people in polar gear skiing past him with great speed. As they dug into the snow above, quickly pushing forward, snow sprayed down to the road below, sprinkling on top of Bill. His hair and bare shoulders were covered with thick white flakes and thin shavings of ice. He screamed up towards the skiers, but no sound emitted, and as quickly as they'd appeared, they vanished into the darkness of the night as the walls continued their flight upward, extending, growing.

Bill felt dizzy as he stared at the shape-shifting walls. They were now more than 20 feet high and quickly getting taller. Bill could see the top edges of the walls, but he couldn't see over them.

The coldness of the road stung his feet, sparking a tingling sensation that started in his toes and gradually climbed upwards, numbing his knees and hips, his stomach, his arms and shoulders, his neck, and finally his face. He was frozen. He tried to walk, but his legs wouldn't move. He was stuck to the road. Losing his balance, he fell forward, catching himself with his hands on the icy pavement. His feet were stuck to the ice, and now, so were his hands. He jerked upward, trying to jar his palms loose, but a sharp pain shot through his wrists and arms. All four of his limbs remained connected to the ice. His back was arched and curved, his butt raised high in the air as if stretching like a cat after waking up from a nap. He was frozen in the middle of the road, and the walls to both sides of him were now more than 40 feet tall and quickly rising.

Bill was dizzy and shivering violently. His arms and legs were turning bluish-gray and swelling, and his back was losing strength. His knees were slowly dropping, inch by inch towards the ice, and his back didn't have the strength or the leverage to keep him afloat. His entire body shook with tension and strain, not only from the cold, but also from his inability to maintain balance.

It was painful to do so, but he raised his head upward, peering down the road ahead of him. It had no ending. He lowered his head even more so that he was staring upside-down and between his legs at the road in the other direction. He was a minuscule dot on an infinite line. Everything was silent and dead. No sounds of any kind echoed between the massive walls.

And then suddenly, Bill heard something machine-like rumbling in the road in front of him. Two bright lights blinded his vision. Like a deer caught in headlights, he was stunned, couldn't move, and was still frozen to the ice. His knees were inches from the ground, and his back and shoulders were oddly contorted.

At first, the machine sounded like a truck, but the closer it got, the less he thought so. The lights were too high above the road and the noise was just too loud. It was approaching very quickly, only 20 yards away and showing no signs of slowing. Desperately, Bill pulled his left hand from the road, and immediately blood surfaced at the lines where warm flesh gave way to frozen flesh.

The sound was louder, the lights brighter.

Ten yards away. The pain in his hand was unbearable. He still couldn't move his feet.

He heard the screeching of brakes. The vehicle came to a sudden stop about five feet away from him. The lights dimmed.

Bill now recognized the vehicle to be a Bobcat, and it was rumbling, the idling engine echoing off the walls of ice that surrounded him. The front grill of the Bobcat was a giant mechanical mouth with metal gums that held knives as teeth. The knives vibrated, shivering, clinking together just as Bill's body was doing only a few feet away.

Laughing, the driver leaned out the side window and waved. "Looks like you've seen a ghost, Bill. Go on now. Get out of my way or I'm gonna hafta run ya over."

Bill took one good look at the Snowman. Staring at the crazed man sparked an anger that drove him to pry his limbs from the road; but he wasn't sure if he could endure the pain of leaving his flesh stuck to the ice if he did rip away. He yelled at the Snowman, but nothing came out. Puffs of air filtered from his lips and into the freezing air, but no words emerged.

The Snowman's laughter got louder.

It's a dream, Bill told himself, *it's only a dream. Rip yourself from the road you chicken-shit. Pull yourself free. A dream can't hurt for long.* Bill wasn't convinced. It *was* a dream, but it felt so real. His body was freezing and almost completely numb, and that tingling sensation mutating through his body felt very real. And so would the pain be if he were to rip himself from ice.

Bill screamed again, but again, nothing came out. Only air.

The Snowman laughed wildly. "All voices are mute. Now get out of my way." The Snowman's face was as white as sugar. Like that of a clown, his nose was bright red, as was the lipstick that coated the outside of his Mick Jagger mouth. His head was crammed into a yellow football helmet, and his long white hair jutted out the creases in the back. Matching perfectly with the color of his eyes, he was wearing a light blue football jersey over a set of thick pads, with the numbers 666 printed across the chest, and above the number was written—Team Antarctica—all in clean white letters.

The night air around them was still silent, but the Snowman's laughter continued to escalate, drowning out the sound of the Bobcat's rumbling engine. His head started bobbing like a carousel horse as he spoke. "Better dress warm, Bill. That goes for all of you. Wouldn't want you freezing to death like you are right now. Want me to warm you up a bit. Want me to make you ruuuuun." He banged his hand against the outside of the door, and then ducked his head back inside the window. He popped in the clutch. The Bobcat was on the move again.

Bill struggled to break free from the ice, but after three strong tugs, his right hand peeled away and immediately started to bleed. Several layers of skin were left sticking to the ice. His feet were next.

The Bobcat was nearly on top of him now, and the lights were back on and blinding. His feet ripped away, one at a time, like Velcro, and he took off running down the road away from the Bobcat. Trails of blood poured from the bottoms of his feet as they were reducing themselves to nubs. Streams of crimson blotted the dry ice as it dripped from his palms, some of it knotting and freezing in clots, sticking in the hair on his forearm as he held his hands in the air, waving them in desperation.

The Bobcat was close behind and gaining again, pinching and biting at his heels. The engine roared, and the Snowman's evil laughter thundered through the night air, bouncing between the walls. The wind returned. Bill had felt a slight breeze from his increase in speed, but now the wind was knocking him around, causing him to swerve painfully from side to side. He couldn't run in a straight line. Through the wind, Bill could hear the sound of distant voices crying for help. He ran and ran, afraid to look back. He could feel the rays of light shining upon him, and he could hear the metallic teeth crunching as the Bobcat closed in. He kept his focus in front of him, but then out of the corner of his eyes, he saw something moving inside of the walls on both sides of him. He looked ahead, broadening his view, and he could see that the walls, now stretching hundreds of yards into the dark sky, were shifting and moving. The voices were louder now, and they seemed to be coming from the ice on both sides of the road. The walls were moaning, calling for him, crying for help. He was afraid to look anywhere but directly in front, but the voices were enticing him, pulling him, surrounding him.

He kept running, oblivious to the pain and blood pouring from his torn hands and feet.

The Bobcat was getting closer, gaining quickly, and the voices inside of the walls were louder, calling his name.

Biiiiiiilllll.

Block it out, he thought. *Keep your eyes on the road. The walls are not moving. The walls are not talking. The walls do not need me.*

The walls *were* moving. Something frozen inside of them was squirming, shifting, fighting for position. *Biiiiiiillll.*

The rumbling of the engine. Laughter. Moving, shifting, crying voices in the walls. The metallic clinking of sharp teeth pinching at his scrambling legs and feet. He could feel its vibrations as the mouth of the Bobcat opened and closed. Bill's feet were a bloody mess, and every step taken had its own individual pain. Everything was happening so quickly. The walls were zooming past him in fast motion, much faster than he could have possibly been running. He didn't know what to do. He looked upward at the crack of darkness that could still be seen between the opening of the sky-scraping walls. The crescent moon was following him. He looked down again, focusing on the road in front of him.

Briefly, Bill glanced to his side, staring directly at the walls, and his chin sagged with fright.

People were moving inside the walls of ice, reaching and clawing to get out, fighting for position at the icy surface. Bill could see them all, thousands of fighting people, all trapped inside of the walls on both sides of the road, their arms, faces, knees, legs protruding from the walls like a bas relief. They were reaching for Bill. *Help us Bill. Help us.*

Bill stared at their frozen faces, all sad, long, oddly shaped, filled with the ultimate fear of being buried alive. They screamed for his help. *Go to the Pole. Set us free. Set us free. Set us free from him.* They screamed and clawed, but Bill didn't stop his progress down the road of pleading arms and legs. *Help meeee.* Each voice was different than the next, but they all wanted the same thing. They all wanted out.

Somehow he managed to get a lead, turning his head to get a look at the distance that separated him from the Snowman's machine, but when he turned back around he ran into a wall. The road had finally come to an end. He hadn't seen it coming. He was now trapped in every direction, and the Bobcat was only a few feet away. A frozen arm from the wall against his back reached out and grabbed him around his chest, pulling him closer to the surface. Another arm clutched his neck. The voices were now shouting into his ear. *Set us free. Go to the Pole and set us free.* Bill's heart seemed to stop beating. The lights from the Bobcat blinded him.

The grill's sharp, metallic teeth clinked together as the mouth opened and closed, opened and closed, crunching, voices calling, crunching, crunching, crunching.

"No, no, no, no, no . . ."

Andy heard Bill's voice from the other room.

"No, no, no, no, no . . ."

He ran into the bedroom. Bill was sitting on the floor with his back up against the wall, arms reaching out in front, grasping and clawing at something in the air, screaming, "No, no, no, no."

Andy touched him. Immediately Bill opened his eyes. His voice was weak. "Big, big machine . . . teeth . . . Snowman . . . so cold. Their touch . . . so cold . . . frozen people . . . screaming walls . . . They need my help." He clutched Andy, welcoming the feel of someone definitely real. "I've got to go to the Pole."

Andy helped Bill to his feet. "It's okay, Bill. It was a dream. It's all over now."

Bill looked at his hands. They had blood on them. He stopped. "Oh, God. Just like in the dream. They *are* bleeding."

Andy shook his head. "No, Bill. You ripped your bandage from your hand. You cut it yesterday on the glass. Remember?"

Bill closed his eyes, nodding slowly.

Kathy stood in the doorway, frightened. "What happened? Is he okay?"

"Just another nightmare," Andy said.

Ralph traveled the snow-clogged streets very cautiously, dodging wrecked and stranded cars. The thick and wet snow covered his windshield as fast as the wipers could clear it, making it even more difficult for Ralph to stay inside the dirty slush paths and grooves made by previous drivers. He could hardly see. The roads were so slick that, even in his 4-wheel-drive, an uneven or icy spot on the road could send him spinning, and he couldn't afford to waste any more time getting Kathleen and Mike to the house. Their delay at the police station had been inopportune enough, costing them nearly two hours of valuable time, which could mean lost lives.

He hadn't expected the station to be in total chaos when he'd arrived in the morning. His plan had been to get the Greenes and go, but as with everything the last few days, it didn't work out that way. As if the road accidents weren't enough for the police to worry about, the entire city was in a panic. Grocery stores were bare. Every shovel in the city had been bought as people tried desperately to dig themselves out. Phone lines in the police station had been ringing off the hook the entire morning, and the police officers in the building were in limited supply.

The heavy snow and ice snapped power lines. Electricity had failed in thousands of homes. Pipes burst, heaters grew cold, sending thousands of people seeking shelter elsewhere. The city was in a state of emergency.

Nine more victims had been added to the death list, and radio reports of a deranged serial killer were beginning to surface.

All along, the Snowman was watching, laughing, and waiting as his plan worked itself out beautifully. His two favorite devices were currently working together: snowfall plus chaos. It spelled pleasure.

By the time Ralph was back on the streets it was almost 1:30, two hours later than he'd told Andy he'd be back. He'd tried calling from the police station, but the lines were dead at the house. He knew that it meant one of two things: they were in trouble and the Snowman had already gotten them, or their telephone lines were out.

Checking his rearview mirror, he could see that Kathleen and Mike were sitting arm-in-arm in the seats directly behind him, fidgeting and nervously glancing out of their side windows at the snow piled high on both sides of the road. Ralph could see the fear and confusion in their eyes, and possibly even an inkling of regret, because what they were doing was very dangerous. Kathleen was determined to help, and Bill had been quite certain that she could.

Kathleen leaned forward. "How much further?"

"About six or seven miles," Ralph said, glancing into his mirror again. "At this pace though, it may take another 40 minutes to get there." The Explorer shifted slightly to the left as it hit a slick spot on the road. Ralph straightened the wheel and increased his speed before starting up the incline to the overpass. In the distance, Bill could see flashing, red, yellow, and blue lights.

The Explorer hit the top of the overpass and came to a rough stop. Ralph smacked his steering wheel with his palm. "You've got to be kidding me. What are these people doing out on the roads?"

A five-car pile-up at the bottom side of the overpass had everything blocked in both directions. Three police cars, an ambulance, and two tow-trucks were at the crash sight, but no one seemed to be taking control of the situation.

Ralph checked his watch for the tenth time. "Got your seat-belts on?" he asked.

"Yeah, why?"

Ralph checked his mirrors, then visually measured the distance he had between the Explorer and the guardrail to the right side of the road. "Time to check and see what this baby can do."

"They've been gone for four hours?" Bill asked, obviously worried. He stepped away from the bay window and sat in a maroon recliner across from Andy on the couch.

"A little more than that." Andy checked his watch. "Ralph left around nine."

"Should we try calling the police station?"

"The phone is dead."

"What?"

"Don't worry, Bill. They're probably just stuck in traffic."

Ralph shifted the 4-wheel-drive to first gear and drove up on the tall embankment. The far side of the Explorer scraped against the barely visible guardrail, giving him just enough room to clear the car in front of them. His tires spun violently, digging into the heavy snow for traction, kicking chunks of snow and slush high into the air behind them.

Ralph had only inches to spare on his side. It would be a tight fit rolling the rest of the way down the overpass, but he believed he could make it. He had to.

Passing stranded cars to his left, squeezing past the guardrail on the right, Ralph bounced and slid the Explorer towards the crash sight. He was blocked straight ahead by the cop cars and ambulance. Decision time would be short, but there wasn't much of one to make. He couldn't stop, his vehicle was tilting to the left and bouncing unevenly against the snowy embankment, and the only direction he could turn was to the right, just in front of the cop cars.

About 15 yards in front of them, an old tan Buick pulled out of line and right into Ralph's path.

The guardrail sent sparks flying as the Explorer squeezed closer to it, and now with the Buick out in front, Ralph was blocked in every direction. He honked twice, but the Buick seemed to be stuck, wheels spinning, its back side rotating in a slow circle as the car slid down the overpass.

Metallic sparks lighting up one side of the vehicle, and cars stalled on the other, Ralph looked towards the ending of the guardrail to see if he had enough room to fit through without hitting the Buick.

Pushing his foot down on the gas pedal, Ralph clutched the steering wheel and sped down the rest of the slope, closing in quickly on the Buick. In the back, Kathleen and Mike closed their eyes, arms still embraced, holding on tightly. As soon as the guardrail ended to his right, Ralph quickly turned the Explorer in that direction. The front end of the Explorer clipped the back corner of the Buick, sending it spinning into another car. The edge of the guardrail clipped the passenger's side door of the Explorer, denting it, and shifting the vehicle in mid-air as it plummeted down the rest of the embankment. The Explorer was now airborne, but only briefly. They dropped about five feet before the Explorer's grill smashed into a mound of snow towards the bottom side of the overpass. All three of them jerked forward and were caught by their seat-belts, and the vehicle continued to move.

Ralph gripped the wheel tightly again, tires spinning, struggling to make it up the incline to the open field of snow. Once over the top, Ralph was able to pick up speed again. The crash scene at the overpass was shrinking in the distance as they burrowed their way through the stranger's front yard.

Bill took off his sweatshirt and placed it on the couch. "It's getting hot in here."

Andy stood up. "It is getting warmer," he said. "I just thought of something."

"What?"

"The force we're dealing with here is totally unpredictable. That is what makes this so frightening. He could strike at any minute, and even though we might be waiting, it doesn't mean that we'd be ready."

"And?"

"Defense. I feel like we're on our heels against this Snowman guy. We know he's coming, but what can we do to prevent it?"

"I don't know."

"We take the offensive."

"How?"

"He's the Snowman. He evidently feeds off cold weather, sub-freezing temperatures, snowfall, ice. We can use the forces of opposition against him. We can turn the tide and totally surprise him when he arrives. We know he's coming, but we don't know when."

"Soon," Bill mumbled, "You can bet on that."

"And not only will we be waiting, but we'll also be ready. We can make the climate in this house the total opposite to what he's used to. We can turn up the heat as high as it will go. I saw two kerosene heaters in the back room. We can turn those on and stick them next to the front door. Candles, flames, fire. Bill, we can heat this place up."

"You think it can work?

"It's worth a shot, and it's better than waiting with a gun up our asses." Andy was interrupted by Kathy running into the room.

"What is it, Kathy?" Bill ran towards the bedroom.

"It's Amy. She's talking again."

Turning onto Bardstown Road, Ralph was only two miles from the house. The wind was frantically blowing drifts of snow against the car, making it almost impossible to keep the wheel straight. Visibility was near zero, and he had no choice but to reduce his speed. The Explorer had been damaged from their cross-country adventure, but it was still moving along. The grill was bent, the door dented, and something underneath the hood clinked and banged with every right turn; yet the vehicle slowly cruised along, passing through the snow like a tank.

Bill grabbed Amy's hands. They were clammy and cold, yet her forehead was sweaty. "Honey, it's me. I'm right here. Say something. Please, say something."

Amy's mouth parted slowly, her lips were dry and chapped. "Pi . . . Piektuk."

Bill squeezed her hands, wanting badly to try and understand why his daughter was so lost. "Amy. What is Piektuk?"

"Monster of my dreams. Snow drifter." Her voice was faint.

"What does he want with you?"

No answer.

"Amy, can you hear me? What does he want?"

"Wants to be continued. Wants rejuvenation." An icy tear formed out of the pool of water in her eye, rolling slowly down her right cheek. "Using me for ultimate union. I have that power for both sides."

"What power? Amy, tell me more."

She rocked her head from side to side. "No."

"Why not?"

"He's so cold. It hurts me, Daddy. He's so cold when he's inside of me. So cold."

Bill grabbed both of her shoulders, pressing against them gently, staring into her eyes. They were transparent and glossy. "Amy. Can you tell us what is happening here in Louisville?"

She didn't respond. Her eyes were glass pebbles. Her chest fluctuated rapidly, as tiny breaths of air escaped.

"Amy?"

She closed her eyes.

Bill stood up from the bed and looked towards Andy. "We lost her again, she—"

"I can see him," Amy screamed. "I can see him and the others."

Bill jumped towards the bed. "Who?"

"They're getting closer."

"Who is getting closer? To where?"

"My hero. My saviors. They're coming to save me. They're coming to set us all free." Then she lost consciousness again.

"What was she talking about, Bill?"

"I don't know." He found himself thinking of the skiers that had appeared in several of his dreams. He wasn't sure why, or how, but he knew that they meant something. They were somehow important to them. "I don't know, Andy," he said. "But I'm starting to get the feeling that this is never going to end."

He was right. Just then they heard someone coming in through the front door.

Kathy crouched down in the corner of the bedroom. "Oh, my God. It's him."

Bill froze.

Andy pulled his gun, slowly approaching the doorway to the bedroom. "Who is it?"

After a brief pause, someone shouted from the front room. "It's me. Ralph. I've got Kathleen and Mike with me."

Chapter 35

2:35 P.M. Antarctica

With more than a three-mile head start, Leroy had been able to distance himself by at least two miles from the rest of his team. He was five miles away from the South Pole, but his lead would not last long. He was old, tired, and physically exhausted, running now mostly on the pure adrenaline of avenging his daughter's death. Holding his hand against his chest so that he could feel his rapidly beating heart, Leroy stopped and slumped over, allowing himself a few minutes of rest. He'd slowed down considerably from his early morning pace. His aching body was quickly breaking down. He was aware that the team would soon be upon him, probably within the next few hours, but he couldn't keep going without resting. His vision was blurry, and his head ached.

Leroy shifted his goggles to his forehead, and immediately the cold wind burned his eyes. He felt pressure against his temples, as if something in the air was pushing against his head on both sides. Leroy closed his eyes, thinking, *He's here, in the air. I can feel it. He's watching me.*

When Leroy opened his eyes, he found himself staring down at his shadow. He felt disoriented, and his head was pounding, throbbing, spinning. His shadow was oddly disfigured around the shoulders, as if something was sitting on them. With his eyes still focused on his shadow, he reached up to his shoulders. Nothing was there, but strangely enough, the shadow of a bird emerged from his shadow on the ice. He watched the bird shadow as it fluttered around his own, and he could even hear the flapping of the large wings, and then it flew out of sight. Leroy raised his hands to his temples, and then he heard the voice. *Leroy. Can you hear them screaming? Come to visit your daughter? She's here.* It was the Snowman's voice. He remembered it distinctly.

Leroy fell to the ground with his skis now sticking into the air. He stared up into the bright sky. He was all alone. He looked down at the smooth ice. The reflection of the sun now blinded him, yet he continued to look down. He thought the voice was coming from the ice, or maybe from within. He rubbed his eyes. The voice came out again.

You'll be getting yours real soon old man. You all will. I don't like when people are on to me, and I hate explorers. Always have. And you've sinned both ways, Leroy. Listen carefully. Someone wants to talk to you. I'll allow it just this once.

Leroy waited. Then he heard the shrill cry of a young girl. *Daddy.*

"Honey, that you?" Leroy screamed towards the ice, the sky, and the air all around him.

Go to the Pole. Go to the Pole and set us free. Go to the Pole and watch for me.

"My daughter? Is she alive?"

The Snowman's voice answered. *Wishful thinking, old man.*

Another voice came forth, screaming from the ice. It was the voice of a young boy. *Hey, Mr. Driving Man. The snow is coming again. Set us free. Come to the Pole and look at meeee.*

Leroy jerked his head to the side, trying to clear his head of the voices. He was sure that is from where they were coming. It worked. His head stopped aching. The voices went away, and briefly, evil stopped laughing. Leroy slowly made it to his skis, balancing himself with his two ski poles. He looked in the distance towards his destination. He was ready to move again. The revenge had returned to his heart, as the sweet voice of his daughter echoed between his ears. "Revenge," he hissed, planting a ski pole in the ice, pushing off with a new-born fountain of energy. He'd skied no more than 10 yards when he caught sight of something in the distance walking towards him about 50 yards away. It appeared to be a man.

Nerves turned Leroy's limbs to jello as he first thought the figure to be the Snowman. He reached for the inside of his coat, ready to grab the special chemical weapon he'd prepared for the final showdown. For a second, he thought the time had finally come, but upon further judgment, the man he was seeing was too weak to be the Snowman. The man in the distance was wobbling like a drunk, arms outstretched, and then suddenly he fell to the ice. Leroy set out after him.

The man was large, wearing white pants, black boots, and a green shirt. It appeared to be a uniform of some kind, but regardless, the man was severely under-dressed and badly frostbitten. His forehead, cheeks, ears, and neck were a bluish-gray. His lips were purple, cracked, and crusted with dried blood. Small patches of ice and sprinkles of snow clung to his roughly grown beard and wild, shaggy eyebrows. The man wore no hat, coat, or gloves, and was breathing his final breaths, struggling to speak. "I …I…kill."

Leroy squatted closer to the man, clutching onto his shoulders. "What is it?"

The man's swollen, blue hands reached towards Leroy. The flesh around the fingers was cracking and turning black, the fingernails peeling off. Leroy turned his head away from them, returning his gaze to the man's face.

He spoke again. "Evil …m …man. K..kill …killed… th..them all."

"Where?"

"Am…Amundsen…Scott … c..cave."

"Amundsen-Scott Station?"

The man nodded.

"What cave?"

The man coughed, raising his chest up from the ice. Blood and spittle emerged at the corners of what was left of his lips. He closed his eyes and his chest stopped moving.

"What cave?" Leroy asked again.

The man didn't answer. Leroy found no pulse. He checked the wrist and the neck. Nothing. The man was dead. Leroy looked at his green shirt and saw the letters SCARE on the front. "Oh, no," he whispered. Just under the letters, he saw the man's name stitched in cursive—David Johnson.

David was the last proof that Leroy needed to be sure that the Snowman was here. Leroy got to his skis again and set off for the Amundsen-Scott Station and the South Pole.

On the other side of the world, the Snowman was ready. After killing nine more at an apartment complex on Dixie Highway during the morning hours, he was ready to make his move. The snowfall was close to 20 inches and counting. The center of the storm was now directly over the

Louisville area. It too was ready. The atmosphere was perfect. After so many years, the time had finally come, the setting was right, and the girl was ready.

The Snowman stepped out into the back parking lot at River City High School. The snow was now up to his knees, and it was falling so hard that no one could see more than a foot or two in front of them. The girl would be his eyes. She and the Pole would lead the way. The Snowman lifted his face towards the sky and opened his mouth, filling it with his white pleasure. He swallowed it and then smiled. "Here I come. Lead the way, my love. Be my guide."

The Snowman took off running, plowing through the snow-filled parking lot with ease.

Amy would be his guide. She would lead the way.

Chapter 36

5:00 P.M. Highlands
21 Inches

With the thermostat now set at 87 degrees, the kerosene heaters working by the front door, and as many candles as they could gather spread throughout the house, they hoped their plan of defense would be enough to at least slow the Snowman's power when he arrived. Fans kept the hot air near the ceiling in circulation. The temperature was almost unbearable, but they toughed it out. They were willing to try anything, and it now looked like their hopes would be pinned on this last line of defense because Kathleen's attempts at hypnosis were not working on Amy.

Kathleen was not an expert hypnotist. She was knowledgeable and quite successful at the technique, but this particular case was much different that anything she'd done before and very unusual.

Off and on for the past two hours, she'd tried to tap into Amy's mind, but there was some kind of barrier that was denying her penetration. For the first time in all her years of work, Kathleen was discouraged to the point that she was ready to throw in the towel. The Snowman's hold on Amy was too hard to crack, and seemingly getting stronger as she drifted further and further into unconsciousness. Kathleen had her professional prognosis—patient beyond help.

Bill watched nervously over her shoulder until Kathleen had no more techniques to try. He couldn't help but be pessimistic. Everything they'd tried had failed, and Amy was showing no signs of improvement. If anything, she was gradually getting worse.

Kathleen stood up. "I'm spent. I really don't know what to do, Bill. I've tried everything I know, but nothing is working. I can't even get a reaction out of her. Maybe if I had more time, I could get something achieved, but she's just in too deep for me to help her. Too much pressure."

Bill ran his hands across his unshaven face and chin. "I guess it's in God's hands now."

"I hope he's got strong hands."

Bill paused. "I wonder what they could do for her in a hospital."

"There's only one way to find out."

"I know, but on second thought, I'm almost afraid to move her. I know she's in bad shape, but I feel we'd all be safer here. I wouldn't want to take her out there. Now that I think of it, he'd have the advantage in the snow. The roads are probably impassable by now anyway." Bill scratched his head, yawning, looking towards Kathy who was asleep on a chair in the corner of the room. "Poor girl. She shouldn't be involved in this mess. I just met her yesterday for Christ's sake, and now this."

"Bill, none of us should be involved in this. We didn't ask for this to happen, but it did, and we have to deal with it now. We are the victims. Don't blame yourself for any of it, don't do it."

"She's so innocent, though. Why did she insist on staying? Why didn't she leave? At least then she'd be out of harm's way."

"I don't think anyone in this city is out of harm's way. But she's strong. She wanted to be with her best friend. We can't deal with the what-ifs, Bill. This is what we've got, and unfortunate as it is, she's in the game with us now."

Bill looked through the bedroom doorway and into the living room. Mike, Ralph, and Andy were talking about something as they approached the bedroom. Ralph entered first, with Mike and Andy following behind. "Any change?"

"Nothing," Kathleen grunted.

"If the Snowman is going to get to us, I think we'll be ready. . . " Ralph was suddenly cut off. Amy was screaming.

"But he's already coming," she yelled, eyes wide open again.

All eyes were on the bed.

"The white enemy, he's coming, and you can't stop him." Amy's voice sounded frightened, but confident. She quickly sat up in bed, resting her head against the flimsy, wooden headboard. Her arms stretched out in front of her, reaching for things that weren't visible to the rest of them.

She was pale and trembling all over. Her arms were moving in an in-and-out motion, as if showing someone the way to her bed. She was a puppet, with no control over her actions, and the Pole was pulling her strings.

Bill grabbed Amy's outstretched hands, but she pushed him away.

"Follow my lead," Amy said.

The Snowman hurdled through the deep snow, knees kicking high in the air, eyes focused ahead. Now only a few miles away from the safe house in the Highlands, the Snowman was running with incredible speed, and Amy was leading the way. The Pole was their guide, their instincts, the internal map that linked them together. The Snowman ran hard and fast, not even knowing the direction. He followed her voice as it whispered to him through the wind and blinding snowfall, and he ran for his goal.

Suddenly, the Snowman lowered himself into the snow until he was totally buried beneath its surface. He blended in with it, and then they became one. He was now the snow. He heard the voice.

Follow my lead.

Up above, Zoro followed, gliding through the silent downpour like a black kite.

"Keep running straight my love. Follow my lead," Amy cried out. "I see the power lines. Follow the path of the power lines. Where they go, you go. Where they turn, you turn."

"What is she talking about?" Mike asked.

Kathleen raised her finger to her mouth. "Sssshhh. Don't interrupt her."

Amy continued. "You're doing fine. That's it. Follow the path of the power lines. Like the electricity running through those lines, you can smell my current. You can smell the flowers, can't you? Follow my lead."

The Snowman burrowed through the snow like an underground train.

"Watch the power lines, and follow. When they turn, you turn, and listen. Follow my lead."

The Snowman continued on. He sensed the power lines above, following their course. When they turned, he turned. One with the snow, he moved swiftly and quickly, listening to the voice that was his guide.

"Ralph," Andy barked. "She's leading him right to us. Can't you see that? She's leading him to the house."

"Grab your gun, Andy. Don't let anything inside of this room. It's getting colder in here, and . . . the air is changing."

"It's only around the corner now," Amy said, "Turn right. Only a hundred yards away." Amy began to tremble. Her eyes rolled back in her head.

The air was getting thicker, polluted with a freezing presence that was making it difficult to breathe as evil seeped into the house, bringing its stench with it.

Amy looked possessed. Her head lolled from side to side on the fluffy pillow. "Not much further," she yelled. "Follow the lines."

Andy pulled his gun and motioned for everyone to move to the back corner of the room.

Bill stayed on the bed with Amy, trying to grab hold of her, but her arms evaded him.

The light in the room flickered, and started to dim.

Kathy screamed. Mike held her. Kathleen held Mike.

"Fifty yards away."

"Oh, shit." Andy closed and locked the door to the bedroom. He and Ralph stood in front of the bed, guns poised, ready, and pointed towards the door, preparing for the Snowman's entrance. "Something's happening. The air, it's . . . it's bad, real bad."

Bill finally grabbed hold of Amy. She went limp in his arms, continuing to mumble, whispering into the chilling air. "Forty yards away."

"He's coming," Andy screamed, adrenaline pumping.

The Snowman hurried on.

Forty yards away.

The snow, it smiled, singing, "Over the hills and through the snow, to Amy's safe house we go."

His speed increased. He felt her presence, and smelled it. He listened.

Twenty yards.

"Twenty yards."

Bill pulled her closer. She was no longer resisting his touch.

The bed shook and rattled, bouncing on the floor. Bill held tight. The door started to shake loose of its hinges.

The air was closing in all around them, freezing, suffocating.

"Twelve-thirty-one," Amy whispered. "House number twelve-thirty-one."

The Snowman materialized and quickly stormed out of the snow. He jumped on the porch, looking at the side of the door.

1231.

He tore the front door off and threw it down. He entered the house. He felt the change in temperature immediately, and it slowed him down, drained him, but nothing was going to completely stop him from claiming his ultimate goal, especially now that the goal was calling for him from the next room.

The lights went out, and the entire room shook.

"Oh, God." Andy gripped his gun with both hands, pointing it to the general direction of the bedroom door.

Ralph did the same. "Ready, Andy?"

"Ready."

Amy let out one last cry before losing consciousness again.

Bill held onto Amy as the bed danced and rattled. Even though the room was dark, he closed his eyes. He could visualize the Snowman running towards the room, and just like in his dream, the Snowman was wearing the clown face and the Team Antarctica football jersey. He could see him running full-steam ahead, and the bedroom was the end-zone. He was charging like a bull.

Touchdown. Touchdown Antarctica.

Bill opened his eyes. The Snowman wasn't wearing a football helmet or jersey. He wasn't even inside the room. The darkness was pressing in on the room, and the door was shaking violently. They could feel something coming from the other side. A sliver of light flashed under the door, and briefly the room was lit.

The Snowman charged into the bedroom door, easily knocking it to the floor.

The room went dark again. Ralph and Andy were knocked to the floor as the surroundings continued to shake. The atmosphere in the room had changed. The darkness was different than before, and the air was absolutely silent. Bill thought he was sitting on the bed, but he couldn't tell for sure because he couldn't feel it, and he couldn't feel Amy lying next to him. He felt like he was floating in mid-air, touching nothing. Mike, Kathleen, and Kathy, still hiding in what used to be the corner of the bedroom, also could feel nothing around them. They were all floating in a dark room of freezing nothingness where all senses seemed to be lost.

Only Amy could see and hear. Only Amy could feel. She was in Iceville again, and finally it was real. She was lying on a bed of ice with the Snowman looming over her. She couldn't feel her father's touch beside her anymore. They were all only feet from her bed, but it seemed like miles because none of them could hear her painful yelling. Then she heard his voice, and it was just like the voice in her dreams. She could tell now that she wasn't dreaming. *Don't bother screaming, Amy. Remember, all voices are mute in Iceville. I'm all you got.*

His bright blue eyes were pulsating as his body was filled with sexual energy. She tried to free herself from his powerful grip, but he was just too strong. She was naked, and his cold hands sent chilling shock waves throughout her entire body with every touch. She felt wind, a breeze, his breeze all around her, inside of her. She felt the power closing in on her, suffocating her just as the darkness had done before the Snowman had entered the bedroom. The Snowman laughed his evil laugh, gently running his icy fingers down the sides of her face. He smoothed one of his hands down her side, between, through and over her breasts. Her nipples were erect, not from pleasure, but from her fear and the freezing temperatures. Straddling his legs over her quivering hips, he bent his head down to hers, whispering his breeze into her ear. *Rejuvenation.* His long hair tickled her cheeks. *Keep the family alive. Give birth to fire and ice.* His breath was stale but chilling, as his mouth and cold lips found her own. His eyes were hypnotic and piercing. He placed his right hand under the small of her back, and immediately goose bumps scattered across her bare flesh. Gently, he lifted her dead weight from the ice, pressing her body against his chest.

This won't hurt a bit.

Again, Amy screamed. Her nightmare had finally become real.

The room was freezing, and they were still lost in its darkness, waiting, floating, trying to feel anything around them. They could not hear each other's voices as they desperately tried shouting to one another, but they could hear the faint voices of others somewhere off in the distant darkness. The first was a voice of a young boy.

Hey Mr. Driving Man.

The boy's voice was followed by an entire army of voices, all moaning, groaning, and repeating the same thing in unison. *Go to the Pole. Set us free. Go to the Pole and set us free.*

Bill wondered if he was the only one that could hear the voices. He wasn't. They could all hear them, loudly and clearly as they whispered into the room with the slight wind that was swirling. *Where are the voices coming from?* Bill asked himself. *Who are these people? Where is my daughter? She's right next to me, but I can't see, feel, or hear her. What is happening to her?* To know would have driven him to insanity. *They are the lost people,* Bill thought. *They are somehow channeling us through the Snowman's entrance. His entrance into the room must have opened up some line of communication from here to there. And the people, who are they? Are they dead or alive? Lost or forgotten? How could the Snowman allow them to make contact with us?* Another voice shouted at them from the darkness. *Quickly, while he is distracted. Time is running thin. Come to the Pole and set us free.*

The voice Bill heard next was very familiar. It was the voice of a woman. It was Mary. *Bill? Bill? Are you there?*

"Yes. Mary? Is it you? Is it really you?"

Yes. It is me.

"Where are you? Are you alive?"

I am dead Bill, but you can still save me. You can still save us all. You can help us to rest in peace. Set our souls free. Set us free from him.

"Mary. I don't understand."

Hurry. There is a crew already on the way. You've seen them in your dreams. The skiers. Bill. Amy sees them too, her saviors, her hero. Now you and your friends can join them. Time is running short. I've got to go now. I know I loved you, Bill. Set me free so that I can feel and love you again. Right now we all feel nothing.

"Mary," Bill called, his voice echoing in the darkness. "Don't go."

Hey Mr. Janitor Man, the young boy called out.

"Who's that?"

I'm Bobby, and I'm dead too. Help me just like you did in the hallway. Protect me again from the bully. Your Dad's van needs cleaning. Here he is right next to me. You can ask him yourself.

"What?"

Son.

"Dad?"

Bill. Come to the Pole.

"I don't understand. Where? What Pole?"

No time for questions. He's almost finished. He's about to cut us off. I think he can hear me now. His voice was hurried. *Look. You've got to go to the school. The door lies in the sch—*

Their line of communication was suddenly cut off.

"The school? But why?"

No response. The voices were gone. His wife, father, the little boy, and all the desperate voices were gone. Or did they exist at all? Bill didn't know. It very well could have been the Snowman playing tricks on him again.

The room had stopped shaking, and the wind was gone.

The pressure of the air was returning to normal, and the temperature was on the climb again. The span of darkness had ended, and the lights were back on but still flickering in and out. The tension in the room was decreasing as everything seemed to be returning to normal. But everyone had heard the voices. It wasn't just Bill.

The Snowman's evil presence was gone, but it had been real, and the seed was now planted.

An obvious mystery remained in the room, on the bed.

Amy was gone.

Chapter 37

5:10 P.M. Antarctica
3 Miles To Go

L oreda was closest to Marvin when the earthquake started, and as soon
as the ice had started to rumble, she fell. That is when, only 10 feet
away, she saw the ice open up and Marvin going down. It was a huge,
dark, air-sucking hole that pulled the Colonel down with ease. At first
Loreda thought he was gone, but then she noticed his fingers clinging to
the edge of the crevasse. She screamed for help, but the rumbling ice was
so loud that nobody could hear her. Realizing she was on her own, she
started crawling towards the opening in the ice, and even that was difficult. The skis made any movement awkward, and coupled with the vibrating land, her progress towards the crevasse was very gradual. She had
no idea how Marvin was able to hold on, but she kept her eyes focused on
the edge of the crevasse, and his fingers were still there, clenched and
digging into what little he could grab of the ice. "Hold on, Marvin," she
shouted, slipping her skis off, crawling across the ice. "I'm coming." She
saw that the crevasse was at least 30 yards long and growing, quickly
splintering and cracking across the ice.

She touched his fingers and slipped both of her hands around his wrist.
She pulled herself up to the edge. The crevasse was only about six feet
wide, but just like the one from yesterday, it seemingly had no bottom,
only darkness reaching downward.

Marvin looked up to her and she could see the strain in his eyes, through
his foggy goggles, surprised himself that he was still alive and somehow

holding on. But he was losing his hold. His fingers were slipping. He was heavy, still wearing his back pack and skis, and pulling her down, inch by inch, into the crevasse's mouth, but she refused to let go. She couldn't let him die. Not now. Not on their last day. They'd been less than an hour away from the South Pole and quickly gaining ground on Leroy. Before the earthquake had started they'd seen him skiing off in the distance. It was only a matter of time.

"Marvin." She moved her grip down closer to his forearm. "Reach me with your other arm."

"Can't," he yelled.

She could barely hear him.

"My shoulder. I think it's broken." He dropped down further, pulling Loreda to the edge. "Let go."

Then the quake ended, and the ice stopped shaking. Except for the wind, the air was silent. "Help," Loreda screamed. "Somebody help us."

The edge of the crevasse was now pressing against her chest. As Marvin's weight forced her down, she tightened her leg muscles to stay on top.

"Loreda. Let go." He took a couple of deep breaths. "Too heavy . . . let go . . . pulling you down."

The edge of the crevasse was now against Loreda's stomach, and her grip was slipping on his arm.

Marvin looked down at the blackness of inner-Antarctica below and then looked up at Loreda. He could see her determination, but he couldn't bring her down with him. He wouldn't allow the death of two. He had to get loose from her grip. He braced his skis against the wall and pushed off so that their arms began to sway.

"Marvin, no. What are you doing?" She slipped down even more, trying to find the strength to tighten her grip.

On the swing back towards the wall, Marvin used all his remaining strength to fling his arm and hers against the wall off ice just below the edge. It worked. Their arms crashed into the wall of ice and immediately her grip loosened on his wrist.

Marvin dropped. She stretched for him, but he was too far out of reach. She looked into the darkness and saw him waving to her. Then his body vanished. Marvin was gone. Unlike Gabe from the day before he was not coming back.

"I'm sorry," she whispered, slipping, slipping. And then she began to fall. *Nice try Colonel,* she thought, *but it looks like I'll be joining you anyway.* She closed her eyes.

"Loreda," someone shouted.

Someone gripped her right ankle. "I'm alive," she whispered, opening her eyes. Out of the corner of her eye she saw someone pulling her up. He was strong. His goggles were off and his long red hair was blowing in the wind.

The others were supporting Eric on one arm while he pulled Loreda out with the other. Seconds earlier and they may have been able to save Marvin's life, too.

Loreda started to cry. "I tried," she said. "I just couldn't hold on."

Eric wiped her tears away. "I know."

She forced a weak smile and then started crying again.

Holding her in his arms, Eric joined her.

Colonel Marvin Shard was dead.

Chapter 38

5:30 P.M. Highlands
22 Inches

Bill and Ralph were both hustling frantically through the front room for their coats. Andy was dressed and ready to go, staring out the window at the falling snow. "What door was he talking about?"

"I'm not sure," Bill said. "But the sooner we get there, the quicker we find out."

"What if he's sending us on a wild goose chase?" Ralph asked.

Bill shook his head. "He's not. It all makes sense. The school being so cold, The Dungeon, the feather inside the shop. Everything leads to the school. It all seems to have started somewhere inside of the school. I don't know how, but if we hurry, hopefully we'll be able to find something before anything happens to Amy."

Ralph turned to Kathy. "I know she's your best friend, and you want to make sure she's okay, but we can't let you come with us. It's too big of a risk, and we don't want you getting hurt."

"I'll stay here with her," said Kathleen. "I'm sure we'll be safe. He's not coming back."

Mike grabbed his coat and quickly put it on. "I'm going too."

"No," Bill said. "It's too dangerous."

"I'm aware of that, but I'm still going."

"But Mike."

"But nothing. It's my school. If something this serious is going to happen there, I'm going to take part in it. I'm going to help bring Amy back."

Kathleen was now more concerned than ever. "Are you sure?"

"As long as you are okay with it."

"Just be careful. Please, be careful. Bring Amy back."

"I will. We all will."

Kathleen cleared her tears and locked the door. She joined Kathy over by the bay window so that they could watch them pull away from the house. Kathleen watched as the vehicle's headlights bobbed and bounced over the rough terrain and finally out of sight. It was the last time she would see her husband alive.

Ever since the incident in her father's house the previous day, Amy had been unconscious in Iceville. Things were finally starting to change. Her nightmares had become reality, and now afterwards, she could feel the butterflies swirling within. Something was changing inside of her, as well as all around her. The crying voices were gone. The Snowman's face was gone. His domineering body, gone. The ice and snow were gone. The air was changing and the wind was decreasing. It was still cold, but not as severe as before. Anything felt warmer than her nightmares, where everything was surrounded by ice. She would always feel the ice and remember what it was like to have it inside of her.

For now, everything in her world was black, and she could smell again. It was a new kind of smell that wasn't normal to her in Iceville. Her head felt heavy. She was upside down, her body bouncing up and down, and she felt a large hand holding her just below her buttocks. Struggling to open her eyes, she was slowly returning to the real world. She sensed the Snowman's presence, but couldn't see him. *Where am I?* she thought. *I feel like I'm moving.* She felt a breeze that ruffled her loose hair, and she heard the crunching of footsteps down below, running footsteps in the snow. Her fingertips were freezing and wet. The cold hand was still pressing against her upper thighs as she continued to bounce against something. She could feel something pressing and pushing against her stomach.

Finally, she opened her eyes. She was slumped over the Snowman's shoulder, staring down into the snow as he ran. His boots kicked chunks of snow into the air, and her hands and hair were dragging against the wet surface. Snow flew into her eyes and hair, but she did nothing to let the Snowman know that she was conscious. *Where is he taking me?* Carefully, not wanting to draw his attention, she looked to the side and noticed they were now in the back parking lot at River City High School.

Unlike the morning and early afternoon, the roads were free of traffic. The only cars were the ones left stranded and buried. Because of the conditions, Andy was not able to go more than 15 miles per hour, even with the 4-wheel drive. He could barely see the road in front of him, straining to see past the front of the hood, as his windshield wipers thumped rapidly from side to side. The front left headlight had been broken in the collision with the Buick, so the light coming from the Explorer was far from sufficient.

Slowly, they were plowing their way towards the school, but even on foot, the Snowman was increasing his lead.

Amy was freezing, and it didn't take long to figure out why. She was wearing a soft, silky white nightgown and nothing beneath it. No shoes, socks, or anything to protect her from the cold. The Snowman's pace slowed as he approached the back doors. The drifts were so high against the side of the building that the doors were all but hidden. The Snowman jumped up the snow-covered steps and slipped through the doors, which were already propped open with a small chunk of ice that he'd left there in the morning. He stepped inside.

Pausing on the middle platform, the Snowman looked up the flight of stairs to the gym lobby, thinking that he had heard something. After convincing himself that he hadn't, he started down the lower flight of stairs, past the cafeteria on the right, and towards the boiler room to his left.

Where is he taking me? Amy thought, as her head smacked against his back with every turn he took. She wanted to shake loose and run, but she wasn't confident about her strength. Also, she had nowhere to go. He would catch her within seconds if she tried to go anywhere.

Walking past two storage rooms, the Snowman opened the door to the boiler room and stepped inside. The heat was on, and it hit him hard. He stumbled, leaned against the railing and slowly made his way towards the shop.

Once he was inside the shop, he paused. He felt disoriented and now more than ever, craved the chilling winds of home.

Amy felt his arm slide down from her thighs to the bend in her knees. His grip loosened and relaxed.

The doors to The Dungeon were only 10 feet away. He took a deep breath, inhaling the cold air. It refreshed him.

"Almost there," he whispered. "Almost there."

Almost where? Amy thought. *Almost where?*

Chapter 39

About 100 yards away from the front parking lot, the Explorer got stuck for the final time. The snow was just too high. They would have to walk the rest of the way. Jumping out, each one carried a flashlight. The falling snow was beautifully silent, a perfect disguise to hide the intensity of the battle they were about to fight.

Andy grabbed a blue duffel bag from the back and jumped knee-deep into the snow beside the Explorer. Walking would be difficult. Andy was the tallest and the strongest, so he led the way, plowing a path for the others to follow. After a few minutes, his legs were tired and his jeans were soaked all the way up to his thighs, but he refused to slow down. His flashlight was a tiny beacon shining through the downpour of snow, and eventually the front of the school was in sight. In the distance, the building looked like an old deserted castle. With snow drifts piled 20 to 30 feet high against its walls, the school was virtually buried.

The heat from the boiler room was what Amy craved, but as they approached The Dungeon's doors, the heat was long gone, and its effects were dwindling. Amy began to shiver. The air coming from behind the doors was colder than the air outside. After climbing the four steps leading up to The Dungeon, the Snowman opened the two doors and was greeted by an unpleasant surprise. Desks, and lots of them, were blocking the entrance. Something had caused them to topple over. The Snowman knew who it was, or what it was. The Pole had told him the forces of opposition were working against them. He would win though, and he would have to take the advantage.

The Snowman growled and gritted his teeth. He looked at the mound of desks and then at Amy. Swiftly, he jumped down the four steps and rested Amy on top of the nearest workshop table. He placed her down gently on a cushion of sawdust and wood chips that covered the top surface.

She made her body go limp, and she forced her eyes closed. She felt like a doll the way he moved her around, but it seemed as if she'd fooled him. He hadn't learned of her consciousness as of yet. She moved as little as possible on the table, waiting for him to do something, wondering if he was still standing above her. It was too risky for her to open her eyes and check, so she didn't.

Her question was answered when she felt his hard, cracked lips press against hers. It took everything in her not to make a face in disgust. She wanted to spit in his face, but resisted the urge, thinking and hoping that the kiss would be all he'd do to her. She prayed that he was finished.

He wasn't, not yet.

His cold hand brushed against her right ankle. She felt something swirling inside of her. Deep inside her stomach, something seemed to be moving around. *What is happening to me? What is going on?* It felt as if her stomach was growling in hunger, but it was a slightly different and much stronger feeling. Something was alive in there, growing, kicking. The impregnation had taken place. The seed had been deposited, and it felt like it was cannibalizing her from the inside out.

His hand slid up to her calf and then to her knee. She was freezing, and his hand felt like a slab of ice against her exposed flesh. Now both of his hands were touching her above her knees, and they were ascending. *Please stop, please stop, please stop,* she pleaded in her mind. His hands were two loose glaciers floating up the smooth ocean surface of her body.

Please stop, please stop, please stop, please stop . . .

His hands stopped moving. Amy relaxed, but kept her eyes closed.

The Snowman whispered, "Don't worry my love. This is just a minor hitch in my giddy-up. I'll have the path cleared in a second."

She heard him move away from the table, again climbing the four stairs to the dungeon. She sighed in relief, despite the pain in her stomach. At least now he was away from the table, and his hands were no longer touching her.

The Snowman grabbed the first desk and hurled it against the side wall of the shop. As he lifted the next one from the pile, it created a landslide of desks down the stairs, most of them bouncing against his thighs and shins before hitting the ground. He kicked them out of the way and tossed another desk against the far wall, smashing it into several pieces.

Slowly, his strength was returning.

Amy opened her eyes and craned her neck upward so that she could see the entrance to The Dungeon.

Crash. Another desk broke against the wall.

Quietly, Amy leaned up on her elbows, watching as the Snowman picked through the mound of desks. She was fortunate now not to be wearing shoes. Her getaway would be more silent with bare feet. He wasn't looking her way and wasn't aware of her movement. Now was her chance.

After nearly 20 minutes of trudging through the snow, they finally made it to the school's front entrance. Snow had piled halfway up the two glass doors so they had to shovel it away with their hands before opening them.

Mike's nerves were finally catching up to him as he questioned his macho decision of coming along. He felt like turning back around and making a run for the Explorer, but he couldn't even see the vehicle anymore in the distance, and there was no way he was going to set out alone to look for it. He'd barely made it this far with Andy leading the way.

Together, Andy and Ralph pulled the door open so that the rest of them could slide through the opening and into the foyer. Once they were all inside, Andy pulled the door closed. Kicking off clumps of loose snow from their pants and coats, they walked through the second set of double doors and into the school's main hallway.

Their boots squeaked on the terrazzo floor as the snow melted into puddles.

Andy knelt down, resting his knee in a melting clump of slush, and dropped his duffel bag to the floor. He unzipped the bag and pulled out two revolvers, handing one to Bill and the other to Mike. He and Ralph were already armed.

Bill lodged the gun under his belt. "We ready?"

"I guess so," Mike mumbled, staring fearfully at his weapon. He'd never held a gun before and wasn't quite sure that he liked the feeling.

Andy stood up. "To The Dungeon?"

"That's where all the clues are leading," Ralph said, starting down the main hallway. "Let's go get him."

The four of them started to run.

The race was on.

With the entrance to The Dungeon clear and his power fully restored, the Snowman closed his eyes and deeply inhaled the welcome Antarctic wind as it blew into the shop. His chest expanded as his body tingled with electricity. Staring into the dark and cluttered first room of The Dungeon, he said, "Amy, we're going home." He turned around excitedly, but his mood quickly changed when he noticed that Amy was no longer lying on the table. Her footprints were visible in the wood chips that covered the concrete floor.

Jumping off the small set of stairs, he glanced around the room, checking under the tables, in every corner, behind the cabinets. She was gone, and the Snowman had been fooled. The Snowman stormed out of the shop, stopping just outside the doors as he felt the heat coming from the boiler room. The mixture of hot and cold temperature was making him weak. Next to the shop doors he saw a large metal box mounted on the wall. After breaking the tiny lock on the bottom, he opened the front panel, and dozens of buttons and switches stared him in the face. Within seconds, the entire school was without electricity. No light, and more importantly for the Snowman, no more heat.

Unable to move faster than a crawl, Amy had only gotten to the top of the stairwell when the lights went out. She was exhausted, and it had taken nearly everything in her to make it up the two flights of stairs. Her stomach was very unstable as something continued to move around inside of it.

A cool draft swirled along the rubber-coated steps, turning her bare feet to ice. She felt numb, just like in her nightmares. She rested inside the lobby to the gym, leaning against the gym doors. With her arms folded tightly against her chest, she shivered, closing her eyes, hoping that the Snowman would not come after her for a while. She felt so alone, but it was better than being with him. Her plan of escape had been foiled by her inability to run. The thing inside of her was draining her energy, using it to grow, to feed, to live. She was relieved to escape the Snowman, but she realized that she had no place to go. Her only option was to find a place and hide, but first she had to rest. She didn't have the strength to move anymore. She raised her knees up to her drooping head and held herself.

She started to cry. She felt the tears coming, and they were welcome. They made her feel real in a time that everything else in her life was changing and unpredictable. She'd lost all hope of returning to her former self, especially now that she had something from the Snowman growing inside of her. She'd never felt dirtier in her life.

Then she heard a noise, a clicking of a door handle straight across the lobby. Thin, flashing lights shone through the small glass panels in the wooden double doors.

Someone was coming from the main hallway.

Andy was the first one through the doors, with Bill following closely behind. He was the first to see Amy hunkered down in the corner of the lobby, and he immediately ran to her. "Amy."

She looked up, smiling at the sound of her father's voice. She struggled to stand up, but she couldn't do it on her own. Bill helped her to her feet and walked her towards the doors that they'd just entered separating the lobby from the main hallway. "Where is he?"

"Downstairs."

"The Dungeon?"

"He was, but I managed to get away." She closed her eyes and then slumped down in Bill's arms.

"What is it, Amy?"

"It's him. He's strong again."

"Again? When wasn't he strong?"

"In the boiler room. That's how I got away."

Bill glanced around the lobby. They were all looking at him. "So he's intolerant of the heat?"

Amy nodded, wincing in obvious pain. "My stomach. It hurts. Something is moving."

She leaned forward, pressing her hands against her belly.

Bill hugged her tightly.

Mike looked around the lobby, nervously gripping the gun in his sweaty hands. "We better get out of here."

"The boiler room," Ralph said. "Let's get her down to the boiler room. The heat can work as our shield."

Bill looked up. "It didn't work in the house. Why should it here?"

"Regardless," Mike answered, "We need to hide." He stopped suddenly. "You hear that?"

"What?"

Whoop whoop whoop.

Mike walked towards the cafeteria stairwell, standing just in front of the gym doors. "Sounds like wings."

Andy lifted his gun. "Mike, back away from that stairwell."

Whoop whoop whoop.

Mike heard the wings again. He smelled something bad in the air. The sound of thick, powerful wings surrounded him, and then out of nowhere, a large black bird stormed into the lobby from the dark depths of the stairwell, targeting in on Mike's head.

"No, not the wings," Amy screamed.

Zoro appeared to the rest of them.

"Mike," Andy shouted, "Duck."

Mike didn't duck. Instead, he turned in the direction of the stairwell as Zoro grabbed his face, forcing him against the lobby's back wall. Mike's scream was muffled by the feathers, as his head was lost inside the flapping wings.

Andy stepped closer, wanting to shoot, but waiting for a clear shot. He didn't want to take the chance of hitting Mike.

When Mike slammed into the back wall, he saw stars, or at least it seemed like stars, as blotches of light from their flashlights penetrated through the motion of the bird's flapping wings. The wings were huge and powerful, creating a darkness that was eternal, surreal, and the red eyes focused in on the kill. Mike felt something wet running down the sides of his face, and when he screamed, he gargled it as it flowed into his mouth.

Through the fluttering wings, he was given glimpses of the lobby around him, but in the end it was all darkness. He couldn't breathe . . .

Whoop whoop whoop.

. . . the wings . . . were . . .

Whoop whoop whoop.

. . . surrounding . . . suffocating . . . blinding . . .

Whoop . . . digging . . . *whoop whoop* . . . grinding into his flesh and bald scalp. He felt himself slipping down the wall, getting colder, as his life poured out of his gaping wounds. The bird chirped and screamed loudly as its rough, leathery wings covered Mike's torso.

Whoop whoop whoop.

Bill covered Amy's eyes with his arm, moving her to the far corner of the lobby.

Andy still couldn't see what was going on. He couldn't see Mike's face, so he was afraid to fire at the bird. He couldn't let it eat Mike alive though, so he charged at it and delivered a punch to its body. His fist was momentarily lost in its wings, but he knew that he'd connected. He heard something crack on impact. Zoro was thrown back against the wall, but recovered and quickly flew into the lobby. Mike's body leaned forward, crashing face down on the floor.

In the lobby, Zoro seemed dizzy, crashing into two of the windows, circling the ceiling, frantically searching for his freedom. Andy followed his flight with his gun.

Andy fired, clipping Zoro in the right wing. It made a clear hole but didn't stop its flight. Zoro started to fly towards Bill and Amy. Andy fired again. The bullet missed, but it sent the bird retreating to the back corner of the lobby, landing on top of a Coca-Cola machine.

Perched high up in the air, Zoro watched Andy approach. He had his gun pointed upward at the bird, waiting for the right shot, stopping about 10 feet away from the machine to focus in on his aim.

Zoro's eyes were two raging balls of fire, and the corner of the lobby was glowing, sparkling with brilliant colors of red, yellow, and orange. His talons clicked and scraped like knives against the metal surface of the machine. His head jerked quickly from side to side, tilting, turning, staring at the gun, waiting to strike. Then Zoro lowered his head and extended his wings.

Andy eased back on the trigger, softly, but not yet enough to fire. Zoro leaped off the Coke machine, flying straight towards Andy, his beak was wide open and ready for the attack. Andy stood his ground, raising his gun slightly into the bird's path. When Zoro was only a foot away, Andy shoved the gun inside its open beak and fired two quick shots.

Zoro exploded like a bomb. The head flew backwards towards the Coke machine, splattering against the Mellow-Yellow button. The lower half of the bird disintegrated into a cloud of feathers and bones, scattering all over Andy and the near walls. Torn and shredded feathers drifted slowly to the floor.

Ralph rolled Mike over on his back. He looked up when he saw that Andy had killed the bird.

"How is he?" Andy asked.

"He's dead."

Chapter 40

Leroy stared up at the aluminum geodesic dome in disbelief. A building. A man-made structure. He hadn't seen one in nearly two months. He couldn't believe he was finally here, only 400 yards away from the geographical bottom of the earth. He'd traveled all day long at a rapid pace despite his age, driven by the desire to confront his daughter's killer, and finally the time had come. After remembering what David Johnson had told him, the dome no longer held the same excitement, and he was afraid to go inside.

The wandering man could have been delirious, but the words stuck in Leroy's mind nevertheless. *Killed them all. The cave. I kill.* He had to be ready. The Snowman could be around any corner, behind any door.

After taking off his skis, Leroy entered the dome. The silence inside was deafening. Everything seemed dead, yet his senses were stimulated. Living in the Antarctic landscape and surroundings for so long, the artificial nature of the station was powerful and weird. The smoothness of the floor, the artificial light, the sense of heat, the smell of people, diesel fuel, and food—everything seemed foreign. He'd forgotten what it was like to smell, to see, and to feel.

He checked inside the science building, but found only silenced computers, scattered papers, broken experimental instruments, and a stale box of doughnuts. The earthquakes had obviously done some damage. The building itself was in total disarray, and one of the concrete walls had a huge crack in it. Dust from the ceiling tiles coated the floor and tables. His eyes focused on a picture lying on the floor. He picked it up. David Johnson was front and center, smiling, with his arms draped around the shoulders of two other men that were wearing the same outfit as he. He looked a far cry different from the frostbitten and decrepit man that Leroy had met only hours before. He remembered the broken words, hissing out from the blackened and chapped lips of the dying man, *killed them all.* Leroy dropped the picture and walked out of the science building.

He was again standing alone in the dome, staring into the small dining hall. It, too, was empty and in shambles. Most of the tables and chairs were lying overturned on the floor. The light above, hanging from the center of the dome, flickered and then dimmed. Even the artificial light was dying. He turned and walked towards the communications building, directly across the dome from the science building.

When he pushed on the door, something resisted on the other side. The individual buildings were heated, so as he pushed inward, a strong sense of warmth surrounded him. With his shoulders, he rammed the door, forcing himself into the room.

The smell of death escaped along with the heat and on the floor Leroy saw what had been blocking the door. A large, black man was lying there, partly slumped against the door and side wall with his head turned awkwardly to the side. His blank eyes stared towards the door to the building. Leroy couldn't help but look into them, and he could see the fear they still held. The light in the communication building was also dimming and flickering, buzzing in and out. The air was bad, stale, difficult to breathe. "He's still in here," Leroy noted. "Not physically, but he's in the air. I can feel it." He stared at the shadows on the walls, watching them as they danced in and out of the light, on the floor, the computers, the radio, playing hide-and-go-seek with his mind.

Through the medium of flickering light and darkness, he saw the second man lying on the floor. Leaning down to get a closer look, Leroy caught a glimpse of the mutilated face and quickly turned his head. He could feel the aura of evil seeping through the doors and open spaces in the dome and individual buildings, but he couldn't tell if it was left over or on its way, or both.

Then he saw the third body in the corner of the building, sitting on the top row of the computers, frozen in the dark shadows. His hair and skin were dry, white as ivory, and his eyes protruded from their sockets. He was frozen solid, bracing himself against the back wall with one hand, and reaching out to defend himself against the intruder with the other.

Then Leroy heard a voice. He looked towards the frozen man. The voice had come from him, he was sure of it. He backed away, bumping into the second body. The frozen man in the corner looked his way, and then his mouth moved. An angry voice emerged. "Get out. Get out while you still can. Go to the Pole."

Leroy turned quickly and ran. He would confront the Snowman at the Pole.

The dome's hanging light continued to flicker, licking the walls and corners with glimpses of day and night. Shadows ran wild as the suffocating air pushed him away from the building. He felt something behind him, and it created a breeze. Looking at the wall, he noticed another shadow hovering behind his. It was a bird, and its wings were flapping, stretching all the way across the floor of the dome.

Then the bird shadow pecked his shadow on the head, causing him to jerk forward. Leroy tried to remain calm as he watched his shadow do things that he was not physically doing.

The shadow's wings, leathery and long, sliced through the air. Leroy felt something pricking his neck. He turned around, but there was nothing there. No bird. No breeze. No wings.

He faced forward again, and the sound returned.

The flapping wings were louder, and the bird shadow was still on the wall, following, pecking Leroy's shadow on the head. And then another bird shadow appeared from one of the buildings, and then another.

This can't be real, Leroy thought. *Just mind games. The shadows are playing mind games, nothing more.* Then his shadow raised its arms, trying to get the birds away from him, but the flying shadows continued to peck away ferociously.

Don't lose it, old man. It isn't real. All mind games, nothing more. The birds are not really there.

Leroy was stunned as he watched his shadow get tired of being pecked and finally take off running down the wall, shrinking in size as it turned the curves of the geodesic dome. His shadow was running away, but the birds were still in pursuit. His shadow was running away without him, passing across the walls of the other buildings before disappearing into the dark turns of the dome.

The sound from behind was gone, and so were the bird shadows. Leroy looked towards the far wall, noticing that he no longer cast a shadow. He didn't know what to think of it, and it frightened him even more than having a shadow he couldn't control.

Just mind games, nothing more. Get control and quit looking at that damn wall. Your shadow has already left. Mind games, nothing more than that.

He ran for the doors as fast as he could.

Gabe felt something inside of him growing stronger, a feeling of closeness that he couldn't explain. The girl needed his help, and he could feel that he was getting closer to her. The feeling was making him stronger. The girl was in trouble, cold, and in a lot of pain. The thing growing inside of her was making her feel that way. He had to find her, get to her, connect with her. He had to save her from something he didn't completely understand, yet he was far from afraid of the confrontation. The force of opposition would be strong, but the feeling Gabe was getting was special, and no matter how strong the enemy might be, Gabe felt equal.

Gabe led the way, picking up steam as they neared the Amundsen-Scott Station. The others were having trouble keeping up with him. Gabe looked towards the dome in the distance, and pointed. "Look, it's Leroy. He just ran out of the dome."

Brice stopped skiing. "He's skiing away. Come on, we can catch him."

Chapter 41

7:05 P.M. River City High School
26 Inches

Bill sat down on the drafty floor, leaning against the doors to the main lobby, holding onto Amy. "What now?"

Ralph looked down at Mike's body, shaking his head. "I don't know."

"Ah, he doesn't look all that bad," someone said from behind.

The four of them turned towards the voice. The Snowman stood in front of the gym doors, smiling. "What'd you do? Kill my bird? Unfortunately that won't work on me. I'm like an annoying case of cancer. I'll keep coming back no matter what you do."

They were only 10 feet away from the Snowman. Andy pulled his revolver out and pointed it at the Snowman's head. "Time for your dose of chemotherapy, mother fucker." He fired. Bill shielded Amy with his arms.

The bullet struck the Snowman's head just above his right eye, splattering white dust against the gym doors. The bullet passed through and lodged inside the left metal door. The Snowman didn't stagger, wobble, or even flinch, and there was no sign of blood around the wound, no brains or skull fragments scattered against the walls and doors. Nothing. The entrance hole in his forehead was quickly filling itself back in as his powdery skin molded and fused back together.

They couldn't believe what they were seeing. Andy kept his gun pointed as he watched the Snowman miraculously heal himself. *This can't be happening,* he thought. No one could have survived that shot to the head.

Laughing, the Snowman stepped towards them. "Now give me what's mine."

Andy shot the Snowman again, this time in the shoulder, but it did no damage.

The Snowman reached for Amy. Bill pulled her away.

"Give me the girl."

"Go to hell."

"That's my plan, but I need the girl first."

Andy made his move, jumping at the Snowman. Bill grabbed Amy, opened the double doors and ran down the long hallway.

The Snowman caught Andy by the throat and tossed him face first against the wall. His nose was broken from the impact and blood drained to the floor as he fell down. Andy tried to make it to his feet, but was sent back down with a blow to the back of his head.

While the Snowman had his back turned dealing with Andy, Ralph jumped on his back, trying to force him to the floor. The Snowman was too strong. Holding Ralph high into the air like a wrestler, the Snowman dropped him down, plunging his knee into Ralph's abdomen. Ralph slumped to the floor, grasping for air. He could hardly breathe. With two out of the way, the Snowman took off down the hall after Bill and Amy.

Holding Amy by the hand, Bill struggled down the hall. Amy was slowing down, almost to the point where he was dragging her along. She was in too much pain to move on her own. "Come on, Amy. He's coming. We need to hurry."

She tripped, landing on both knees. "I know, but I can't help it. He's doing it again. Just like in the house."

They were only a few yards away from the main stairwell. "What's he doing?"

"He's taking me over."

"Resist him, Amy."

"Can't." Her eyes fluttered as she struggled to keep them open. "I'm fading out."

"Amy, no." Her eyes had that lost look in them again, transparent, unknowing. She dropped to the floor. "Please, Amy, get up. We've got to get going."

"Hello, Bill." The Snowman stood looming over the both of them.

Bill whispered to Amy, "Resist him, Amy. It's okay."

"You can speak to her, Bill, but she can't hear you. Not where she's at. Hand her over before I kick your teeth through the back of your skull."

Bill stood, slowly dragging Amy towards the dark stairwell next to the main office.

Bill saw it coming, but he could do nothing to avoid it. The Snowman's boot struck him on the side of the face and sent him reeling backwards, stumbling into the first few steps of the stairwell. He was in too much pain to react. His head was spinning, and his mouth was slashed inside and full of blood. Through his blurred vision, he saw the Snowman grab his daughter and run with her back towards the lobby. He'd lost her again.

In the lobby, Andy pressed his hand to his nose, trying to stop the flow of blood. He looked at Ralph who was lying on the floor. "He's got Amy again."

"Where?"

"They just went down the stairwell. Find out where they're going. Hurry."

Andy turned the corner and jumped down the stairs, three and four at a time.

Ralph slowly made it to his feet and looked around for Bill.

Andy's flashlight was still working. It made the darkness passable, but he needed more than a flashlight to get him through the downstairs maze. He needed a map. He'd never been in the school before, so he'd have to listen and feel his way through. He knew to go to The Dungeon, but he didn't know how to get there. The cafeteria door was locked, so he turned in the other direction and went on. He checked two storage closets, and both were locked. Hearing something in the distance, he looked at the boiler room door and opened it. Following the footsteps, he walked in and straight on through to the shop.

The shop was freezing. Andy could easily tell the difference in temperature from the rest of the school. He'd never felt such cold before. He positioned his flashlight on the stairs ahead, just in time to catch the Snowman running to the left inside The Dungeon. Andy followed, stepping over pieces of broken school desks, jumping up the four steps leading into The Dungeon's first room. After climbing a few more desks, he ducked into the north-south corridor and continued the chase.

The Snowman turned the corner to the east-west corridor just as Andy entered the north-south. The light at the end of the tunnel was pulsating, and for the Snowman it meant energy. He smelled the air and could hear the voices whispering to him through the wind. They soothed his soul as he ran towards the light.

"Almost there," he whispered to Amy. "Finally coming home. Oh, how long I've waited."

Andy saw the green light shining into the corridor and ran towards it. The temperature was steadily decreasing and the wind was getting stronger, swirling and flying through the turns of The Dungeon's corridors.

At the end of the first corridor, he looked east, and couldn't believe his eyes. It was beautiful, but at the same time it frightened him. He was looking through the breakthrough point, staring at the ice and snow of Antarctica, amazed and shocked.

"Antarctica," he whispered, watching the Snowman step over the threshold with Amy draped over his shoulder.

Then a strong burst of light illuminated the corridors. Andy covered his eyes and started walking backwards, wiping his bloody nose as his eyes remained fixed on the bright light. "Unbelievable."

Not sure of what to do next, Andy turned around and ran back down the corridor to find Bill and Ralph.

After dropping Mark and Magnus off at the station, the rest of the team continued after Leroy and the South Pole. They were only a few 100 yards away from the Pole, but the land ahead was uneven, cracked, and choppy from the past earthquakes. Skiing would be difficult. Slowly, they were closing in on Leroy, but it was difficult because of the obstacle course in their path.

Gabe pointed to the skyline just over the hill as a bright burst of light lit the horizon. "Did you see that?"

"The flash of green light?" Brice asked. "I saw it."

"So did I," Loreda shouted, flipping up her goggles. "What was it?"

Brice shook his head. "I'm not sure."

Gabe led the way. "There's only one way to find out."

Bill rested against one of the tables in the shop, waiting for a sign or word from Andy. Just then, he appeared at the entrance of The Dungeon.

"Andy," Ralph said, turning away from his brother. "Did you find them?"

Andy jumped down into the shop. "You're not going to believe this."

"What?"

"I found the door. We're going to the South Pole."

Chapter 42

7:25 P.M. Breakthrough Point
Antarctica

As soon as the Snowman stepped foot on the ice, he noticed a change in the landscape. It was a different place than when he'd left it in the morning. The ice was breaking apart, and he couldn't understand how, or why. He'd felt the land beneath him rumbling off and on for many years, but recently it'd been occurring more frequently. He didn't understand how the Pole could allow something this terrible to happen. He wondered if they had control over it at all. He could only guess what was happening. The end of the millennium was approaching. The birth of the One would come soon, probably within the next hour, and the Snowman's physical time on earth would end soon there after. The breaking apart of his land felt like a stab of closure into his dying body. Seeing the cracked ice was unsettling, but at the same time very exciting. It marked not only the ending of a very successful reign, but also the beginning of a new and final reign for their side. As soon as the successor was born, the process would start. The Snowman would live out the final five years of his life in rest, preparing the child for the dawning of a new age, the age of ultimate chaos and destruction, the age of ultimate death, the age where all sinners will finally be pulled towards the center of the earth in a dualistic hell of fire and ice. The age of fire and ice. The end of the world was drawing near, the final piece nearly complete. The Snowman looked at the newly formed crevasses, hills, and cracks in the land not as mistakes, but as signs; signs of his ending and closure.

He had to get Amy to the cave. He could see the cave's opening from the breakthrough point. The scientists' core sampling site still stood directly over it. He couldn't wait to get her into it. It was his home. He'd spent so many centuries constructing it, digging, painting, chipping, carving at the walls. The walls were works of art, icy frescoes, reliefs and carvings depicting hell in its truest forms. They were his masterpieces, and he couldn't wait for Amy to find pleasure with them. Jumping the cracks and scattered crevasses, ridges and holes, the Snowman traveled the 50 yards from the breakthrough point to the cave within seconds. He stared down into the cave's darkness and smiled. Carefully, with Amy secured in his arms, he crawled down into the ice.

Andy stepped down from The Dungeon. "I know that Antarctica is on the other side of the world, but believe it or not, and for whatever reason, it's also under this school." He walked to the corner of the shop and grabbed three dusty wool bags. "Let's get packed."

Bill hobbled down from the table and zipped his coat up to his neck. "Andy, under normal circumstances I'd say you were crazy, but after what I've seen the last few days, I'd believe anything."

Andy grabbed their weapons and tossed them into one of the bags.

"Andy," Bill said. "What good are those going to do? We've already seen that they don't hurt him."

"True, but it's all we have. At least we can try and slow him down if we have to. I see no other way of getting to him. I don't know of any other way to slow him down."

"The hell that is ice," Ralph mumbled, staring around the room.

"What's that, Ralph?"

"How does one get rid of ice?"

"Rock salt," Andy said, not intending to be funny.

"No, it's obvious." Ralph waited for their reactions, but they said nothing. He went on. "We melt the bastard. Opposites wipe each other out. Fire and ice. The way you get rid of ice is by fire." Eyeing a box in the corner of the room, he walked over to it. It held eight blue canisters, each about two feet long and three inches wide. He read the label on the side of one of them: PROPANE GAS TORCH. "Perfect," he said, filling the wool bag with the canisters.

"Ralph?" Bill called from across the room. He was ignored.

"Bill, do you have any matches?"

"Yeah, a whole box in my desk, why?"

"Okay, now I need," Ralph paused, walking around the work tables, rubbing the tips of his fingers together, thinking, "I need something . . . something . . . got it. Bill, where's the Endust?"

"Endust?"

"Where do you keep the spray cans of Endust?"

"In the closet," Bill pointed, "Over there in the corner."

"What's he up to?" Andy asked Bill.

"I don't know for sure, but I think I've got an idea."

Less than 10 minutes away, they were all on foot, even Eric. The snowmobile had been left at the station with Mark and Magnus. Even the skis proved to be useless on the uneven land. Gabe led the charge as the feeling of the girl grew stronger with every step taken. He could tell they were getting closer to each other.

Leroy was pushing slightly ahead, taking advantage of traveling alone. He was able to maneuver around the obstacles without having to check over his shoulder to see if everyone was making it safely. He had only himself to worry about. Still, they made sure they kept him in their line of sight. They were closing in on the South Pole, and if something was going to happen, they suspected it would be very soon.

Then the ice started to shake, rattle, and roll again.

The quake caught the Snowman off guard. After placing Amy down on the floor of the cave, he lost his balance and smashed into one of the side walls. There was no sense of stillness. He rammed his fingers into the wall and braced himself until the shaking was over.

Amy was lying in the corner, shaking along with the ice, awake again and wondering where she was. Hidden in the darkness of the back corner, she couldn't see much of anything, but she felt the earth moving, and the motion was painful. Her stomach was pounding as something continued to shift and turn inside of her. Leaning against the back wall of the cave, Amy pulled her nightgown up over her stomach, and saw that it too was changing. A small amount of light was shining through the opening to the cave, so Amy was able to see a slight bulge down low on her belly that hadn't been there a half hour ago, or at least she hadn't noticed it then. Now it was moving. Beneath the skin she could see something pressing against her flesh. She started to cry when she saw the indentation of a small hand pushing against her belly-button. Her skin seemed very thin and flexible, like flimsy rubber. The creature inside of her wanted out.

When the quake ended, the Snowman pulled his hands out of the wall and approached Amy. Squatting down to one knee, he ran his hand over her bare stomach and smiled. She flinched as if she'd been shocked, but noticed with the touch of the Snowman's cold hands that the thing inside of her had settled down. It stopped moving, for now.

He whispered into her ear. "I'll be right back."

She watched him move out of the darkness and into the light that was shining down from the opening. And in that light, for the first time, she saw the walls.

The last quake was short, and luckily nobody had been hurt. Brice stopped about 100 yards away from the South Pole, and he stared in confusion. They'd been told by past explorers that a small brass pole marked the location of the geographical South Pole, but instead, they saw something different, much different. A black rectangle about eight feet tall and six feet wide rested on the ice like a paper-thin doorway. From the front it was a tunnel of darkness, but from the sides it was barely visible it was so thin.

"Is that supposed to be there?" Eric asked.

"No." Brice shook his head in disbelief.

"I wonder if that's where that burst of light came from," Loreda said.

Brice stared at the dark rectangle and then at Leroy in the distance. Leroy was closing in on the doorway.

Gabe yelled for him to stop, but Leroy couldn't hear him. The wind was picking up again. "Let's go check this thing out."

They started to run.

The Snowman felt the pressure of explorers from every direction. He cursed himself for not killing them earlier, but his lust for Amy had clouded his judgment. He was seemingly immortal, but he was still a man. He remembered the skiers. The feeling in the air was strong, they had to be close. Turning in a slow circle just outside of his cave, he surveyed his land. Through the broken chunks of ice and small hills, he saw them, five of them coming his way, running towards the breakthrough point. Evidently they hadn't seen him.

"Welcome," the Snowman said softly.

Then suddenly, the Snowman was hit in the right shoulder with a bullet. He looked to his left. A man charged at him with fury and rage in his eyes and a gun in his hand, yelling, "revenge, revenge," at the top of his lungs.

The Snowman's shoulder was blown apart, seemingly starting to melt and corrode. He turned towards the charging man. "Leroy, it's been a long time."

All four walls were filled with carvings and pictures, all alive inside the cave of ice. Images of thousands of people dying, devils flying, serpents swimming, phantoms roaming, and souls preserving, all stretched along the walls like the animals in the ancient Lascaux cave in France.

Amy was terrified by what she was seeing, as terrified as she was of the creature growing inside of her. The front wall near the cave's opening was filled with symbols and letters, none of which she recognized. It was as if they were messages from an ancient and unknown language, preaching in words she could not understand. One of the side walls was a depiction of the Hell that is Fire, and it was filled with scenes of boiling pits of fire, people burning, melting, and drowning. Amy focused on the gold, orange, and red center of the wall. At the bottom was a sea of boiling blood, fire, and lava, and out of the middle emerged a Devil with flames shooting off in every direction from his body, melting and scorching everything in its path. This Devil was the Snowman's father and first son of Satan. He was the evil being that ruled the earth during the first Millennium from the Hell that is Fire. His eyes were two fiery suns, and his extended tongue licked flames of amber onto the drowning people below. Up above the swimming serpent demons and outstretched Devil was a long rope. The rope extended all over the wall like overgrown vines. Many of the lost souls were suspended in the air, hanging from the rope, dropping from different sections of it into the sea of boiling fire and blood. Their faces were filled with fear and agony. Their thoughts were in their eyes. The end of the rope continuously descended towards the fire-burning hands of the half-submerged Devil. The souls dropped into the fire, one by one, falling into the clutching hands of everlasting evil.

Amy forced her eyes away from the center of the wall. She followed the scene as it wrapped into the wall of unknown words and then into the white, black, and azure wall on the other side of the cave. Two scenes halved this wall. The top was a picture of a town buried deep in snow, with a visible slide running through the middle of the accumulation and into a rectangular, black doorway. The slide had hordes of people trampling and crushing each other with futile effort to avoid getting sucked towards the black doorway. A black bird perched on the top of the door watching as the lost souls passed through. It was the last to see the eyes that screamed as loudly as their mouths. Why? What had they done to have such evil brought upon them? On the lower section of the wall and on the other side of the black doorway, the souls were all frozen and landing in piles. There, the Snowman stood, packing them inside the ice, forcing their lifeless bodies into a wall, until they became the wall. Inside were thousands, no, tens of thousands of souls, frozen and preserved inside the ice. Parts of their bodies protruded from the wall like a bas relief. They were sinners, statues, frozen forever inside the wall, but not yet fully dead. They were the people in Amy's dreams, the ones she could hear screaming for help. She saw them now inside the picture on the wall, but knew that outside the cave they were very real. Their pain was real, and she could hear their voices again faintly, hovering through the wind and down into the opening of the cave. She looked at the side wall again, the Hell that is Ice, and stared into the Snowman's blue eyes. The Snowman in the wall pointed towards the back wall of the cave.

Amy slowly turned her head towards the back wall of the cave and was shocked to see her Easter picture hanging at the top of it. The wall itself had no other depictions or scenes. It was blank except for a few words. Under her picture, Amy read what had been carved in the wall, colored in black—The Final Dimension. Under that it read—Fire Meets Ice. Fire was in red, ice in blue. Amy backed away from the back wall, crashing against the wall of unknown words. She looked down at her stomach again, feeling the bulge with her trembling hands. Fire and Ice was starting to kick again.

Bill, Ralph, and Andy turned the corner and faced the far wall of the east-west corridor. The air was bitter cold, and they knew too well that they were not dressed for the Antarctic temperatures. The pulsing light was nearly blinding, but out of the light they saw two red dots quickly approaching—two flaming eyes. Hissing, the black cat jumped up towards Bill's face. Andy intercepted it with one blow from his massive fist. The cat dropped to the ground and didn't move again. It was dead.

Andy looked at the Anderson brothers. "The Snowman is next."

They continued into the light. They could hear someone yelling.

"Revenge," Leroy screamed, closing in on the Snowman, firing his last few bullets. He was filled with such intensity that he couldn't even tell if his special-made bullets were working. He'd spent years creating the lethal de-icer and explosive bullets, which fired simultaneously from his homemade, double-barreled .45 caliber revolver. One bullet encased potassium chloride, sodium chloride, and magnesium chloride, and was set to explode like shrapnel upon impact, reacting like rock salt on ice. The second bullet encased toluene (the colorless and flammable petrochemical used in the explosive compound TNT) and a mixture of concentrated sulfuric and nitric acid. Upon firing, the latter bullet was to ignite during flight, scorching the target in the form of a flying ball of fire.

The bullets had worked on the ice sculpture he'd created back home only three months ago, but now they seemed to be doing only minor damage to the Snowman, whose shoulder was quickly fusing back together. Several of the bullets turned out to be duds, and Leroy's unsteady hands sent half the bullets flying off past the Snowman and into the ice surrounding his cave.

Out of bullets, Leroy threw the gun to the ground and continued running towards the Snowman with outstretched arms. He jumped.

The Snowman swung his arm forward, connecting with Leroy in midair, knocking the old man backwards and onto the ice.

Leroy landed hard, smacking the back of his head against a small slope in the ice. He looked up, dazed but not ready to give in, now leaning up on both elbows.

The Snowman closed in on him.

Amy was dizzy, partially because the walls all around her were shifting; and also because the creature inside of her was pressing against her stomach again, making her nauseated. She could smell the bodies burning on one wall and feel the crackling sensation of ice on the other. She was freezing on the outside, but the thing was burning from within, and the pain was growing with each passing minute. She could feel the wind swooping down into the cave, caressing the bare skin under her flimsy nightgown, and with it whispered the crying voices. They weren't coming from the walls, but from the air outside the cave. *What is happening to me? I can't go on with this. I've got to do something to stop the growth, but what?* There was nothing she could do to stop it. The thing inside of her already had a mind of its own, and it wanted out.

They ran as fast as they could to help Leroy. The strange man with the long, flowing hair was closing in on him. Gabe peeled away from the pack.

Brice yelled. "Gabe, where are you going?"

"I know where the girl is," he answered.

"Who?"

"I can sense her. She's in that cave. I'm going to the cave. She needs my help."

Brice let him go, and they continued towards the Snowman, hoping to get there before Leroy was killed.

Just then, another blinding burst of light shot out from the doorway. When the light cleared, they saw three people step through the black rectangle and onto the ice of Antarctica.

The Snowman stopped his approach towards Leroy, turning towards the three that had just crossed the breakthrough point. Then he heard someone screaming from behind. Explorers were closing in on him from every direction.

Brice cupped his hands around his mouth, watching the Snowman run at the three strangers in front of the doorway. "Loook Ooout." Tuuuurn Arrrooooound." He hoped his warning was in time.

The thing inside her was pulling and tugging against the lining of her womb. Her stomach distended to the size of a basketball, and the pain was beyond endurance. She couldn't go through with this any longer. She couldn't let it happen, she just couldn't. *What can I do? I've got to think of something.* And then she did. Under the opening of the cave, next to the wall of unknown words, she saw something bright and sharp lying on the ice. She would have to hurry, and be brave. She hoped she had the strength to do both.

Crawling across the cave's floor, her arms and legs numb and barely moveable, she could hardly feel the ice beneath her. The first ripping sensation hit, and she doubled over in pain, clutching her stomach until it went away. She looked back at the floor and slowly made her way to the object.

Briefly blinded by the strong burst of light, Bill, Ralph, and Andy were vulnerable to whatever awaited their arrival at the doorway. They heard the man's voice screaming at them, warning them, but it was too late. When the light dimmed, the Snowman was already upon them. Andy and Ralph ran to the right of the doorway, and Bill went to the left, ducking behind a large wave of recently formed ice. He heard someone scream. He followed the sound until he noticed the cave off to the left in the distance. "Amy?" The Snowman wasn't following him, so he took off for the cave.

Amy screamed again. Bill picked up his speed. He was now more worried than ever. "What has he done to you?" He could tell by the sound that it was not a scream for help, but a scream of pain.

The Snowman followed Ralph and Andy, quickly catching up to them. On a sudden change of direction, Ralph slipped on the ice and stumbled to the ground, and the next thing he knew he was being lifted in the air.

Andy stopped when he heard Ralph go down, and when he turned to help, it was too late. The Snowman had already grabbed Ralph, clutching him in one of his long arms, holding him above the ground in a bear hug. Ralph kicked and struggled to break free, but the Snowman was too strong. Ralph couldn't move his arms.

Holding Ralph with his left hand, the Snowman lifted his right arm high in the air, and grabbed a two-foot-long sliver of ice.

Andy saw the wetness of the weapon, and could easily see it piercing Ralph's body. Slowly, he unzipped the bag and pulled out his gun. "Don't do it," he screamed towards the Snowman.

"Yeah, right." The Snowman laughed, and then swung the icicle down in an arch towards Ralph's chest.

Her head was spinning, but she could still hear the voices from everywhere. Under the opening of the cave, the light from outside shone upon her. She reached down and grabbed the icicle from the corner of the cave, and with unsteady hands, she held it high above her head.

Leaning with her back up against the wall of unknown words, she tried not to pause or hesitate. The thing inside her had to die.

She screamed again. Sticking out between her legs was a small hand, and the grotesque fingers were smeared with blood and wiggling as the yellow claws scratched and ripped her inner thighs. "Oh, my God, my God." She was hysterical. The beastly creature inside her growled, pushing more of its arm out into the swirling air and freedom of the cave.

"Please, God, give me the courage," she whispered.

The light from the opening of the cave was blotted out by something, a figure, a man. Amy gripped the icicle taut, glancing up towards the opening. She saw the face of a man, a familiar but also mysterious face. The man in her dreams. "My hero," she whispered. "Save me." And then she closed her eyes. She couldn't bear to look as she swung her arm downward, jamming the icicle deep into her womb.

Bill watched as Gabe jumped down into the cave. He was a stranger, but at the same time, Bill felt that he'd seen him before. He had to trust that he was going in to help Amy, nothing else. Bill heard the pain in her voice, desperately wanting to be the one to help. He stopped about 20 yards away from the cave as he came to a crevasse in the ice. Too long to run around, he would have to jump at least six feet to clear it. He believed he could make it. He had to.

After hurling his bag across, he backed up about 10 feet and prepared for his leap of faith. He made his run and pushed off at the edge of the crevasse. Flying in the air, he felt like a bird, but after seeing that he might not make it, he wished he had wings. Somehow he kept going. It was a clumsy landing, but he planted his right foot on the edge of the other side and tumbled forward. His hands hit the ice first, briefly supporting his weight. His wrists snapped backwards, and his elbows buckled as he went into a roll. Staggering to his feet, he brushed off the loose snow, amazed that he hadn't fallen into the ice. Now facing the cave, he saw that the rest of the way was flat ice. "Amy," he called. "I'm coming."

Andy fired at the Snowman's hand. The icicle exploded just before reaching Ralph's chest. The Snowman stumbled backwards. Ralph tried again to break free, but he still couldn't move his arms. The Snowman squeezed tighter.

Ralph and Leroy glanced at each other, both wondering who the other was, and what they were doing here.

Andy faked defeat and dropped his gun. Both Leroy and Andy could see Brice sneaking up behind the Snowman with a ski in his hands, ready to swing.

The icicle stuck deep down into her stomach, piercing the alien creature inside. She felt it moving, squirming, writhing like a moth stuck with a pin. It screamed and slammed against her womb, trying to get out.

Blood soaked Amy's nightgown and spilled out in a pool to the floor of the cave, mixing with the liquid that was already freezing against the ice. Despite the pain, she jammed the icicle down further into her womb until she heard something pop. Removing the icicle, she watched as her stomach decreased in size. *What happened?* she thought, watching with horror-filled eyes.

Staring up into the light again, she squinted as Gabe grabbed her hands. Her savior. He was whispering. "Put forth your hand and touch anything he has. O Lord, behold, all that he has in Your power, only do not lay a hand on this person." The words flowed naturally from his lips, although he seemingly had no control of them. He was the connecting force, so he allowed the power and strength to flow freely through his body. Without pausing or hesitation, he continued to speak, he continued to pray.

Amy soaked the soothing words in, trying to not look at her deflating stomach. After hearing the popping sound, she hadn't been able to look down. Atop her red and oozing blood now fell a thick, dark green, liquid. The pollutant poured out between her thighs and over the exposed arm. Tiny claws continued to wiggle as the creature inside of her tried to free itself. The green fluid continued to gush, forcing the creature out, inch by inch. Only the words of the man in her dreams could bring her peace.

"Cast out the demons who dwell within and stir up those who are possessed. The violent struggle against the ultimate Adversary. O Lord, keep us and protect us always from the evil generation. Let not the fallen angel and tempter take another soul. You saved us from the burning fires, now save us from the preserving ice. These children of men are caught when the evil time falls suddenly upon them. Listen . . ."

Nauseated by the blood and what was pouring out of her, Amy was barely able to keep her head still. She wanted nothing more than to pass out. She screamed again, banging the back of her head against the wall of unknown words to balance the pain. The creature forced the top of its head through her vagina. She couldn't breathe. She squeezed Gabe's hand, listening to his prayers.

"Break the strength of the wicked and the evildoer. Punish their wickedness; let them not survive the eternal battle . . ."

Amy saw a bright light at the top of the cave. The glare off the ice blinded her again, but the calling voice was pleasantly familiar. "Amy."

She tilted her head to the light. She heard the voice again. "Amy?"

Amy couldn't find the strength to answer.

His swaying legs emerged from the light in the opening. Bill landed unintentionally on Gabe's right ankle and fell backwards into the Wall of Ice.

"Dad," Amy whispered.

"I'm here, Amy." He reached for his flashlight as it rolled across the floor of the cave, giving brief glimpses of the walls. He didn't notice what was on them. He hadn't noticed the Snowman's work. Looking at the mumbling, praying stranger that leaned over his daughter, Bill asked, "Who are you?"

Gabe didn't answer. His words continued to flow.

"My savior," Amy whispered.

Bill grabbed the flashlight and shone it towards Amy, starting with her face. He saw that she was sweating, despite the freezing temperature, and her tears were of the worst pain imaginable. Slowly, he moved the ray of light down her body, to her neck, her upper chest, stopping when he caught sight of her stomach. "Oh, dear God."

The Snowman turned to see what had their attention. Before he rotated his head, Brice started his baseball swing and smacked the Snowman across the face with the side of his ski. His grip loosened, and Ralph was able to wrestle himself free. The Snowman stumbled backwards, arms swinging and arching for balance, until he stopped his fall with his hand.

Jumping back up to his feet, he raised his right hand and rocked his index finger from side to side, staring with violent anger and rage at Brice.

Brice panicked, watching the Snowman as he lifted the ski off the ice and pointed in his direction. He turned around and started to run, but he didn't get very far. The Snowman threw the ski at Brice from about 15 feet away and impaled him through the lower part of his back. Like a skewer through a piece of meat, the ski cut through his back, forcing its way out the front of his stomach.

He staggered, futilely grabbing the end of the ski with both hands. His body went limp and he fell face down on the ice, forcing the ski back through his body. The Snowman turned to face the other three, but they were nowhere to be found. Then he heard Amy's cry mixing with the wind. He turned towards the cave. *It's happening*, he thought. He heard her scream again. "She's ready," he smiled. "Fire and Ice is coming out to me."

The Snowman ran for his cave.

Andy, Ralph, and Leroy stepped out from behind the doorway, wanting to check on Brice, but they knew they had to stop the Snowman first.

Ralph pointed. "He's heading for the cave over there. It's where Bill is."

"We better find a way to stop him. Bill's a sitting duck in there," Andy shouted.

Ralph put his hand on Leroy's shoulder. "You wait here by this door. There's no sense in you getting killed over this."

Leroy held up his hand, stopping Ralph in mid-sentence. "The name is Leroy, and I'm in this no matter what. I don't know your situation with this man, but I'm well aware of mine." Leroy started to walk. "You two run around and swing a big arc so he can't see you. Approach the cave from the back side," Leroy said. "I'll distract him. Hurry, go."

Knowing that it would do no harm, Leroy stormed towards the Snowman. It was a suicide mission, but it was the way he preferred to exit the world. He wanted his revenge.

Ralph and Andy felt like they were running in slow motion against the wind as it smacked hard into their bare faces. They'd dressed for the Louisville temperatures, not the Antarctic.

"The Snowman. He just stopped running," Andy yelled.

Ralph stared in the distance at Leroy. "What the hell is that old man doing?"

"I don't know, but I think we're going to make it. If he can hold his attention for a few more minutes we'll beat him to the cave."

Watching Leroy, Ralph couldn't help to be amazed at the old man's courage. He was one of the bravest men Ralph had ever seen, charging at the Snowman as he was, but he was also probably the dumbest.

Eric stood up from behind the broken wall of ice, watching as Leroy charged wildly towards the man with the long, white hair.

Loreda grabbed his arm. "Where are you going?"

"To help Leroy."

"Brice told us to stay right here."

"I know, but he's dead now. I can't let Leroy fight this thing on his own."

Eric stepped out from behind the wall and ran towards the Snowman and the cave.

"Amy, what is happening?" Bill asked, dropping to the floor.

The monster between her legs was fighting for its freedom, now fully exposed to its waist.

Amy couldn't answer. She dug her fingernails into the ice. It felt like the cave was coming to life, and it sounded like the walls were shifting again. Bill pointed his flashlight at the walls and his heart skipped a beat. The Wall of Fire was in motion. One by one, the lost souls on the wall were dropping from the flaming rope and into the sea of boiling fire, and the Snowman's father was rejoicing. Bill could smell burning flesh and could hear the popping and cracking from the boiling, red water as a fine mist of smoke began to funnel into the cave from the wall. He switched directions with his flashlight and pointed it at the Wall of Ice, and the icy slide dumped soul after soul through the black doorway and into the land of ice and snow.

Although he still held onto Amy's hand, Gabe's attention was now on the walls. He could hear the crying, pleading voices. "Cast you out," Gabe said, "Be strong. Do not fear the one that kills the body, for he can not get rid of your soul. The state of souls after death shall be returned, for your time in Hell was not brought upon you by your own doing. It's not what you did during life, but it is what you *didn't* do that makes you sinners in their eyes. You are not sinners. You were taken against your will. Satan cursed the world with his first son in the Hell that is Fire, and he was defeated. His grandson will be destroyed now in the Hell that is Ice. Satan's dualistic arms will . . ."

The monster between Amy's legs was hissing and stretching. It was a light purple color and the top of its head sprouted tiny white hairs. Then Fire and Ice turned its head towards Bill, showing off its sharp, pointed teeth. It wasn't the teeth that knocked Bill back on his butt. It was the eyes.

Its eyes were different colors. One was a light shade of blue, and the other was dark red, and both were glowing.

"Think . . . I'm dying," Amy whispered.

"No, Amy. You are not going to die."

"So cold."

"No, Amy. We won't allow it to happen to you."

The cave was filling with smoke and a freezing mist.

Amy closed her eyes.

They then heard a tiny, hissing voice. "Hell has many dimensions." It was the baby, the creature, and it was nearly out. It turned its head towards Bill again, eyes glowing. "Fire meets Ice."

Gabe let go of Amy's hand and grabbed the icicle. Amy was rapidly losing blood. With his free hand, Gabe motioned the sign of the cross on his forehead, shoulders, and chest, and then over Amy's stomach.

Bill gently lifted Amy's head up off the ice. "Kill it."

Gabe raised the icicle high above his head. "In the name of the Father, Son, and Holy Ghost, I cast out the wicked being." He closed his eyes and brought the icicle downward.

Eric plunged his shoulder into the Snowman's back, knocking him to the ground. As soon as the Snowman's head hit the ice, Leroy drove the tip of his boot into his temple. Eric straddled the Snowman, throwing a continuous string of punches to the stranger's throat, and Leroy did the same with his kicks, but lower down on the Snowman's body.

The Snowman torqued his body far enough to lift his right shoulder off the ground, and he freed his arm from Eric's weight. He caught Leroy's foot on the next kick and squeezed hard, cracking several bones inside. He twisted the foot around nearly full-circle and tossed Leroy to the ground. He then brought his knee up, hitting Eric in the lower back. Eric flew off the Snowman and toppled to the ice next to Leroy.

The next thing Eric knew, he was being lifted high off the ground and spun in the air. The Snowman threw him a good 15 feet until he bounced against the ice and was knocked out cold.

Leroy was persistent. He hobbled on his good foot and wrapped his arms around the Snowman's neck. He tried, but couldn't find the strength to choke him. The Snowman grabbed Leroy by his forearms and flipped the old man over his head, plunging him head first down on the ice. Leroy's neck snapped, and he didn't move again.

The Snowman looked at the cave. Ralph now stood in front of the opening, waiting.

Just as Loreda inched her way out to help Eric, she was tapped on the shoulder. "Who are you?"

"No time for questions," Andy said. "Just do what I say, and when this thing is over I'll be more than happy to make your acquaintance. As soon as the coast is clear, make a run for that black doorway over there. Believe me, it's much safer in there."

"Where does it go?" Pam asked.

"I'll explain later, please, go." Andy stood up and, seeing that Ralph was alone at the cave, he took off running to help him.

"What now?" Pam asked.

"We go to that doorway." Loreda grabbed Eric by one arm and Pam grabbed the other. "He's unconscious, but still breathing." Together they dragged Eric to the doorway.

Gabe brought the icicle down and jabbed it into the creature's neck, pinning it to the cave's floor. Fire and Ice screamed in pain. It kicked and squirmed, swinging its tiny arms in a helpless attempt at protection. Gabe removed the icicle and brought it down again, and again, and again, until the head disconnected from the body. It rolled awkwardly across the floor of the cave. It was the child set to end the world with Fire and Ice, and now it was dead.

Gabe dropped the icicle. "And the Devil will be seized by the hand of God, chained up for a thousand years, thrown into the abyss so that no one's soul can be led astray."

Bill grabbed Amy and pulled her close, trying to keep her body warm. The smoke and mist surrounded them, swirling around all corners of the cave. He noticed a shadow blocking the cave's opening. He was surprised to see it was Ralph.

"What's going on up there?"

Andy joined Ralph at the cave's entrance as the Snowman closed in on the both of them, now about 30 feet away and quickly gaining ground. Ralph yelled down into the cave. "Just stay calm."

"We've got to get her out of here," Bill yelled. "She's bleeding to death."

"Just a little longer, Bill."

"She's freezing and dying. She needs help."

Ralph took off his coat and dropped it through the opening. "Wrap that around her. It will have to do for now. Use it to staunch the flow of blood."

Bill kicked the headless creature away from Amy, holding her tightly, directly under the opening of the cave. Smoke filled the air, and the back wall was starting to vibrate and rumble. "Something is happening down here. Hurry."

The Snowman stopped about 20 feet away from the cave, angry that the two men were blocking his way, but also excited that he was going to be able to hold his son very soon.

Ralph and Andy reached down into the bags between their feet. Ralph pulled out one of the propane canisters. Without taking his eyes off the approaching Snowman, he whispered to Andy, "Get the matches out."

"There's no way they'll light in this wind."

"We don't have a choice."

The Snowman was about 15 feet away, taking his time now, teasing them, taking one large step after another. He knew they had nowhere to run and certainly nowhere to hide. They were on his turf now.

Ralph turned the knob at the top of the canister, and the spout hissed as gas was released through it.

The Snowman stopped, holding his hand to his chest. "Not another gun. It worked so well the last time."

Andy struck the first match. It lit, but the wind immediately blew it out. He quickly tried another.

Same result.

The Snowman took another step forward. "Shouldn't play with matches. Kids who play with fire wet the bed."

Ralph moved the canister's spout closer to Andy just in case he did manage to keep a flame burning for more than a second. He had the line of gas in position to ignite.

Andy struck another match against the side of the box and again the wind blew it out.

With his eyes still focused straight ahead, Ralph reached down into the opening of the cave and grabbed what Bill was lifting up to him. "Come on, Andy."

"It's too windy."

The cave was a mixture of hot and cold temperatures as the mist gathered around the floor, walls, and ceiling in a thick blanket. Bill couldn't see Amy, although he knew he still held her in his arms. He couldn't see Gabe either.

Gabe could hear what was going on and what was being said outside the cave. He felt his way to the opening, extended his hands upward towards the light, and closed his eyes.

"Ralph, I'm trying, but . . . hold it, the wind . . . it stopped." Andy struck another match. It lit. Andy shielded the tiny flame with his extended hand, positioning it over the propane spout. It ignited with a swooshing sound.

Ralph adjusted the flame to about six inches. "Come on. Come to papa," he said, pulling the creatures head from the opening of the cave and placing it near his feet. He then reached into the bag for the can of Endust.

The Snowman saw that the wind had stopped, and he didn't understand how it could have happened. "Kids who play with fire wet the bed." He was only five feet away from them. "Men who play with fire get killed instead." The Snowman leaped at them with his arms sprawled wildly out in front.

Holding Fire and Ice's severed head by its thin white hairs, Ralph threw it at the Snowman. He quickly raised the Endust can and pressed down on the button, spraying the mist into the sliver of fire that was coming from the torch. The result was an explosion of fire and it scorched the Snowman in mid-air. Ralph stumbled against the front wall of the cave because of the heat, but he kept his blow torch pointed out in front at the Snowman. Andy backed away, shielding his face from the flames.

The Snowman caught the object that was thrown at him as the flames from the torch reached his clothes. In his melting hands he held the head of his only son—Fire and Ice. Satan's final solution had been thwarted in the end. There would be no heir. The Snowman choked out a gargle-filled scream as he stared down at his son's boiling face. The eyes were no longer glowing red and blue, but now dull as pennies. "Damn you! Damn you, God!" Within seconds his entire body was engulfed in flames. He dropped to the ice clumsily and fell to his knees, ripping at his clothes and skin, bellowing loudly in pain.

The wind, getting stronger, blew some of the flames back into Ralph's face. He kept the Endust button pressed down as he stepped closer to the burning and melting Snowman. The propane and Endust created a thick string of fire that extended to about four feet in length. Ralph's shirt caught fire and it quickly spread up his sleeves. He held on though, inching his way towards the Snowman, determined to keep the fire on him until he was dead, even if it meant his own death.

The Snowman's hair burned as if each strand of hair was a single wick. His entire body was covered in flames and he rolled on the ice in a desperate attempt to smother it. The Snowman's face melted like wax, his skin dropping in clumps to the ice.

Ralph kept blowing the torch until he too was engulfed in flames with the Snowman. Ralph was burning himself alive.

Andy looked around for something to put out the fire but couldn't find anything. Water would have worked, but everything was frozen.

The Snowman's face and upper body were quickly reduced to bones and boiling flesh as piles of him dropped to the ice. Above, a funnel of black smoke spiraled into the Antarctic sky.

Andy took off his coat and wrapped it around Ralph's burning body. Ralph was dead.

Suddenly, the ice started to shake and rumble again. The earthquake had returned.

Andy slowly made his way back to the opening of the cave. When he got there, he heard Bill yelling something from below as smoke and mist poured out.

Then Andy heard a huge cracking noise and, no more than 30 feet away, he saw a crevasse split the ground and a huge slab of ice popping upward, roaring like claps of thunder. Ralph's charred body started rolling down the incline towards the crevasse together with the Snowman's bones. They fell into the abyss.

Andy looked towards the doorway. It was getting smaller, now about a foot shorter on all four sides. Pam and Loreda were almost through, dragging Eric behind them. Andy heard Bill calling from inside the cave.

Andy reached down the opening. "Grab my hand." He couldn't see anything through the rising smoke.

"What's happening, Andy?"

"Earthquake."

"I'm sending Amy up first," Bill yelled. "It's getting warm down here. Something weird is happening."

Andy felt around the opening until he touched Amy's arms. "Everything is breaking apart up here." He pulled Amy up and out of the cave, resting her on the ice beside him. She was unconscious again.

Bill then reached up his arms and grabbed onto Andy's hands. "The Snowman?"

"He's dead and gone."

"And Ralph?" Bill called out as Andy pulled him out of the cave.

Andy closed his eyes and gave a hesitant answer. "He's dead."

Bill didn't respond.

Loreda and Pam had been only 15 feet from the doorway when the earthquake started, and the ice began breaking apart. It was by far the worst earthquake yet. They wondered if Leroy's theories had been right. Dragging Eric, they stopped just before entering the breakthrough point. They could now see what was on the other side—some kind of underground tunnel. They were reluctant to pass through, and then they remembered the man's words. *Trust me. It is much safer on the other side.* They were convinced now, wanting absolutely no part of anymore Antarctic earthquakes.

They walked through the breakthrough point and entered the east-west corridor.

Bill was amazed with what he saw upon exiting the cave. The ground was now totally uneven and unstable. Everything underfoot seemed to be collapsing. Huge chunks of ice, like icebergs, were popping up from the ground and floating. Water was beginning to surface from below, and much of the ice was now afloat. The ice core was melting from below.

After Gabe was pulled out of the cave, Andy lifted Amy off the ground and cradled her in his arms. Blood still dripped from her open wound. Eyeing the shrinking doorway, he said to Bill, "Let's make a run for it."

Bill nodded, nervously observing the splintering and cracking ice all around them. About 30 yards past the doorway something exploded beneath the ice causing an opening. It was in the shape of a perfect circle. From the circle, an enormous burst of light hurled into the Antarctic sky. The light went on as far as the eye could see, stretching up through the clouds and beyond. It seemingly had no end.

"What is it?" Bill yelled.

"I don't know," Andy said. "Keep moving." They moved towards the doorway, but they couldn't take their eyes from the vertical tunnel of light.

Just then they saw something floating upward inside the light. It was in the shape of a human, but very transparent and surreal. The apparition waved to them and then continued on floating upward into the sky. In a matter of seconds, the tunnel of light was flooded with apparitions rising from the circle in the ice, and they were all waving. Most of them seemed to be smiling and crying, but it was obvious that they no longer felt pain. They were being set free from the ice. Thousands and thousands of apparitions poured out of the ice and upward until they were lost in the clouds and could be seen no more.

Closing in on the doorway, Andy turned to Bill. "They look like ghosts. Do you believe in ghosts?"

"I'd believe in just about anything right now."

"They're actual people. Or at least they were. They're transparent, like ghosts, but people nevertheless. It's as if the light is a vacuum, and its sucking them from the ice. Where do you think they're going?"

"I don't know."

Gabe did. Despite the ice cracking and breaking off into the rising waters that surrounded them, he stopped and stared at the tunnel of light, and at the thousands of souls that were inside of it. "Be free." He knew where they were going. "You can finally die," he dropped to his knees in exhaustion, "in peace." He fell to the ice as the power drained from his body. The connection was leaving, task complete.

"Come on." Bill grabbed him under the arm, helping him to his feet. Gabe looked and felt normal again because he felt vulnerable like everyone else.

After minutes of continuous flow through the tunnel, the apparitions thinned out.

Bill hadn't been able to find her, but he knew Mary was in the tunnel floating upward with the rest of them. The thought of it made him smile. It was the only thing that could possibly bring a smile to his face now that his daughter was hours away from death. Mary was finally free.

The tunnel of light was nearly empty and dimming, when the last apparition appeared from the hole in the ice. It was a young boy, 10 to 12 years old. He was shivering, but his smile told all. He was finally free, and he waved. If Bill had been closer to the light source, he would have seen the boy mouth the words, "Thank you again."

As soon as the boy was out of sight, the tunnel of light disappeared and the hole in the ice vanished down into the icy waters. The oceans that surrounded Antarctica seemed to be surfacing and somehow storming through and across the ice.

About 10 feet away, a fresh crack formed in the ice and followed them. They ran. The doorway was shrinking.

Eric opened his eyes. The corridor was unfamiliar, but much more pleasant than the ice. He was relieved to see Loreda's green eyes gazing down at him. "Where are we?"

Loreda giggled.

"What?"

"I don't know."

"You don't know where we are, or you don't know why you're laughing?"

"Both, I guess. It doesn't matter though. We're safe."

"As long as you say so."

Pam joined them. "How do you feel?"

Eric grunted. "I've felt better."

A bright burst of light flashed through the corridor, and three men emerged from the breakthrough point. One of them was Gabe. The other two they didn't know. The taller one was a black man, and he held a young woman in his arms. The other one was holding onto Gabe's right arm, helping him along the corridor. Behind them, they could see through the doorway that the remnants of Antarctica continued to shake, rumble, and melt away.

"You don't have to tell me now," Loreda said to Andy and Bill. "But eventually will you, if you can, of course, tell us what just happened." She extended her hand. "I'm Loreda. Loreda Cranfield."

"I'm Bill Anderson, and this is Andy Evans. The girl is my daughter, Amy. We need to get her some help as soon as possible."

"What's wrong with her?" Pam said.

Bill took Amy from Andy and headed down the hall. "Let's go upstairs, and I'll try and explain everything." He wasn't sure what they were going to do. They were still trapped inside the school until the snowstorm passed. The open doorway made them nervous, but at least now no one was chasing them, and it didn't seem as if any of the melted ice and snow was coming through the breakthrough point and into the corridor. If they had to wait a day, Bill thought Amy could survive. Away from the ice and snow, she was already showing signs of improvement. It was visibly noticeable as he stared down at her. The color was returning in her cheeks. The blood seemed to be clotting, the wound closing. He first had to get the power in the school working again, and then he'd call for help.

Eric slowly got to his feet, and he held onto Loreda's arm as they walked down the corridor.

"Bill," Loreda said. "Where are we?"

"Louisville, Kentucky. Underneath a small Catholic High School."

Gabe thought it was appropriate.

"Louisville?" Loreda asked. "But how?"

"Through the doorway."

She was confused. She never expected her trip back to the States to be this fast. She shook her head. "This has probably been the longest day of my life."

"It's been the longest twenty years of mine," Bill sighed.

After . . .

At 6:30 Saturday morning, the breakthrough point disappeared. The doorway was closed, and would never be used again, not in Louisville, not in Antarctica, not in any city in the world.

The blizzard of '94 was the worst in Louisville history. It dumped nearly 35 inches of snow in less than 24 hours, and the entire city had been buried for almost two weeks.

Eric and Loreda did manage to go out on that first date. By then it had felt like they'd known each other for years, and it ended up being the first date of many. Several months later they were engaged, and within a year they were husband and wife. Magnus and Mark miraculously survived the last earthquake. The dead bodies in the research station had been lost deep down in the ice, but the two managed to hold on, taking shelter for several days in the skylab.

The other bodies were never found, and the occurrences on Antarctica went down in the books as unfortunate and unexplained. The papers mentioned nothing about a mysterious doorway, or a Snowman, claiming that the survivors were rescued by ski planes just as the earthquake had started. The doorway was non-existent. End of story.

As for Antarctica, the earthquakes stopped as soon as the breakthrough point vanished, barely in time to save what was left of the melted continent. After all the quakes had ended, nearly a quarter of the two-mile thick base had melted into the three oceans surrounding the continent, and it didn't take long for the southern coastal nations to feel the effects with abnormal high tides and floods. Much of the land and surrounding waters had already started to refreeze within weeks, but scientists are currently working on finding the causes of the sudden meltdown.

Antarctica still remained Antarctica, the coldest place on the earth, but it wasn't without significant changes. The topography of the land had been altered drastically, with a much more rigid and mountainous landscape than before. Temperatures fluctuated but remained relatively normal, for Antarctica, that is, but the strangest occurrence of all was the momentary sprouting of plant life around the South Pole. It was as if during the earthquake part of the continent had been turned inside out, and what had been underneath the ice for so many years was finally given the chance to breathe and grow again. An unexplained phenomena, much like the crop circles and UFO sightings, it seemed to happen in one night.

Most of the South Pole Research Station had been lost under the ice, but a new one was due for construction in 1998. The government and SCARE wanted nothing to do with it. The National Science Foundation would again have control over the research in Antarctica. With the tragedy still weighing heavily on the minds of many explorers, the next Overland Expedition was not set until the year 2000. The only people to be stationed there would be scientists and researchers, all trying to figure out what had happened to the ice and the land underneath it.

It was Christmas of 1995, and Andy Evans was due for two-weeks paid vacation. He was the youngest police chief in the history of the LPD, and the raise in pay had been significant. At first he'd been reluctant to take over Ralph's old job. Ralph would have wanted him to take the job, and Andy knew that, so after a week of internal debate, he did.

He was heading to Florida to visit his old friend, Bill Anderson, who was living in Miami as a bank teller with his daughter. Amy was engaged to be married to a man named Gabe Mulloy. Both she and Kathy were graduate students in biology at the University of Miami. Lisa was to arrive in Miami in two days with her baby, Ralph Jr., and Kathleen Greene was scheduled to arrive the day after with her kids. No one wanted to be in Louisville for Christmas. A snowstorm was expected for the weekend.

Andy clamped the last buckle down on his suitcase and headed for the front door. His flight was scheduled to take off in an hour, and he didn't want to be late. On his way out, he stopped at the fireplace and picked up something from the bricks on top. It was a bone, a small bone from a foot. He wasn't sure why he'd taken the time to pick it up off the ice that night in Antarctica, and he sure didn't know why he'd kept it. He didn't need any physical proof to remind him that the Snowman was dead. He clutched the bone in his hand, went into the kitchen, and tossed it in the garbage can.

Andy left.

He did not see the garbage can glow with a faint green aura.